Beyond Christianity – To The Christ

Beyond Religion – To The Source

By George E. Fandt

Bob,
Blessings on your
Journey!
George E Fandt

ISBN: 1-4107-1025-4 (e-book)
ISBN: 1-4107-1026-2 (Paperback)
ISBN: 1-4107-4255-5 (Dust Jacket)

Library of Congress Control Number: 2003090023

This book is printed on acid free paper.

Printed in the United States of America
Bloomington, IN

First published in 1999 by Koinonia of Chautauqua, 119 W. 2nd St.
Suite 506, Xenia, Ohio 45385

1stBooks – rev. 06/21/03

Table of Contents

Acknowledgements.. iv
Preface v

Chapter...Page
1. The Nature of the Tao—Followers of The Way..................... 1
2. Personal Journey—Spirit and Religion 45
3. The Quality of God—Prologue to John................................ 71
4. Being Born Again—Enlightenment 97
5. The Biblical Library—Spirit and Law................................. 109
6. Spiritual Libraries—Ancient and Modern........................... 159
7. The Power of Silence—The Unity of Spirit 199
8. The Future of Faith—Being Right or Well.......................... 225
9. The Nature of Healing—The Energy of Life 237
10. Heirs of God—Epilogue 253

Glossary 273
Bibliography and Recommended Reading 275

Acknowledgements

There are many thanks due, to the dozens who encouraged me to make this effort. Those from the congregations I served as Pastor/Teacher, classmates, friends, students, and members of various study groups. My thanks also, to the many who read early manuscripts and made suggestions, especially to our friend Rebecca York, for so much helpful feedback and extensive editorial help, along with her ability to chide me into making needed changes.

I am grateful for the advances in technology, which make the writing process so much easier than in the past. Without a home computer, word processor and speech recognition software I doubt seriously if I would have been able to finish this project.

For encouragement, advice and technical support in the computer process my thanks to our good friend H. Dale Morse.

I am grateful to the inner resources of Spirit that have supported the writing of this book. I am learning to trust the Tao (Way) and its resource of effortless accomplishment, (the meaning of the Chinese words *wei wu wei*). While I admit to inner resources and the help of Spirit, this is not channeled material. The unfolding has been entirely conscious and I accept full responsibility for the concepts, both original and derived. Sometimes while proof reading, I have been caught up by the flow of words and realize that there is more here than meets the eye.

I wish to thank the many sources I have drawn upon in this work. I was not very familiar with copyright procedures, but in correspondence with several authors and publishers found that my usage invariably fell under the provisions of 'Fair Use'.

Inasmuch as I have for years collected short quotes and verse I have only knowledge of the original source and not where I was first exposed to them. I thank those to whom I may be indirectly indebted. I know that ideas are not subject to copyright but I am indebted to the many over the years, who through lectures, sermons or writings have challenged my thinking and increased my fluency of thought. To those who have contributed to this awareness, my sincere thanks.

Preface

Our notion of god seems very much dependent on our personal political framework. We who belong to a democracy see god and religion differently than those who believed in the 'divine right' of kings. In the culture of the Roman Empire the political structure of the Western Jesus Movement was not viewed with a democratic viewpoint but rather as a part of the empirical hierarchy. A prime insight achieved in the writing of this book is the development of an historical awareness of how the political struggles of the Roman Empire played a most important role in the formation of the present day Christian Church.

When Constantine converted to Christianity, it changed the Western Jesus Movement, conforming it to the political structure of the Roman Empire. Modern Christianity is much more a product of the politics of the Roman Empire than it is a result of the teachings of Jesus. It was not so much that the Romans were Christianized, but rather, that Christianity was Romanized. The Roman Western Church approached the story of Jesus with a literalistic historical view and seemed unable to recognize the mythological teaching stories abounding in the gospel accounts. It was the Gnostic Eastern Church that attempted to keep the actual teachings of Jesus alive. Unfortunately the Roman literalists won the battle; I can only hope that the teachings of Jesus will ultimately win the war.

It was politically expedient to structure church rule like the Empire. The Emperor received his authority from god and was sometimes even considered divine himself. The relationship of Emperor and Empire also became a model for the institutional church with heritage passed on by birthright. Priests in this period were not required to be celibate, and many had children who were favored to replace their fathers in positions of privilege. Because priests and parishes were able to accumulate a great deal of wealth the church eventually imposed the rule of celibacy. In the case of a celibate clergy the birthright was passed on through the legacy of apostolic succession and the laying on of hands. The church saw itself as a stereotypical political structure. At the top was god, and then came the bishop of Rome (Pope), other bishops, followed by priests and deacons, and at the lowest level, the laity following life serfs in a feudal system. Within such a system, the concept of the kingdom of god within each soul became both political and religious heresy. By the fourth century with the help of the Roman Empire all parts of the Jesus Movement not in sympathy with the 'official' church were now being labeled as heretics and either pushed out of the mainstream or physically eliminated.

The most notable casualty to the sounding prophetic voice in the ascendancy of 'officialdom' within the early Roman church was the suppression of Gnostic Christians. The meaning of the Greek word *gnosis* is to know. This name was applied to those who maintained that salvation was internal, individual, and accompanied by knowledge correctly applied (wisdom?). The position they adopted toward the outer world as an illusion was not treated favorably by the political/priestly alliance. As a result, Gnosticism was suppressed as heresy. Modern church historians were in the dark for centuries about Gnostic beliefs, for the only records available to them were condemnatory writings and judgments against the Gnostics and their movement. An accurate picture of one's religious and spiritual outlook does not come undistorted from an adversarial opposition party.

Religion and politics are both externals and when god is viewed as an objective other, god is perceived as one would regard an Emperor or King. When god is understood as an internal Principle then god is experienced as belonging to one's own consciousness or gestalt, or as Jesus called god, the Father within. Because of the vast distinction between an inner authority of acceptance and an external one of judgment, we must make the decision, "Is god an inner ally or an external judge?"

Because I have a firm faith in the democratic principle of the 'priesthood of all believers', please understand this work as a *testimony* of my faith and not a *test* of yours.

One reason for writing this book is the decision to leave a tangible inheritance to our grandchildren. Hopefully, I will leave them with some sense of what the 'old man' stood for. Some of them have already read early drafts, and some are just learning to read. So, a secondary dedication of the book would be to them and their children: Chandra (and great grandson Cody), Stephanie, Adam, Desiree, Jessica, James, George and Taylor.

The primary dedication is to the memory of my father Elmer Walter Fandt, who taught me how to think, and to my companion and wife for over half a century, Lillian Nelson Fandt, who taught me how to love. They symbolize my journey, the path of the head, and the path of the heart.

Chapter One—The Nature of the Tao
Followers of The Way

Tao Te Ching

There is a being, wonderful, perfect;
It existed before heaven and earth.
How quiet it is!
How spiritual it is!
It stands alone and it does not change;
It moves, but does not on that account suffer.
All life comes from it, yet it does not demand to be Lord.
I do not know its name, so I call it Tao, the Way.
And I rejoice in its power.[1]

Movement of the Spirit

The *Tao* (way, means) is the Source from which all energy springs. The *Te* (power, virtue, integrity) is that which springs from the Tao. Te is the self-aware *intention* of the Tao. The expression of Te is derived from Tao alone. This same meaning of way and power are conveyed in the opening verses of the Gospel according to John.[2] In John 1:1, Tao can be understood as analogous to god and Te to *Logos* (word).

To allow Spirit to work as *intention* within our lives is to understand the subtle difference between expectancy and expectation. Expectation is to have in mind the goal or plan that we have predetermined to be our path. Expectancy is an intention of openness toward unfolding that which we have not prearranged. It is to will the will of god without needing either to know or control that will. In the words of Diane Kennedy Pike, widow of

---

[1]Tao Te Ching, Section: 25, by Houston Smith in 'Jesus at 2000' Pg. 110
[2] See Chapter Three:—The Quality of God

1

Episcopal Bishop James Pike, our lives are to be lived with no expectations, but great expectancy.

This is a book about religion and its effect on the spiritual journey, essentially the Christian religion; and from what I have read of other World Religions, the issues addressed are relevant to them as well. It is also a presentation of a particular worldview and the story of a Faith Journey.

Because my worldview involves allowing unfolding to take place and inner guidance to control what is beyond my personal knowledge, this book follows minimum external design. I have made little attempt to compartmentalize ideas and insights by category; for most could be placed in a variety of contexts. Some concepts can be tied to a textual source, but none will be truly understood until integrated into one's own life journey.

The basic premise of this book is Jesus' insight and instruction that the kingdom of god is within us.[3] Religions, as a matter of creed and ritual, exist outside of us. All too often, they are a hindrance rather than help in finding the inner Joy and Peace of god that Jesus taught was the quintessence of the spiritual journey.

I am aware that the term 'kingdom' is judged by many to be a sexist term and, therefore, politically incorrect. Although I could substitute words like 'reign' and 'realm', they do not have the acceptance of the centuries of use developed by the more familiar translation of Jesus' words. In the rush to be politically correct, asexual terms have begun to proliferate. Unfortunately, the aftermath has all but obliterated the distinction of centuries, if not millennia, of significant mythology. The Sky above is Father and the Earth below is Mother. The Sun and Rain make provision, the Earth Mother brings forth abundance. Unlike many languages, English does not give its nouns gender, so we tend to judge our generic pronouns as having sexual preference.

Other confusing aspects of correct language usage exist. When writing about god as Source, I find it expedient to alter the standard convention with regard to the capitalization of the word, 'god'. I have reached the conclusion that god as an experiential reality exists; but god as an object or thing does not. The word 'god' capitalized in our language gives to it the status of a proper name and as a consequence supports the word 'God' as objective and separate. For that reason I choose not to capitalize the word wherever feasible. The word 'god' not capitalized, rather than the word 'God' capitalized, accentuates the non-object or subjective nature of Spirit.

The reverse seems to be true of other English words not normally capitalized; words like Spirit, Father, Intelligence, Principle and Way when

---

[3] Luke 17:20-21

capitalized impart movement away from object status as common nouns. The sex of pronouns in reference to god is also very misleading and if for no other reason than effect I will attempt to use the neutral pronoun 'it' wherever feasible. 'It', also suggests an aura of impersonality, which I feel will be helpful in conveying the idea of god as Impersonal Principle. The personal or ego self is at the root of our culture, it is part of the space/time illusion and the main reason for our belief in spiritual separation.

The concept of god as a person is by definition, objective; and as such, is subject to space/time limitation in the same context as the personal self (self not capitalized). Only an Impersonal God and an Impersonal Self (Self capitalized) can share limitless, timeless, and spaceless spiritual identity and unity as Impersonal Life.

One could say that Impersonal Self is the internal and eternal reality of Spirit; and personal self is the ego's identification with the bodily form of space/time. The spiritual Impersonal Self is in union with god as All-That-Is. Individuated self, in its identity with one's body, separates from all else, and recognizes god only as being outside and distinct. At the level of the Reality of god the real Self exists and the ego self must be understood as part of the illusion of space/time.

For me, understanding Self and self is more like an awareness of polarities that we choose for orientation. We are able to experience a sliding scale of reference with our identity placed either toward the unconditional oneness of Spirit or else focused on a conditional 'otherness'. That which we choose in our awareness, we become – Self or self. When we truly pray, "Thy will be done on earth as it is in heaven," we mean, "Let or allow god/Spirit to manifest as us." We thus choose not to be identified with the individuated self of separation, fear, defense, and attack. Because the body lives in space/time, we must accept the temporal and physical relationships of space/time. Birth and death are but space/time interruptions in eternal awareness. Even as we function in this temporal world, we can know that at the absolute level of Spirit, we are not separated bodies but pure Spirit unified with All-That-Is. When we experience *oneness* rather than *otherness*, we learn to pray, "Thy will be done within Self, as it is in god." As Jesus taught, "We are *in* the world but not *of* the world."[4]

One other word of definition and explanation needs to be stated. Much will be said with regard to the word 'illusion' as the way in which we perceive our physical world. Because we are usually not seeing with the eyes or heart of Spirit, we do not see what mystics call the *real* world. What we come to perceive as our world outlook or gestalt depends upon our

---

[4] John 17:11-16

mindset and our particular belief systems. This is not the case of 'seeing is believing', but rather 'believing is seeing'. We will see what we expect to see for belief is the means by which we perceive.

This statement raises the question of the basic relationship between our minds and their relationship with the whole. Appearance suggests to us that what is outside is separated from our mental awareness and attitude, when in fact the 'outside' is a projection of the way in which we expect it to appear.

Our mind is cause and our perception is the result. This in spite of a cultural bias that suggests the other way around, i.e. the world out there is the cause and we, and our experience, are the effect. In the unity of wholeness there is no separation; and unitive consciousness results in an integration in which we realize ourselves as a vital part of the whole and the whole a vital part of us.

Illusion is a label we need put upon apparent phenomenon. A way of interpreting the world we see. We can not truly claim to understand fully the connection between illusion and reality, but we can be aware that these dualistic aspects of our experience are not identical.

Perhaps we can grasp this concept best, by examining our personal view of god. If god is Spirit, then god is not a separated 'other' that exists apart, capable of vocalizing as a personality to us, a thing distinct from the unity of the whole. The voice for god is not separated from Its expression; it is integral within it. God did not create a Universe apart from Itself, and then step back and communicate with the creation as an entity apart. The Word of god is not a vocalization from a separated personality that we call the creator. The living Word is the living energy and the loving intelligence, which is expressed as our Impersonal Self, and is the reality underlying the illusory, separated space/time world.

Reality is unity and god is one with the whole. This concept can be framed in the sense that god is one with All-That-Is. All-That-Is, includes our mind and what we perceive as all minds, indeed the whole in the sense of the total Cosmos. All minds are joined, and this unity is not destroyed by our failure to perceive this fact. Recall the words of Jesus, "That they may be one as we are one." "The Father and I are one." And so we are; all of us.

It is well to be aware that unity is not limited to what we like to call sentient beings; it is a unity that includes the whole expression of god. The energy underlying the apparent universe and its variety includes that which we compartmentalize into plant, animal and mineral kingdoms.

In our mind is the power to produce many belief systems with greater and lesser identity with the whole. In many if not most of our established religious beliefs, we view god as having a personality expressed in an objective other. God is not an object! God is Spirit and whole (Holy), All-

That-Is. Belief systems, which support a fracture between the Source and Its expression, make the phrase, 'Word of God' a form of idolatry. The unity of the Holy (Whole), bonds only to the Living Word.

Let it be understood that there is a variety of belief systems that seek to express this living unity. These have in common a unitive philosophy of wholeness as well as holiness.

The "Shema Yisrael", from the Hebrew scriptures, moves towards this unity; "*Hear, O Israel*, The Lord our God is one." The religious problem of course, stems from the legend that we have eaten fruit from 'The tree of the knowledge of good *and* evil', led to that fate by the *god of appearances*, the satanic; thus our unity *supposedly* has been destroyed.

The Unity of god, of course, has not been destroyed! It is *still* reality for those who exercise the vision to see it. Spiritual vision comes from within, not from a god, supposed to be without. This 'hidden splendor' is available to all, for it is the core of our reality.

It is intriguing to note the variety of visions which can come from an awareness of the integrated whole. Profound appreciation arises from the observation, that when consciousness is unified with the whole, in spite of the different approaches, somehow at a practical level they all seem to work.

These include the philosophy of Buddhism, the teachings of The "Bahagavad Gita", the unitive wholeness and non-dualistic teaching of Shankara, the path of the shaman with its animal guides, the teachings of Swedenborg who saw god as man to the Nth degree, the Sufi teachings of Indris Shah as well as the metaphysical views of New Thought and expressions of New Age such as "A Course in Miracles" and other writings.

To be vital, a spiritual path must reflect the Hippocratic oath 'to do no harm'. It must also honor symbols of the Impersonal Self experienced by others and forgo the need to be right, in order to be well.

When I was in high school in the early 40's I accepted without question the scientific law of the conservation of both energy and matter. Matter and energy, according to the science of the time, could not be destroyed and were both considered immutable.

The atomic experience changed all that. Matter could now be seen as a construct of energy; atoms of matter were not conserved but converted to energy. A small amount of matter could translate to vast amounts of energy. The view is now accepted that in primordial time unimaginable amounts of energy were converted into the expression of matter (The Big Bang).

The perception of scientific law has been markedly changed by the atomic event but religious thought has been relatively unaffected and religious ideas have done little to catch up. Energy and matter are still seen as separated and *the energy of god is still viewed as creating a world separated* from Itself. When it comes to this clear witness of modern Physics, for the most part, today's religion doesn't have a clue.

Science now views matter as a transmutation of energy. We need to consider that matter is a form with an underlying relationship to the energy of god. The illusion of space/time results because of our failure to recognize this connection. Matter expressed from energy only appears separated from its source. Apparent matter and invisible energy are one.

To expand our view of physics and switch from the material world to the Spiritual, we need to look at basic laws regarding matter. The quantum level of energy is at the heart of all things. The paradigm shift required, is to become aware that the energy of the universe is intelligent! The material appearance of objective space/time is mistakenly viewed as a reality when we perceive matter standing alone by itself.

A paradigm is a framework of understanding. Each paradigm may have certain aspects of clarification and usefulness; it may also have a patent lack of application as well. Paradigms become outdated and at times are no longer relevant or helpful to the understanding of our world. It once served well to view the earth as the center of the universe; it no longer is helpful to do so. Old wineskins are incapable of holding new wine!

The illusory world appears a fact to our sensory experience because our bodily senses are keyed to the space/time experience. The reality of an object is not its form; the source is rather to be found in the intention of timeless Mind/Energy, which supports objective appearance. The spiritual journey leads us away from the dogma of externalized space/time religion to the underlying energy and intelligence of Spirit. It is creative intelligence, which results in the coherence of the material world. This intelligent energy the Sages have called Love.

Expectation is prejudicial, for with predetermined judgments we mold our perceived world according to our beliefs. With prejudiced memory we see the past in our present. Scientific experiments show that the field of optical illusion is rife with illustrations of seeing what we expect to see rather than recognizing what is actually present. Many subjects, given a deck of playing cards with the Ace of Spades colored red, were unable to detect the change. Our visual experience is often fooled by expectations.

Everyone has had experience with the limitations of language. Words are but a symbol of our thoughts; and what we think we said is frequently heard differently, based on what the listener habitually expects to hear. The same principle of expectation holds true for all of the interpretations we place upon others. Acts of innocence, because of prejudgment, may be seen as indications of guilt. We need to look beyond our belief systems and change our perceptions and expectations. One must use spiritual vision, in order to see with the heart beyond material appearance.

At times the words 'illusion' and 'hallucination' are confused, for both terms refer to seeing something that is not real. Illusion is an erroneous appearance still connected to reality. Mistaken perception is always an interpretation of what is in essence invisible to us. Hallucination is a delusion with no connection to outer experience. It is usually a result of chemical triggers in the nervous system, induced by a mind-altering substance, or caused by some form of sensory deprivation.

Perhaps illusion is best grasped when we understand the effects produced by stage magicians. When an elephant is made to disappear from our view, it is most likely accomplished with mirrored surfaces or hidden panels. The elephant is in fact still there when it seems to disappear. The trick of course, is that we can no longer see it. In illusion, reality is still there; we simply have temporarily lost the ability to recognize it.

Since childhood, we have been trained by our culture to discriminate between the form of objects and occurrences at different times. Because our present belief systems focus on material or space/time reality, I refer to this view of the world as the illusion of space/time.

This illusory perception prevents us from recognizing the meaning that underlies and sustains all that appears to be: the existence of Spirit and Logos or Mind/Voice as the true Word of god. What we see as we look at the world of space/time is the perceptual illusion of space/time. This apparent world seems to be both here and now and also to possess both a future and a past. Our present physical adventures in duration give little clue to the existence of timeless Spirit or eternal values. Because of belief in the temporal as reality, we are not yet competent to see with the timeless eyes of Spirit. When we expect to see the durational effects of time, we will not see the Timeless. There is no 'forever' to be found within the temporal!

We have been educated to think in subject/object form. It is the nature of our intellect to use words in order to classify our thoughts. Unfortunately, there is no possible way to convey, by word-symbolized thoughts, non-thought or non-object awareness. To know our spiritual awareness we need to be apprehended by Spirit, the meaning of which words cannot contain.

The mystery of this reality will be fathomed as we grow in the knowledge of our true being; but the labels we apply, as descriptions of the event, will always be woefully inadequate to describe its reality. This is the primary reason why mystics refer to mystical experience as the silence, stillness, or even the void. It is the still, small (silent, subtle) voice of spirit.

When by the power of mind, spirit expresses itself into form, spirit is expressing from oneness, but the resulting diversity we perceive, is illusion; a product of mind now split from the awareness of spirit. The reality of spirit does not express the illusion of form; illusion is expressed through the channel of our collective minds. Form, to us, is an illusion, whereas, the intelligent energy of Love is the essence of the reality behind the form.

We may try to coerce spirit to intervene in our illusion in order to effect physical and/or mental healing. The confusion of trying to manipulate the Law of One to do our bidding at the level of mind and body results in distortion. Some so-called 'spiritual healing' is a misguided attempt to change physical conditions; whereas, effective spiritual healing is evoked by appropriate belief and thought at the level of spirit. We can use mental law to remove mental roadblocks and allow spirit to express. At the level of body and body-mind we do not and cannot manifest spirit, for only at the level of unified Mind and Impersonal Self is Spirit known. An attempt to coerce the reality of Spirit to appear is not the nature of true healing; healing is rather, to undo the unreal and remove our blocks to seeing Spirit's reality. We are not perceived physical bodies of appearance; we are free of space/time, for our reality remains as an extension of god's reality.

Level confusion results by trying with mental law to manifest spiritual expression. At the level of spirit we are spirit and spirit manifests of itself. When we remove the blocks to the awareness of love's presence, we are not doing – we are undoing. We are undoing something that is not real; we are undoing the split mind. The blocks are not real; they are simply false meanings we have given to outer appearance.

Remove false meaning and judgment (the power we have given away) and the blocks will dissolve into the nothingness from whence they came. We will have discovered the voidness of the full, and the fullness of the void. On the path of spirit allow spirit to be in control. Let its will be done. Allow spirit to solve the decisions of the mind – a hard lesson. Allow spirit to express in matters of matter. Few of us, it seems, have learned that trust.

A major factor in following the Way or Tao is knowing that god as Spirit permeates the whole universe. God has not created apparent material form, but rather expresses itself as coherent Wholeness and Unity. God is not visible form, as in the concept of pantheism (all is god). God has infused the whole Cosmos from its being, more closely suggested in the word panentheism (god is in all).

The Way or Tao is based on the understanding that space and duration (time) is not reality in form, but that only in its *essence* is space/time an expression of spiritual reality. The illusion of the ages mistakenly perceives space/time expression as source. The source is spirit; and matter, the result of its expression. The Way or Tao knows reality is at the level of spirit, and that material form is the space/time expression of the unity of spirit. To believe material space/time appearance is reality is the root of illusion.

Ken Wilbur refers to basic laws regarding the levels of spirit, mind, and matter. He suggests that the operative level of the law at these levels is different. At the level of spirit the law is one, whole without separation. The level of the mind introduces interpretation and perception, varying according to our belief systems. The law at the level of matter is complete diversification, separation, and classification.

At the level of matter is diversification.	Things
At the level of mind are beliefs and thoughts.	Perception
At the level of spirit is oneness.	Knowing

Knowledge is found Only in Silence of the Mind.

The Way or Tao is the way of looking past the world of form and ideas to the vision of spirit. Spirit is a way of knowing that god is, and that god is in the world but not of it. God did not make the illusion, we do. We do so by misdirecting the law of mind that god has expressed through us. Level confusion results when we seek to bring about healing, by focusing on the external illusion of form instead of the internal reality of spirit.

God as spirit expresses the universe into form. This we perceive in the traditional form of animal, plant, and mineral kingdoms. All these kingdoms have intelligence, and cohesive molecular awareness. The mineral kingdom is perhaps least understood as having any degree of sentient awareness. It is only recently that we have developed an understanding that the plant kingdom has awareness at a kind of emotional or feeling level. Plants can respond to the projection of human emotions. Dividing the world into plant, animal, and mineral kingdoms makes no sense at all from the viewpoint of spiritual awareness.

Mountains may move, stones may cry out, but god does not move the mountains; it is changed perception. The Absolute Energy of Love supports the cohesiveness of the material world. Rupert Schelldrake's morphogenic theory makes it apparent that the cellular and molecular levels of the human body respond to ideas, beliefs, and emotions held by the human mind. The genetic DNA that is held identically by each cell in the body, does not determine how each cell chooses to function in the body. There is an underlying intelligence that guides that formation.

We speak of language as a tool for communication, when in fact, language and words are devices of separation. The 'I am' statements that we make are indicative of our state of awareness. They should be statements of being not doing. When *we seek to become*, we in fact, deny

9

the reality of what *we already are*. We seek, when in fact, in our core we are that which is sought! However, it is in spite of the language of separation that the Holy Spirit must awaken oneness. 'I did' or 'I do' are ego statements, a division of our world into physical components.

The ego is not a monster, it is not evil, it is not negative, it simply is not. The ego is our construct for survival in the space/time world of body and thought. To judge the ego as evil is to construct a negative awareness of its supposed reality. It is not another reality; at the level of the Real it simply does not exist.

Jesus was not a political savior; his role was not that of saving *per se*. His was an expression of a life of healing and wholeness. He is not *the way* to god; in his Christ awareness he *shows* the way. To believe that his experience and awareness is vicariously our own is incorrect. It is *our* experience and awareness that is the way. Jesus did not bring salvation to us; rather, he demonstrated healing in his life, which we need to demonstrate in our own. Jesus said, "God is spirit" and "God is love"; follow his lead.

In the religion *about* Jesus, as regards the nature of god, there are least two grand oxymorons (logical contradictions). The first contradiction is 'objectified spirit' and the second is 'adversarial love'.

Objectified spirit is the concept of god as an object, thing, or separated entity. It is a picture of god as other, separate from creation. The concept of spirit as *pneuma* (wind) is not accidental. The wind blows where it will and we know not the source thereof.

Adversarial love is seen in the religious ideas of judgment, condemnation, and separation, as acts of god. The worst possible illustrations of this contradiction I can possibly imagine are statements in the book of Revelation referring to 'the wrath of the Lamb' and the Psalms that curse one's enemies such as "Happy shall they be who take your little ones and dash them against the rock."[5] I cannot possibly imagine what a wrathful Lamb would look like nor can I believe that god would curse our enemies by destroying their children.

Love is the ground of all being, and as such, the idea of separation from god is in opposition to reality. God is not just all power and being; god is the only power and being. Omni means all and only, all energy, all intelligence and all presence, at the root of All-That-Is, One!

The Holy Spirit (Christ) does not speak with words for there are no separations, classifications, or categories in spirit. Spirit speaks as physical and mental stillness! Spirit is wholeness; complete, holy and pure being.

---

[5] Psalm 137:9

Spirit is not the process of healing but the oneness of the whole. Wholeness can be felt; not explained.

Words as symbols inherently separate and categorize in order to function. They cannot be used to state what cannot be cataloged, except to describe dimly what can't be said. Words cannot state the mystery, but only be used to point in the direction of its meaning. Words are symbols, designed to cope with a tangible, material world. They are designed to compartmentalize, divide, and place precise boundaries on objects being described. For all their power in the visible material world, they are of extremely limited help in dealing with the invisible and boundless dimension of Spirit. When I speak of timeless and spaceless, I am trying to dissolve boundaries, not create new ones. Language and grammar offer little help in this dilemma. If I am trying to speak of dimensionless Spirit, the grammatical articles of our language are useless. If I say *the* Spirit, then by using a definite article I have created a defined object. If I say *a* Spirit, then I raise the question of the existence of other spirits as well.

Religion at its best, is the expression of Spirit through the community witness of art, poetry, music and faith. Religious congregations have the capacity to broaden real fellowship through the sense of extended family. For those whose nature is more sensory, beauty may also be expressed in ritual and architecture. I feel no need to criticize these positive aspects of religion.

My intention is to bring a healing message to those who have been harmed by the negative aspects of religion, especially within the organized Christian Church. As I write this, there are members of the Sikh religion in India, who have killed each other over the issue of whether they should eat their fellowship meal at tables or while sitting on the floor.

Ambrose Worrall and wife Olga were very effective healers. Ambrose worked as an aeronautical engineer at Martin Marietta Corporation in Baltimore, MD. Olga was director of a healing clinic at a Baltimore United Methodist Church; neither accepted payment for the healing work that they did. In their excellent book, "The Gift of Healing", Ambrose and Olga Worrall tell the story of a dream Olga had, and the unfolding of its meaning.[6]

Olga dreamed of being in a hospital corridor when she heard a baby cry from a burning room. Others tried to tell her that the child was dead; destroyed by the fire. She rescued the lifeless infant from the flaming room, entered a room without fire, and prayed "Please, dear Lord, heal this child,

---

[6] The Gift of Healing, Ambrose and Olga Worrall: pages 24,25

give him back his life." The infant began to stir in her arms. The dream carried powerful emotional content for her and she couldn't shake it off.

That evening they were making a social visit in the home of a business acquaintance of Ambrose whom Olga had never met. Olga, as a sensitive, saw the spirit of an elderly woman sitting on a sofa across the room, holding an infant boy upon her lap. Only Olga saw this and heard the woman say that her name was Mamie, that she was the mother of the husband, and that the sofa had been her bed during her life on earth. She pleaded with Olga to tell the family that she had the baby with her, and that it was in perfect health.

Olga hesitated, wondering what the couple would think if she relayed the invisible woman's message. When she did, the wife cried out with great joy, "My baby, my baby – he's not burning in hell – he's alive. Thank god, thank god – you are giving me back my baby."

After the wife grew calmer, the husband explained that his mother's name was Mamie and that the sofa had been her daybed, removed from her apartment following her death, some months prior. He went on to explain that their infant son had been scheduled to be baptized at the age of six months but had suddenly died when only five months old. At the funeral service a pastor told them that their infant son was conceived in sin, died in sin, and that being unbaptized, would eternally burn in hell. Olga's message from the mother brought them hope and life. Her earlier dream had been precognitive of the events of the evening.

It is unfathomable to me how a pastor could believe that god is Love and at the same time, accept the foolishness that this same god of Love would condemn an unbaptized infant to roast in everlasting hellfire. I recall someone taking the Surgeon General's warning about tobacco and making a play on the words, suggesting "Warning! Religion can be hazardous to your spiritual health".

The danger of religion is not in its beauty or in its group support, except of course when the group yields to demagoguery and becomes a negative force in society. The danger of religion comes about in its zealous exercise of usurped moral authority. Because of political power attained in its historical development, a particular institution of religion may begin to falsely assume it is now obligated to become the guardian of truth. People, in need of structured external authority, will unfortunately demand from their institutions claims of infallibility. It takes a willing buyer and a willing seller. Note the role of religion in the Palestinian conflict.

The cause for some of the greatest scourges on earth has been the belief that religious institutions should preserve and control faith. The Crusaders in their Holy war against Moslems, the Conquistadors conquering the New

World, the tortures and horrors of the Spanish Inquisition, the burning of witches or condemned heretics such as Joan of Arc, and the Salem witch trials of New England, as well as the more recent terrorism of 9/11/01 are illustrations of this behavior.

The dangers for the individual are assumptions that the knowledge of god is presumably handed down in succession to those who claim they have the answers. The benefits from this 'truth' are then restricted exclusively to those who submit to authority. To be 'saved' one must 'belong'.

The development of the tradition surrounding the story of the 'Keys to the Kingdom'[7] provides an illustration of how a simple spiritual teaching can be distorted to meet political and religious ends. Peter had stated that he believed Jesus to manifest the Christ. Jesus blessed him for this knowledge from the Father within and further stated that this insight regarding the inner kingdom was the key to understanding the mission of one's own inner Christ. Subsequent Church History suggests that the spiritual dynamic of the story did not survive very well.

One must remember that the story came into its present form, after the political formation of the Western Jesus Movement and its alignment with the Roman Empire. Tradition had already positioned the deceased Peter as the first Bishop of Rome (Pope). No wonder the story was distorted to mean the Pope held the Keys to the Kingdom (now outer keys rather than inner). When admittance to the kingdom of god is recognized as the exclusive province of an external institution, such as the early Roman Church, any specific individual attempt to access awareness of the inner kingdom is rigorously denied. The 'official church' is the only vehicle of salvation.

We too often think in terms of an exterior kingdom, which will exalt us in the world, and appreciate who we are. The fact is, that it is the appreciation and experience of this internal kingdom that enables us to see our own exalted inner reality.

It is certain that we will not find an inner kingdom in the world of outer appearance. Jesus spoke of the spiritual awareness of the inner kingdom as a great treasure hidden in a field. To purchase the field it is necessary to sell all that in which we have previously invested. "We must remove our self-constructed blocks to the awareness of Love's Presence."[8]

The struggle between inner authority and external authority is a central issue of this book. The best illustration of this conflict is Jesus' teaching in regard to the difference between the letter of the law and the spirit of the law. Jesus referred to the Spirit of the Law when he spoke about helping a

---

[7] Matthew 16:16-19
[8] A Course in Miracles: Text: Introduction

man who fell into a ditch on the Sabbath day. Jewish Law decreed that no work was to be done on the Sabbath. Stringent legalists would not extend help if it involved what they believed to be work. *The literal letter of religion must surrender to spiritual common sense, exemplified in the Law of Love and Freedom of the Spirit.*

Religious institutions are the bulwark of the letter of the law and for many of them the ideology of power through authority is the main reason for their existence. The spirit of the law finds itself in the awareness of individuals who have discovered the inner kingdom, the domain of Spirit and its guidance. The spirit of inner law proceeds from Spirit and is the source of freedom of conscience and freedom of will; "For you shall be free indeed!"[9] Jesus did not say learn the truth, he said know the truth!

There is no larger guilt trip laid on our society by the present-day Christian Church than that placed on persons who have experienced divorce. Few institutional churches offer a safe haven. The basic religious problem of divorce in contemporary Christianity stems from the words attributed to Jesus in Matthew 19 and Luke 16, stating that man must not divide what god has joined and whoever marries a divorced woman or man commits adultery. This follows also in the Roman Catholic view of marriage as a sacrament. This paradigm at times serves to preserve the marriage contract but is unsupportable when continuing a marriage is a mistake.

Some marriages are designed to graduate from. One or both of the partners may have learned the lessons their marriage was designed to teach. I am reminded of a woman who became divorced because of an abusive relationship and then married a man of similar religious convictions as her own. The second marriage could have worked well for them except they were both biblical literalists and each time they confronted the words about divorce in the gospels, she inevitably suffered a nervous breakdown from the turmoil and tension created in their interpretation of that passage. She had frequent episodes of this conflict and invariably ended up in the mental ward of a local hospital. She perceived herself as an adulterer and nothing could dissuade her from viewing herself as under the judgment of god.

When are we going to be able to discover the lesson that if a religious belief is crippling us, Spirit is trying to teach us to let go of it, rather than make debilitating attempts to conform to it. Again, Jesus did not say learn the truth, he said know the truth!

This is the record of a spiritual journey. It is the story of personal experience in the development of my awareness from ego's outer material

---

[9] John 8:36

world to knowledge of a life imbedded in spirit, a passage in awareness or consciousness from personal self to Impersonal Self.

To readers who may be deeply ingrained in religion I can only offer the advice of a friend and pastor, Edward D. Angell, who, as I left a very conservative college to attend a more liberal graduate school of theology, offered me this advice: "You will be exposed to many new ideas, but don't worry about it; if you keep your mind focused on trusting god, anything you lose will be worth losing and whatever is worth keeping, you will never lose". At the time I had no inkling that a very similar statement would one day become the exact foundation of a very helpful metaphysical text in regard to experiencing the peace of god.

Nothing real can be threatened
Nothing unreal exists.
Therein lies the peace of God.[10]

By implication, if something can be threatened, it can not be real.

It is notable that the phrase 'Followers of the Way' is an expression descriptive of many on the spiritual path. This accolade, at minimum, applies to philosophical Taoism and the earliest followers of the Jesus Movement. The Way, or Tao, is the path of Spirit and if we understand Jesus as a role-model or Way-Shower, then this perception of him falls into the context of the working of that Way. The Chinese word Tao, much like the English word Way, seems to function both as a noun and as a verb. It can be understood as means or as path. The Tao as demonstrated by Jesus was the mystical experience of the inner sovereignty of god.

Unfortunately, it did not take long for some in the early Jesus Movement to ignore his teachings about the nature of god and replace them with their own simplistic messianic agenda. At the time of Jesus, there were expectations for a Deliverer from god who would set up a worldwide political and religious kingdom, over which Israel would rule.

Because of Jesus' untimely death, the messianic hopes that some in the Jesus Movement held for god's intervention into the world were deferred or postponed, and converted into beliefs about his imminent second coming as a belated Messiah.

The fact that kings and emperors were given absolute authority over life and death helped create a world of such messianic expectation. It followed naturally from this particular political awareness that god could be no less authoritative over the people than their own rulers were. Unfortunately, rulers were often despots and at times even insane, i.e. the Roman Emperors Caligula and Nero.

---

[10] A Course in Miracles, Introduction

It was not that unusual for indefensible concepts of god to follow this kind of leading. It has only been with the relative success of modern day democracies that people have developed the personal freedom to question these terrible and untenable autocratic pictures of god.

Many early Jewish members of the Jesus movement did not perceive Jesus as one who was simply trying to communicate the true nature of god. The context of Jewish heritage interpreted and understood his crucifixion and death as some part of god's divine political plan. In their need to explain the death of Jesus, there were those who formed an amalgam of the Jewish tradition of blood sacrifice with the crucifixion.

The sacrificial system of Judaism, which included the legalized concept that there could be no remission of sin without the shedding of blood, became incorporated as an explanation of the death of Jesus. The crucifixion of Jesus was interpreted as a fulfillment of prophecy by these legalists, linking Jesus to Jewish ritual sacrifice. In this stringent, Jewish based orthodoxy, the death of Jesus and god's supposed need for sacrifice, come together in this mechanistic theological framework as one and the same.

"Why did god have the need to require Jesus' death?" or to put it more bluntly, "Why did god need to have Jesus killed?" are questions that are unanswered by a sacrificial paradigm. Some theories suggest substitution: the idea that we are supposed to die but Jesus took our place. Older theories of sacrifice were simply payment to god for favor. Is god really so angry it wants to kill us, or is god so pliable that it can be bribed? Belief that without shedding blood there is no redemption from sin, is simply not true.

I can understand how a primitive society, in an occupied territory of the Roman Empire with its legions, could focus on a political Messiah and interpret the tragic death of Jesus in the way that many of them did. But how can the church today still base its institutional life on the premise that Jesus died for our sins as a human sacrifice? The Vikings practiced human sacrifice to the god Thor. Is Jesus' sacrifice a substitute for multiple pagan sacrifices? Do we still believe in a god like Thor?

If this kind of supposedly Christian theology is valid, then Jesus' teaching of the nature of god as Love is made a mockery. God is intrinsic to the world and not an interventionist! An interventionist god denies the reality of god's presence in the here and now! We have made of god what some have called the 'ultimate extraterrestrial'. C. S. Lewis said, in the book "Shadowlands", "If god controls then god is a vivisectionist".

Religion is a system of supposed or assumed beliefs. Spirituality is a knowing inner awareness of the Real. We behave according to our belief systems. It is our concepts and ideas that separate people. If we look at the heart and the experience of love, we will discover a much larger family than we are now able to recognize.

To a sinner healed by grace, "God be merciful to me a sinner" speaks of a world condemned already. Guilt is already rampant. It does not come from god, it is inherent in our sense of separation. We are not sinful but simply mistaken in the nature of our source. We come from the energy of holiness and love, but we may not yet be in touch with that fact.

Traditional Christianity is cursed with the belief that the majority of the world's people are going to hell because they do not accept its religious dogmas. We are taught that we have been abandoned by an angry god and should fear his wrath. Thus, we believe we will be punished as errant children and enemies of god. This results in a need for god's pacification; for we believe in a god of wrath and not a god of love. We have not yet heard Jesus' teaching that god is Love.

Karen Armstrong, an author of several excellent books on Biblical material, and a former nun, states "I had to leave the God I knew who dragged around with him the rags of my own past life with all its mistakes and misconceptions before I could really find him again. I had created this 'God' in my own image and likeness and in the likeness of a mistaken system. Now I had to let him go so he could become himself for me. If I wanted to find him I had to lose him first; this is – and I should have known it – a law of the spiritual life."[11]

If we want to find the real, we must undo the unreal! She tells a heartfelt story in her two books dealing with leaving the convent and then adjusting to life as a secular person. Her story reminds me of my own experience of backsliding to grace. "Straight is the gate and narrow is the way and few there be who find it." Some of her thoughts on religion: "The Church says that the way is obedience to religious vows. Kill the body, kill the mind, kill the heart for only the dead find god. Spirit says provide for the body, challenge the mind, open the heart, find life and find god."

My college pastor Edward D. Angell said repeatedly, "There is no pain like the pain of a new idea." This is true for people coming from fear, but in the context of love a new idea may be the 'aha' of confirmation.

God is not found in our concepts. God is found in our hearts. The difficulty is that our belief systems often act as barriers to the experience of the heart. The pain of a new idea is most often the pain of a bruised ego, for we can believe that our ideas and concepts represent who we are. Thoughts are things and they can be a revelation about the hidden treasure within or can be a wall blocking the awareness of its presence. The reality of Love is

---

[11] Beginning the World, Karen Armstrong—page 122

not an idea. It is an experience of the heart, knowing that there is no boundary between us and others or god and us.

When at the level of the intellect harmful concepts are confronted, this circumstance is often judged by the ego as an attack, for we may believe that what we think is what we really are. While it is true that our thinking will reflect what we have experienced as our reality, the real Self that is god extension is far greater than our thoughts or concepts about it.

The head will never understand the heart, for the meaning of Love is far beyond definition. It is much more important to *be* real than to *do* clever.

It is perhaps impossible to criticize what appears to be a harmful concept without engaging the ego's defense mechanisms. A child may be playing with a butcher knife, but if they are holding it by the blade, one can not safely yank it out of their hand. Perhaps a solution is to offer a toy, which will be much more appealing or compelling so that they will drop the knife to pick up the greater prize.

Jesus' comment on such a situation had to do with new wine in old wineskins. A new idea may first demand a new paradigm. I am slowly beginning to recognize that in order to suggest to a fundamentalist that god did not write the bible, one must consider that their paradigm about a personality type god must first shift, before the possibility of an historical, critical approach to the scriptures will be accepted. The paradigm about the nature of god must shift before a new concept about 'god's word' can be accommodated. The Bible is multiple layered material from many different sources with differing insights and opinions. A century or two from now, with a new paradigm of god, people may be ready for this new idea.

Walt Whitman comments, "We consider Bibles and religions divine – I cannot say they are not divine, I say they have all grown out of you, and may grow out of you still. It is not they who give you life; it is you who give them life."

A Sanskrit saying teaches: God sleeps in the minerals, Awakens in the plants, Walks in the animals, And thinks in you! There is no reality where god is not. God is not in the illusions; they are our own. God is Presence; god is not a person, *let alone three persons.*

Soap opera consciousness demonstrates outer dependency. We can own causality or we can dissipate it into an external with statements like "You did it to me". We can give our power to external authority as cause, such as to parents who won't let go, relationships that demand conformity and to religion, in such things as the power given by fundamentalists to the Bible. We give our center away and lose the personal power of the 'I am' within.

Personal power is not from separated ego, it is from an experience of holistic Unity. It values cooperation over competition. Only we can overcome separation, by changing the meanings and beliefs we ourselves project upon our world. It is a sickness of our fractured lives when we lose wholeness, and in doing so the awareness of our holiness as well.

Understand god? Hell no! God is an awesome mystery far beyond our capacity to comprehend or define. Experience god? Absolutely! We can know awareness that god, the source of the universe, knows us, and cares. When god finds its being in us, we find our being in god. There is nothing to acquire in the spiritual life, for there is nothing to acquire it. The real Self already is our spiritual life and the ego self has no capacity to add All-That-Is to the nothingness of its dream.

Logos is the energy source, but appearance is a result of our judgment. Appearance alone, is a false and mistaken world. Spirit is the Source of the real world. As in the Legend, Adam named the creation and then ate of the knowledge of good *and* evil. A world of fear, death and violence is the result of the meaning we have given it. The Buddha found that which had never been possessed and has never been lost. The Tao stands alone and does not change.

When I was a fundamentalist I used to think that I knew god; but over the years god consistently, greatly exceeded my expectations and I was often forced to forgo my limited concepts. Religion has to do with form, spirituality with content. Devotion to god is not a solitary withdrawal to focus on a distant other. It is the awareness of god as the underlying reality of all that appears to be. Understand the no-*thing*-ness of god. The whole contains the part but the part also contains the whole. As a piece of a laser plate contains the full picture, the dewdrop does absorb the ocean. God does not make the world we see, we do.

The 'better way' is a subtle thing; part of the dilemma we face is that cultural Christianity is based on Paul's conversion experience; not upon what Jesus taught. Paul had valid insights into his own conversion but he had little if any exposure to the teachings of Jesus. As a result his brand of Christianity was based upon both his legitimate insights and his historical need to connect with Jewish traditions.

Roberto Assagioli wrote in the context of transpersonal psychology about experience of the Superconscious. In his book "Friendship with god" Neil Donald Walsh assumes a voice for god and states, "The Supraconscious is the name given to the level of experience reached when the superconscious, conscious and subconscious, are all rolled into one – and then transcended. This is a place above thought. It is your true state of being, and this true state is who you really are. It is unperturbed, unmoved, unaffected by your thoughts. Thought is not first cause. True Being is."[12] Thomas Merton, a contemplative of our own generation, taught that god is in the world in Solitude. In our silence we discover we too are that same Solitude. Turning within is not isolation and contraction when it is expansion and connection with All-That-Is.

Blessed are the pure in heart, they shall see god; not eventually but actually; when we realize purity in heart we will learn to see with the heart and become of transparent character without judgment. We need not bodily die in order to discover that Spirit returns to the god who gave it.

It puzzles me to hear people speak of the peace of god and then teach about the wrath of god indicating that their 'god' is not at peace. It is patently obvious that if god is able to give its peace to us, god must first possess it. We must make the connection between the peace that god has, and the peace that god is supposed to give. The vision looks to the peaceable kingdom. The lion and the lamb led together by the innocence of a child. This is a greater and vastly different meaning of the peace of god.

A symbolic Trinity may be helpful, but it is time we lay aside a literal concept of three gods. Even parts of the early church tried to do this with a sense of triunity. On the other hand, the argument that the Holy Spirit proceeded from the Father *and* the Son, divided god artificially. The One Force and Intelligence of the universe extends as the real world, and is the true Sonship. God and Sonship are identified with and identical to the underlying content behind the appearance of all form. Perceiving form as having a unique reality of and by itself is the starting place of illusion. The symbol of the Trinity is delusional, for to see Jesus as a unique son is to miss the point. The man Jesus died 2000 years ago; it is the Christ as the Holy Spirit, which is intrinsic to his and our reality. To believe Jesus is god is to inescapably deny god as Spirit. If Jesus is god as a distinct person, then it follows god must be a person (object) as well.

The Jewish religion taught that there is no remission of sin without the shedding of blood. The Bible says things that are true and things that are not true. Blood atonement seems to be one of the untruths preserved by the religious tradition of biblical infallibility. Why did Jesus die?

Jesus may have died because of so-called human sinfulness and was willing to die for his message; but Jesus did not die for our sins. "If god could require the death of this good man; then what might god require of us? This awareness has led many people to be bitterly fearful of god."[13] The bible calls god a jealous god. Why should god be jealous, of what, of

---

[12] Friendship With God, Neil Donald Walsh—page 245
[13] A Course in Miracles: Text—page 32

whom? Is god not All-That-Is? What other gods could be placed above this god?

The narratives we now have in the gospels about the death of Jesus and the events of the week prior to the crucifixion, are in many cases based more on details of Jewish prophetic expectation than actual history. The upper room meal, with Jesus and the disciples gathered together, was most likely a celebration of god's inner reign with emphasis on the joy of *koinonia,* translated as fellowship or communion.

Certainly the upper room meal was not a memorial service recalling Jesus' death, for he was still with them. The familiar benediction referring to the fellowship or communion of the Holy Spirit comes much closer to the mark. "May the grace of our Lord Jesus Christ, the love of god, the Father, and the fellowship (*koinonia*) of his Holy Spirit be with you all."[14]

Where is the communion in the communion service? "This is my body." In Jesus' prayer of expectancy in John 14 he expressed "That they may be one as we are one". This statement offers a better explanation of the symbolic meaning of the celebration of the Last Supper of Jesus with his disciples. With the words "This is my body", he took the one loaf and distributed it to all present. The bread did not become the body of Jesus. Jesus' life is to be understood as the bread we eat. *All* were instructed to eat of this symbol of oneness. It would be a most accurate symbol to suggest that the bread of his spirit was going to be made from the oneness of all of us. When he later said, "receive the Holy Spirit" this was a direct application of his prayer that all would be one. Jesus in his distribution of the bread and cup was demonstrating the oneness that we all are and the consciousness of the oneness that shall return to us.

Rather than the traditional symbolism of the conversion of bread and wine into his body and blood it is more accurate to understand this meal as a symbol that his work was to be shared by all. The symbol was a conversion of his body and blood (his life and work) into bread and wine, the sustenance of our lives and now understood as our food and drink.

He used his life as a metaphor of the bread that sustains us in our life and work. It was not the miracle of wine and bread into body and blood but the other way around. We are all to become one body and life. Perhaps this is the next leap in the divine plan of evolution visualized by de Chardin and others. The coming of the noosphere predicted by Teilhard de Chardin is an ultimate evolutionary goal of global humanity. Humanity will be as one consciousness, One Mind. (mind – *nous*). Communion (koinonia) with god has no proper symbol other than the fellowship (koinonia) of the Sonship.

---

[14] II Cor. 13:14

As referenced by Elia Wise in her book "Letter to Earth", we are already joined in the One Mind. We are not yet fully conscious of that fact.

Jesus in his Christed ministry, demonstrated in the world the Christ consciousness or Holy Spirit that in time would become the consciousness of global humanity. In consciousness we are now becoming truly one world. It is resurrection and not crucifixion that accomplishes atonement.

Apparent disasters such as September 11, 2001 strip the illusion of separation from our eyes and open us to the awareness that we are the one that Jesus prayed we would become. The bread and wine do not symbolize his death but our life. When we eat the bread and wine of the Christ Life, we understand the symbolism of the oneness of Christ as the global body.

This is not the formation of a world religion or just another attempt in devising an illusion. It is rather the awareness that we are all participating in the same Mind and the wholeness of the same Spirit. The Holy Spirit has become the Whole.

One needs to remember that Paul's writings predate the gospel records. It is also important to note that the only time Paul ever refers to something Jesus may have actually said was in reference to the so called words of institution, "Eat this bread and drink this cup in remembrance of me."

In their rituals many churches place great emphasis on what is now called the Lord's Supper, Mass, Eucharist or Holy Communion. Some denominations observe this symbolic meal every day, others every Sunday, and others on a quarterly or occasional basis. Some refer to it as a sacrament, which means that observance carries sanctifying grace, a belief that merely eating assists one in becoming holy. Very few actually consume a fellowship meal, for the symbology is now sacrifice and blood atonement, rather than fellowship or communion. (*koinonia*)

Real communion is found in the presence of Spirit, when Spirit bears witness with our spirit and we come to know that Spirit is One. To be in Spirit, and to worship in Spirit, is not a question of proper form or correct ritual. Real *koinonia* with Spirit demands the silence of the personal self so that the transcendental or Impersonal Self may make its presence known.

For many, if not most, in the church today, the service called Communion is simply an attempt either to replicate, or to memorialize, the supposed substitutionary sacrifice of Jesus for the world's sins. Never mind the contradictions of replication, for those who claim Jesus performed the supposed sacrifice also claim to believe he did so once for all time.

There is a sacramental belief that the material objects of the communion meal have been endowed with transformational authority and carry the capacity to instill grace and forgiveness. This sacramental power has also been accompanied by the fear of damnation for those who eat or drink in an unworthy manner. The significance has been lost that the *koinonia* of the communion service is understood as fellowship, not sacrifice. I suppose that one positive consequence of current mythology about the communion service is that in ancient religion it was god who drank the blood of human sacrifice, whereas, it is we who now symbolically drink the blood of god.

In the Upper Room memorial the symbolic bread and wine represented the real presence of the universal Christ. They are the 'I am' statements translated into form. "Unless you eat the flesh of the Son of Man and drink his blood you have no life in you."[15] These are words referring to a symbolic level of spirit. Take my Spirit as your Spirit.

This whole gospel puzzle is complicated by the fact that there was a time lapse of from twenty to sixty years between the events of the gospels, and the recorded form in which they now appear. The material, as oral tradition, went through the telling of many editors, each of whom had opportunity to revise, add, delete and interpret ideas and events according to their own worldview. This situation presents a fundamental problem in reading the gospel accounts. Which are teachings *of* Jesus and which are teachings *about* Jesus? In the biblical record, what is the religion *of* Jesus and what is the religion *about* Jesus?

The prophet Micah had asked the profound rhetorical question centuries before, "Does god require burnt offerings, the blood of thousands of rams, ten thousand rivers of oil, or the sacrifice of my firstborn, the fruit of my body for the sin of my soul?" His answer to that question was that blood sacrifice plays no role in the relationship between god and god's people. Rather, "What does god require? To do justly, to love mercy, and to walk in humility with your god."[16]

It is amazing to me that the powerful and sublime words of Micah carried no weight at all in the developing theology of the western or Roman part of the early church: the part which survived politically. Perhaps politics, in the structure of the Roman Empire that demanded sacrifice to the Emperor, favored imperial authority and rejected individual expression.

This concept of human blood sacrifice, a major fault inherent in traditional Christianity, is based on the assumption that Jesus died for our sins. The theory that Jesus was a required blood sacrifice for our sins substitutes the notion that something happening outside one's own experience has become central to the gospel, rather than the need for inner transformation. This phenomenon is a prime example of religious teachings *about* Jesus overshadowing the teachings *of* Jesus, who emphasized the

---

[15] John 6:53
[16] Micah 6:6-8

internal happening of new birth, "You must be born again." It is unfortunate that with the advance of time the Christian church became a force for a religion about Jesus, rather than emphasizing the teachings of Jesus.

The developing political church, indeed, makes the natural exposition of the words 'born again' refer not to an internal process of growth and awareness springing forth to new life, but rather, to the sanctioned possession of a legalistic birth certificate. If we are willing to accept the blood sacrifice we will receive the 'new birth' certificate. The new birth is seen and understood as a legalized and externalized occurrence. "He paid it all", is a phrase that makes an external Jesus rather than internal Spirit the means of our unfolding awareness.

Most traditional Christians equate being born again with being saved. In our culture, being saved is an outside event. God changes the books. New birth is an internal experience. Those who believe they have been saved, for the most part don't seem to have a clue as to the real meaning of being born again (new birth or enlightenment).

The message has now become *saved* rather than *healed*. The Greek word root *sozo*, to make well, is translated as salvation but can be rendered into English either as healed or saved. The preferred usage *healed* suggests inner change. The traditional rendering in translations of the New Testament has become predominantly *saved*, suggesting being rescued, or change of outer circumstance. With this interpretation, salvation is now understood as an external legalized event rather than an internal experiential one; we are rescued not healed. Spiritual birth is like human birth, an entry into new life. It is also the metamorphosis[17] into a new being, like transforming the chrysalis of a cocoon into a 'butterfly' of Spirit.

Beyond Christianity – To the Christ

Moving beyond Christianity, to the Christ/Spirit, is accomplished in part, by developing an awareness of the limitations of traditional Christianity's religion *about* Jesus compared to the fullness of Jesus' own teaching about the kingdom of god within us all. Jesus' teaching about the inner kingdom and the Father within, are in many ways echoed in Paul's references to the universal Christ/Spirit.

Christ is a term that refers to having been anointed. Anointing is often seen as something that comes to one from outside, but the actual anointing of god comes from within. "The Spirit bears witness with our spirit that we are the children of god."[18] The people of Jesus' day were looking for an

---

[17] Romans 12:2
[18] Romans 8:16

externally 'Anointed', military, political Messiah. Jesus attempted to redirect their search to the discovery of an inner kingdom and inner anointing. In Colossians, Paul refers to the great mystery hidden from many, now made known, which is Christ in you, the hope of glory.[19] The universal Christ/Spirit is not properly understood as Jesus within.

Many, by tradition, use the words Christ and Jesus interchangeably because the church has taught that Jesus was the expected Messiah. For reasons of clarity I prefer to use the name Jesus to refer to the historical teacher and the term Christ or Christ/Spirit to point to the internal and universal Spirit of god that anoints and energizes all beings, and all things. Jesus taught and demonstrated this inner Christ/Spirit. His reference was not only to the Father within, but also to Son of Man, as well as son of god. This awareness is the *Keys to the Kingdom*.

It needs to be understood that there are those who may miss the letter of the name and still possess the spirit of the same. One can possess the spirit of the Christ and still refer to it as Jesus within; or for that matter, Krishna or Buddha within. I may fault such about their choice of words, but I would be amiss to question their spirituality because they choose to speak traditional words, or words of a different tradition. It is also understood that there are those who, although they may experience little religious conflict with orthodoxy, and seem to have no apparent reason to challenge tradition, nevertheless are still able to center their lives on love and possess a deep sense of spiritual unity. There is a danger in judging others simply on their intellectual and theological framework, a cursory judgment of words and surface ideas. In the presence of Love, regardless of outer appearance, love will still be effective even in spite of what I might judge as inept vocabulary.

The effect of divine law still remains; we will reap what we sow and as we have sown. It is not that we simply reflect god in our lives (as if god were outside), it is that god is the very light of our life and we are become the light of the world. The light does not have to be ignited, but the bushel that covers it must be removed. The obstruction not only prevents the light from shining; it also obscures our awareness that we are that light itself.

The Christ of god was within Jesus, or rather, was recognized by Jesus as the quintessence of his own being. The Christ of god in us is of identical essence; and is properly understood in the expression of god living as us, and will if we allow, be recognized as such by us. There is no way that the personal self of Jesus can be realistically understood to be the Impersonal Self, or Christ/Spirit, living in and through us all.

---

[19] Colossians 1: 26,27

In worshipping Jesus as god, the church dissipated the meaning of the Christ. In its Trinitarian theology, the church cast out any hope that we could replicate in our lives what Jesus accomplished in his. There is an imperative need on our part to move beyond the traditions of the church and discover a living faith by *means* of the inner presence of god's Christ/Spirit. This is the Way. This is the Tao. We need to move beyond Christianity to the Christ. Christhood or Buddhahood cannot be attained. It can only be recognized as what we already are in truth.

It cannot be over-emphasized that, *that which we already are, is not something to be accomplished.* We cannot achieve what one already has or is; we must merely and simply, recognize and realize, in order to function from that Reality. In real healing we do not create or bring about anything, we merely develop the awareness of the pure being we already are. We remove the attitudes and beliefs that block the inner awareness of god's vision of our true being.

If we think that salvation is to be attained, or worse yet, depends on something outside, such as 'Jesus saves', then we already have erected a block or barrier to understanding who and what we are. There is no need for a mediator to be involved in who we already are. How can there be special beings that save, and ordinary beings that need to be saved, when the One Reality of the entire universe is the Same?

May we come to the point where we realize that even a concept of Jesus as Savior can be a stumbling block. The germane, allegorical expression of Buddhist teachers is, "If you meet the Buddha on the road, kill him." The Buddha is never Other; it is always and only one's own true Self. If you meet Jesus as an 'external savior', kill that concept, for your true savior is your experience of the Christ of god within.

We need not struggle *to know reality*, but we may seem (to ourselves) to struggle in an effort *to undo the unreality* we have labored so hard to construct and accomplish. The blocks we have erected seem so real and so permanent precisely because we are the ones who have constructed them. We are, in effect, always wading through our own garbage. Because we are conditioned by our materiality to seek reality in outer form, it is in the outer that we think we will find our own Christ/Spirit nature. We could not be further from the truth. We undo the unreal by letting go the struggle, letting go the blocks, and letting go the past. This is the real nature of forgiveness. We are not in a struggle to forgive what is real, but to undo what is unreal. *True forgiveness or undoing, is the awareness that there is in reality nothing to forgive.*

Jesus said, "My yoke is easy and my burden is light."[20] That is a spiritual truth; it is religion that makes the yoke hard and the burden heavy. The English word yoke has root in the Sanskrit word yoga, which carries the meaning of 'union'. The yoke of Jesus was focus on the enlightened awareness of oneness with god. When our yoke or focus is our awareness of being one with god, then it naturally follows that we are coming from a place of peace and joy and there is no question that we will experience our burden as 'light'. It is not the world's weary yoke or heavy burden we are experiencing when we take this advice; it is our own inner strength that god is expressing through us. "Come unto me all ye that are weary and heavy laden and I will give you rest. Take my yoke upon you, and learn of me for I am gentle and humble of heart, and you will find rest for your souls." AMEN!

The traditional church, as with most religion, thinks in watertight compartments. It teaches that the world, supposedly created perfect, has fallen by the means of sin and is under judgment and condemnation. The Creator has become prosecutor/judge; humankind, as a result of Adam's fall, is both depraved and condemned. In this view, Jesus, because of sin, had to die and shed blood for man's redemption. He became a human sacrifice to meet the needs of god.

In a simplistic theology about Jesus as 'The Lamb of God' who takes away the sins of the world, the question still remains unanswered: "What kind of god needs this blood sacrifice?" The answer: None!

I believe it is an act of supreme arrogance to presume that we have been able to destroy the creation of god by our 'so-called' sins. They do not alienate the god/Source from us. Because they cloud our perception, these 'sins' are best understood as mistakes. As these mistakes are corrected, the awareness of our oneness with god will increase proportionately.

The New Testament offers several views and religious interpretations concerning the meaning of the life of Jesus and his teachings. There is *little* doubt that the teachings of some of Jesus' religious contemporaries and editors within the Jesus Movement caused their ideas and concepts to be attributed to Jesus in the gospel records. This ascription is somewhat the opposite of plagiarism. There is also *no* doubt that after Christianity became the official Roman religion, the political structure of both empire and church had a major influence on the ideas that were preserved in the New Testament record.

One approach to the problem, "What did Jesus really say?" is proposed in the 1993 publication "The Five Gospels" a Scholars Version translation

---

[20] Matthew 11:30

(SV) linked to The Fellows of the Jesus Seminar. This translation also includes the Gospel of Thomas. The Jesus Seminar attempted to select by vote which sayings of Jesus in the gospels were most probable. In his book "Honest to Jesus" the author Robert W. Funk as spokesperson for the Jesus Seminar, sees Jesus as limited to a political and economic based prophetic ministry, primarily concerned about this world and justice. All of the 'I am' statements of Jesus are considered to be interpretations and additions by the early church.

Funk claims, "It is unthinkable, in view of the parables and aphorisms, that Jesus said many of the things he is reported to have said. He certainly did not make claims for himself. To have done so would have contradicted his fundamental disdain for arrogance and hypocrisy and run counter to his rhetorical strategies, such as the reversal of roles so common in his parables. Sayings like those we find in the fourth gospel could not have originated with Jesus."[21]

There are, I agree, many statements attributed to Jesus in the gospels that he simply did not say. However, while Funk asserts that Jesus did not make claims for himself, I believe that this does not substantiate an argument that Jesus would not make claims for the inner kingdom that he was announcing. The limitations of the Jesus Seminar are made clear in the United Methodist scholar Houston Smith's lecture, "Jesus and the World's Religions" published in the book "Jesus at 2000". Houston Smith points out that the Jesus Seminar discounted the mystical aspects of Jesus' experience from consideration and as a result, many of Jesus' authentic statements based on his mystical awareness were expunged by the Seminar.

These deletions are very much in reference to statements attributed to Jesus in the fourth gospel, such as "I am the light of the world, I am the way, the truth and the life. No one comes to the Father unless it is through me."[22] If one considers the 'I am' statements as arising from Jesus' own mystical experience, then the 'I am' statements Jesus made are his explicit directions for the discovery of an inner kingdom and are not referenced to his ego personality. I believe that there is a Way within us all, and that it is true that no one finds the Father within, except by means of discovering god's inner Presence. To limit the words "No man comes to the Father but by me", to the historical Jesus is the distortion of the spiritual faith of Jesus into a religion about him.

In regard to the words of Jesus, "I am the way, the truth and the light". Jesus did not say these words merely to apply them to himself but, rather, to

---

[21] Honest to Jesus, Robert W. Funk: pages. 162-3
[22] John 14:6

emphasize that each one must discover this truth from within their own Higher Self. I have read no more cogent words than those of Robert Conklin, who in his delightful little book "Reach for the Sun" states, "The source for such words could not have been the Great Exception but, rather, the Great Example."[23] I whole-heartedly concur. The basic problem with the doctrine of incarnation is that we have particularized it to refer only to the personhood of Jesus of Nazareth. We have failed to understand that the Spirit Jesus manifested in his life, he knew would inevitably unfold in us.

I have no argument with the divinity of Jesus; but I do believe that what was true for him also holds true for the rest of us; and I believe this is what he tried to teach. Jesus was son of god and so are we! The reality of Jesus was not his space/time personality but his inner oneness with the father, which he claimed as a reality for us all. By placing Jesus on a separated pedestal we have eliminated him as a pattern for our own lives.

Any *form* of god embodied in rituals of worship is counterproductive. God as Spirit cannot be known in materiality. God conceived as an object or 'outside other' defeats the inner opportunity of experiencing the overwhelming sense of spiritual oneness. To move from liturgy to Spirit, from isolation to oneness is what the transformative experience of new birth is all about. Nirvana, as the Sages of the East call the encounter of spiritual birth, is experiential knowledge of the One Self. Enlightenment, or new birth, is the awareness of the One Life and recognizes that our true Self has its source in the unity of Spirit. Our *real* life and the life of Spirit are one and the same. The Spirit is expressing as us. An experience of enlightenment is not just to claim new birth but also to realize it (*make it real*). Disease is cured not by naming the medicine but by taking it. The true laws of god are not written on paper but on the heart. Our true being is not just *in* god; it is also *of* god.

Lao Tzu, legendary founder of Taoism, is the credited author of the "Tao Te Ching" (Classic Words of Way and Virtue). The opening assertion of his eighty-one short sections is "The Tao that can be told is not the eternal Tao". There is a restatement of this principle by the sage in Section 56, which correctly understood provides insight into the basic problem of conveying the ineffable within the confines of language. "He who knows does not speak, He who speaks does not know" or "He who knows cannot say. He who says cannot know." An expanded rendering would read, "He who knows (the Tao) does not (care to) speak (about it), He who is (ever ready to) speak (about it) does not know (it)."[24] Those who claim to believe

---

[23] Reach For the Sun—Section: 5
[24] Translation—James Legge

say it. Those who attain to experience have no need to say it as they have moved beyond concerns and beliefs.

Underlying Spirit is the energy that is the foundation of the universe. The universe responds to intent and event. The relationship of Spirit and universe is avowed in the words immanence and transcendence. God as transcendent, wholly other is impossible to be labeled; it energizes the world by immanent Spirit and that Spirit is variously called Krishna, Christ, Logos, Buddha, Holy Spirit, Way, Brahman or Tao.

Healing action does not try to know the will of god as a separate ego in order to claim authority to do that will. It is understood best in the Chinese expression *wei wu wei* (do not do) doing by not doing, *allowing* the Will of Spirit by being centered in it, an easy yoke and effortless accomplishment. Both intent and attitude are involved in will: Will as purposive or active (I want or intend), and Will as allowing or passive (I permit or am open to). Our intent needs be, to allow. To desire to *know* the will of god is an ego power trip; i.e. *show me* your will so *I* can do *it*, or so *I* can tell others what *it* is. What is required is a simple willingness to allow Spirit to unfold according to its good purpose, *whether we understand it or not*. We need not push the river.

In an experience he called "The Disposable Church", Hugh Prather used as a spiritual exercise the children's ditty, "Row, Row, Row, your boat…". Reflecting on the words "gently down the stream", "merrily, merrily", and "Life is but a dream", one can perceive a profound parable that speaks to our condition, even though we seldom have recognized these words as such. One can also imagine our usual experience as expressed in a parody, "Push, Push, Push your load, roughly up the slot. Grumpily, Gruffly, Grouchily, Fearfully; this is all we've got."

The limits of verbal expression make it necessary to 'point toward', rather than explain Spirit. We are compelled to do this, in spite of the discernible contradictions of language. Paradox in any language is the name of the game. "He who seeks to save his life shall lose it, He who is willing to lose his life shall save it."[25] Jesus taught that god is Spirit, notwithstanding that Spirit is impossible to define or categorize.

God as Reality is sometimes understood as the Ground of Being, rather than Being Itself. Being is considered by some to imply objective substance, whereas 'ground of being' does not. The term 'godhead', the essential nature of god regarded abstractly, is a similar attempt to deal with the same problem. God is to be understood as Principle and not as an encapsulated source.

---

[25] Luke 17:33

God is Love as essence but there is technically no objective god that loves, and it can confuse our awareness of the Law of One, when we say objectively that god loves. God is both principle and love, but god expresses principle and love *as* us and not *apart* from or *toward* us. God as principle is not understood as simply detached natural law without awareness – god is principle, as Source, Love and Consciousness, and so are we. The principle as Love is not apart or separate from us. God is Love and so are we. Pure Being is our own Essence. What god is – is our reality as well.

God is Truth, but having no defined substance, god has no need to defend or protect any concept of objectified truth. Truth and the Real have no need or ability to judge or condemn error; in fact one could argue accurately, that Truth doesn't even know that error exists. Error, as with darkness and cold, is not negative energy in competition with truth, light and heat; but rather is simply an assertion of lack or absence of energy. Error as an absence does not, in itself, even exist. This foregoing statement can, of course, only be made at the level of the Absolute. This is a better understanding of the phrase, "God is too pure to behold evil"[26] for evil has no reality for god. God is the only Presence, the only Power, the only Knowing.

Evil does not exist as a dualistic power in opposition to the One Source. What we call sin is an inversion of god-energy or simply the absence of love. But Love cannot be absent, so sin becomes a mistaken illusion of our own awareness. Sin as a mistake can be corrected by letting it go in forgiveness, as an awareness of love's presence.

The consequences of an unbalanced checkbook can lead to suffering because of an over-drawn account, but the principles of mathematics are not attacked or offended as a result; least of all, does the principle hold any malice toward the one making the error. Mathematical principle only waits for the error to be corrected in order for an accurate balance to be restored. An unbalanced checkbook does not judge or condemn the one making the mathematical error. It only waits for the error to be corrected.

The mystery which is god, stated as either being or non-being perhaps can be approached in the way a physicist faces the dilemma of stating the nature of light. Light energy is understood as wave or particle depending on the viewpoint of the observer. So too, it may be that the nature of god will be understood, depending on our observation point, as principle or as pure being, neither, or both.

---

[26] Habakkuk 1:13

There is, by nature of our space/time awareness, a need to understand the distinction between the absolute level of values (their reality) and the hierarchy of values (their application). One can rightly perceive god as love and god as truth. At the absolute level (of god) it is understandable that these values will be given equal weight. However, to do so at the space/time level leads to inescapable confusion, for at the level of material or temporal application they will inevitably come into conflict. If at this level truth is given equal value to love and both are considered absolutes then one must maintain the stance that telling a lie would be a 'sin' against the truth.

There will arise occasions where in order to value love, truth must be sacrificed. I have always had a profound resonance with the story of "The Diary of Anne Frank". Christian friends hid her family and other Jews in a hidden annex attached to the rear of their place of business. To do so it was necessary to lie to the Nazis who would have killed them. In fact when a traitor told the 'truth' they were apprehended and most of the annex residents found death in the Concentration camps. In this scenario it was love that told the lie and fear and greed that told the truth.

I concur with the act of love and find despicable the actions of those who told the truth. At a temporal level there is no question in my mind that love is a higher value than truth. When they come in conflict, the lower must yield to the higher. We must choose between being right and being well.

Truth is a value – but to do no harm is a greater value. The principle of love is the only absolute value that can be maintained at the temporal level. Even then, the statement to do no harm, has its own limits and pecking order. In the temporal order we are often faced with a choice between greater and lesser good, or perhaps greater or lesser evil. For instance given a situation where a maniacal gunman has indiscriminately killed several people and is threatening the lives of more, is an officer of the law justified in killing the gunman in order to prevent further bloodshed? To me, the answer is obvious, which gives rise to the question of situation ethics. In the temporal world we are faced with a myriad of such situations and some of the answers are not easily forthcoming. What is justice? Again I am reminded of the words of the prophet Micah. What does god require? To do justice, love mercy and walk in humility with god.[27]

One problem with religion is its authoritative need to speak in absolutes. Because the Bible commands us not to bear false witness, there are those

---

[27] Micah 6:8

who consider any deviation from the truth a sin against god. Perhaps there is more than meets the eye in the phrase, "Speak the truth, in love."

I have wondered in courtroom dramas, where witnesses are required to take an oath, to "Tell the truth, the whole truth and nothing but the truth" why attorneys on examination often silence a witness with the phrase, "Just answer the question." Haven't they sworn to tell the *whole* truth?

If we think we possess the truth about god, we need to be more aware of our amateur standing in the matter. We need to hold open minds, as there are yet infinite possibilities beyond our finite grasp. There are profound negative implications and limitations when we think of god in terms of an object or thing. Yet in terms of our personal, practical relationship with Source, we must understand that divine Principle is not cold, distant and separate from our own experience. Jesus, as a teacher working within the limits of culture and knowing that god was the Principle of our lives, still chose to refer to this Principle as our Father. However, the Impersonal God is not personal, as we understand another objective personality.

The Impersonal God is, as the poet Lord Tennyson said, closer than breathing, and nearer than hands and feet.[28] The Impersonal God is in direct relationship and correspondence (the act, fact, or state of agreeing or conforming) with the Impersonal Self. The personal self is an illusion and is the major block to experiencing the Impersonal Self or the kingdom of god within. To experience our correspondence with god is called enlightenment, or new birth.

In fact, our belief systems about the nature of god are at the very heart of how we experience the world. The world, not withstanding its appearance, has only the same apparent reality that we in separate bodies do. Whether we presently perceive ourselves as spiritual beings *in* the world, or material beings *of* it, we eventually must come to understand that the energy underlying material appearance is the same spiritual reality underlying us. There is but One Source of all that appears. What we really are corresponds to what god really is. As god is *no thing* so also is the real Self that is one with All-That-Is. The real Self is not an object. To paraphrase the Buddhist saying about god; the real Self is, *as subject* but *as object* the real Self is not.

Humankind has a way of taking spiritual insight and congealing it into outer ritual and form, with the hope of preserving it for future use. Like the manna in the wilderness and the bread of the Lord's Prayer, spiritual intuition is valid only as an inner experience of the now. The past and future have no place in the vision of Spirit; for Spirit is the realm of the

---

[28] The Higher Pantheism, Alfred Lord Tennyson—Stanza Six

time-less. *We need to learn how to move beyond the religion of past and future to the now of Spirit.*

We may believe we have a personal history as personal selves; but this illusion of a past is only a stumbling block to the experience of the impersonal, universal and eternal now. Yet, Spirit preserves the real creations of the Impersonal Self, even those from the apparent history of the personal self. At the level of reality, I am; at the level of illusion, there is obviously no me.

Whether Eastern or Western, American, European, African, Hindu, or Oriental, it is helpful to recognize that from illusion's viewpoint religion in any culture of the world's people, is basically discerned as an expression of ritual and form. With a primary focus on these religious structures, religion unfortunately can become a means of stultifying the Spirit. It has been said that religion is like a vaccination against spiritual growth. History demonstrates that the political, religious and ritual structures of Buddhism, Taoism, Vedanta, Judaism, Islam and Christianity are products of their own entrenched belief systems. Muslims are currently involved in a struggle with Fundamentalist leaders imposing their interpretations of The Koran as political law with civil punishment. These beliefs become dogmas that dominate and control the framework of theology and ritual, both in regard to one's perception of god and one's mode of worship. Fortunately, there are those who in undoing the tradition are enabled to find the Presence.

In a not so strange way, religion and inner spiritual awareness have the same kind of understood relationship as do sexuality and intimacy. Intimacy as a deep experience of shared oneness may or may not be linked with sexuality. Religion, comparably, at times may have no link at all to spiritual intimacy with god. Many who exploit sexuality do so from a deep need to discover and experience intimacy. They fail in the attempt to achieve this goal, because the form their sexuality takes may lack the trust, commitment and responsibility that intimacy obliges. As well, many who follow religion do so from a deep need to discover and experience spirituality. They fail in the attempt to achieve this goal, because the form their religion takes may lack the trust, commitment and responsibility that spirituality obliges. Spirituality must move beyond the structures of religion for it is at the level of Spirit that ultimate intimacy is achieved. At this level of deepest human intimacy, we know as we are known.

In sexuality, we often begin by wanting to unite with another by possessing them. They now belong to us. To possess another is to obliterate their identity and intrinsic worth. Religion has a habit of being very possessive. To love another is to know the true value of their person. To like another is to respond to personality and presence. True intimacy accepts the origin and experience of the other as equal to one's own. Spiritual Intimacy arises in the transcendental awareness that there is no personal self and no *other*. In the intimacy of oneness all boundaries dissolve and the original desire for union (*koinonia*) is fulfilled.

Spiritual awareness will bring us to a point where we are able to give up our irrefutable judgments and our unrelenting grievances, which are our strongest ties to the illusory outside world. We will then begin to learn that all of our experiences with the apparent external world are but lessons. These lessons are instructions that will help us internalize the full grasp of Spirit upon our lives. When in our relationships with others, we determine to learn from our colleagues who search with us, as well as our detractors who may be clinging tenaciously to belief systems we no longer support; we will accelerate our learning curve.

On the whole, religion teaches us to strive to become what we ought to be. Spirit understands the essential fallacy of *trying to become* what we already are. In order to be at home in/with Spirit we need only to know that, in our reality, we have never left home. When the prodigal 'came to himself'[29] there was no distance to travel and even the perceived gap was abolished when his father ran to meet him. For the Father within, there is no distance to travel.

The Principle we call Love is best perceived not as a person who loves us, but as the ground of life itself. Yet Jesus, knowing that god was Love as principle, still chose to refer to god as the Father within. I marvel at his words, "I do not say to you, that I will pray to the Father on your behalf; for the Father himself loves you."[30] To me, this is a powerful lesson in the nature of effective prayer. We do not need to try to involve an immanent god that is intrinsic to the process. True prayer like Spirit, is a non-thing and in the Silence of god, is participation in the flow of the universe. True prayer is not the doing of words; it is the intent of being, and thus becomes prayer without ceasing.

The concept of a mediator between god and man is based on belief in a god who is separated from humankind. Protestants hold Roman Catholics in disdain for relating to Mary as mediatrix but cling tenaciously in the same fashion to Jesus as mediator. Neither viewpoint perceives the accessible unitive reality of god. When we accept the principle Jesus taught as the 'kingdom of god within', *we have no need for a mediator because there exists no separation.*

---

[29] Luke 15:17
[30] John 16:26,27

As we discuss the question "Where in the world is god?" it is well that we examine the wisdom of Jesus. God is Spirit. God is the reality underlying the world of appearance. We become aware of the fact that to Jesus god is not something *other*. Jesus was aware of the fact that the world of appearance was indeed, an illusion. If there is one aspect that I take for granted regarding the life of Jesus, it is the fact that Jesus was an enlightened Mystic. He knew the nature of the reality of Spirit. He knew the illusion of the world of appearances. He understood that his own reality was identical with the reality of god. From this basis, he said, "The Father and I are one" and spoke from his inner reality when explaining to his disciples that there was in truth, only the one reality we all share.

Jesus made many *I am* statements; I am the light of the world, I am the way, the truth, and the life. What he was stating to his disciples is the simplicity that we too, really are the way, the truth, and the life. The inner spiritual reality of us all is identical and is as well the reality of god.

As a Mystic Jesus had come to the awareness that there was one central reality underlying all of the world's appearance: Spirit. Spirit is the core reality of all that appears to be. It is the most common of errors to suppose that the appearance of things is their reality. From this flawed assumption we conclude that each and every separated appearance has its own separate reality. Thus from this faulty understanding we believe we live in a world of separation, full of boundaries. This mistaken outlook forces us to miss the simplicity of the unity of Spirit. Spirit is One; in Spirit there are no boundaries and there is no separation.

When Jesus spoke of his own spiritual core reality he referenced his own being as an *I am* statement. These are best understood as simple statements meaning this is what *I* really *Am* and this is what *we* all really *Are*. This is what *god* really *Is*, without boundaries, without separation, and because there are no boundaries there is no opportunity for judgment. *In oneness what I am, we are, and god is.* Accepting this premise of Jesus' core mystical awareness, we are able to reconstruct the life of Jesus somewhat differently than the life we find in the gospel narratives.

Jesus was a man who discovered an inner truth, appropriate to all humanity and common to the total phenomenon of world appearance. His main mission was to demonstrate and teach this concept of the kingdom of god within us. The Christ was in Jesus. In the depths of Jesus' spirit there was only the one, and at that still point the Christ was one with him as it is one with us.

The religion *about* Jesus in the New Testament, the so-called apostle's creed and other church creeds are not at all what I would sense as being the main concern of Jesus' own creed.

A Jesus Creed

I believe god is Love, Light, and Spirit.
I believe that the residence of Spirit is the reality within us all.
I believe that we are One with our Source.
I believe we are the Salt of the earth and the Light of the world.
I believe that experience and knowledge of the Kingdom within,
    Will demonstrate that within us is the Way, Truth, and Life.
I believe that the inner Realm is the only Way or Means to life
    And no one will experience god's Reality except from within.
I believe the Way (Tao) is within us all.
I believe that we are a unity of energy and spirit.
I believe that we are one with god and one with each other.
I believe that Love is the core of god, the universe and of us all.
I believe that the Christ of god is one with me, one with us all
    And one with the reality of universe.

From this perspective, stories of a miraculous birth and the apparent tragedy of Holy Week as literal accounts do not stand on their own merit.

There is no need to conclude that as a teacher of mystical truth the life of Jesus began any differently than any of our own lives. We may simply assume that he had a father and mother like us all. We also may come to an understanding that the ending of his life was not drastically different from the death of other prophets and sages with a radical message of inner peace.

In our own generation we have experienced the senseless mission of national and international terrorism. Is our military prowess and our huge defense budget just a contemporary form of Messianic hope? Can we really hope to deal with events like the destruction of the World Trade Center from a spirit of anger and the outworn ethic of an eye for an eye and a tooth for a tooth? To follow this law in response to others, is to end up with a blinded society, gumming its way through life.

It is evident from the prevalent religious view of Jesus day, that there were many people seeking to discover a militaristic messiah who would meet their needs by throwing off the tyrannical yoke of Rome. The followers of Jesus break down into two basic factions, those who sought to understand his teaching, and those who hoped to see him as a Messianic force needed for the overthrow of the excruciating conditions of their world. Two basic ideologies came to the fore as a result: one emphasizing the teachings of Jesus; the other, a religion about Jesus.

In the early church these two theological perspectives caused an historic split between those who tried to understand the teachings of Jesus and those who perceived him as fulfilling the role of Messiah, as religious figurehead and sacrifice. One 'teachings' group later characterized as heretical were the Gnostics, responsible for the Gospel of Thomas and in great part for the Gospel of John. The messianic group became the religious and political leaders of the Western church, suppressing Gnostic teachings and giving support to the Roman Empire.

Those who looked for a messiah and perceived Jesus as fulfilling that need were disheartened and disillusioned by his untimely death. This religious group scrambled for an interpretation based upon Jewish scriptures that would explain to them the reason for their Messiah's death. As a result, they perceived the death of Jesus as connected to the Jewish sacrificial system, the shedding of his blood for the remission of sin. They saw their messianic hopes as simply deferred to an impending second coming at which time the Messiah would finally fulfill their political expectations.

An offering made in the Jewish sacrificial system was to be without spot or blemish; and the religious opinion of human personality at that time held that it was deeply blemished by the theological concept of original sin through Adam. Jesus as an ordinary man could not have met the qualifications for a completely perfect offering and thus fulfill a sacrifice for the sins of humankind. Speculation suggested that Jesus did not come into the world in the same way as the rest of us. He had to be free of Adam's transgression. Biblical attribution interpreted his freedom from sin and the resulting perfect sacrifice, in two basic ways: he had no earthly father in Joseph and thus was virgin born; and his mother Mary was immaculately conceived by her mother Anne. Thus, Jesus was the perfect sacrifice because he had no taint of original sin from either his mother or father.

The New Testament mythology of the beginnings of Jesus' life and his death are founded deeply upon interpretation of the Jewish Old Testament. These after the fact prophecies were considered to be actual events.

The stories of Passion Week do not fit well with an understanding of Jesus as someone who knew that he was one with the Heavenly Father and the Holy Spirit. The passion prayer regarding the cup being passed, in the garden of Gethsemane, is most certainly a dialogue between two separated entities, a Father distinct from His Son. The narratives of Passion Week: trials before Pilate and Herod, the scourging and crown of thorns and the denial of Peter, speak not so much of history, but an invented cost of the supreme sacrifice Jesus was willing to make for our sins.

It is important to understand that the pagan festivals of the Roman World centering on the winter solstice and the spring equinox became a central part of the celebrations of the Christian year in traditions surrounding Christmas and Easter. Christmas, its gift giving, the reversal of the sun's track and the lengthening of days, is the joy of new beginning. Easter, a celebration of the rebirth of life with the Easter Bunny and Easter eggs is more closely connected to the particulars of the Vernal equinox than to the passions and crimes of Holy Week. Religious people often complain that the Easter Bunny and Santa Claus have taken over these Christian celebrations when apparently the opposite is much closer to the truth.

Stories about Jesus find a home as projections of a worldview. "Jesus Christ Superstar", a powerful musical, hinges on the struggle between the messianic expectations of Judas and the vastly different views of Jesus.

The Holy Week stories of the New Testament are attributions of events or supposed events that arise from a different age and culture. They project a Jesus based upon their individual and group beliefs, and our generation does the same. I recognize that my own viewpoint is based on a Jesus with an awareness of mystical enlightenment. His was a worldview of unitive energies and purpose, in contrast to humankind's divisive projections of separation from each other and from god.

Religion, in its history of past encounter with spirit, believes there was a time when god once spoke to men; but religion at present seems now to demonstrate only that its institutions have forgotten how to listen. Perhaps the tradition of an overt communication of a literal, audible voice for god had to be invented; at any rate, institutionalized form seems to have lost the spiritual awareness of the inner voice.

Stillness is the Source; and we must let go of the world in order to hear the sound of silence. In order to remember dream awareness and its feelings upon awakening, one must be still in body and thought. As one begins to stir physically and to use the mind in discursive thought, one loses contact not only with the dream state but also with the very memory of the dream itself. As in retaining memory of the Dream State, stillness is the matrix of the unheard voice of silence. When we think of the still, small voice we must remember that the word 'still' means both motionless and silent.

Recovery of the Inner Silence is a discipline much like the experience of trying to remember what appears to be forgotten. We often strive to recall a word or name without success but only when we relax and let go of our striving, indeed we may even have forgotten about our search, when all of a sudden the word or name surfaces in our consciousness. In a similar fashion, we must indicate our intent to Spirit and must allow Spirit in its own time to accomplish its own purpose in revealing the kingdom. It is the Father within that does the work! Revelation does not occur according to our plans.

There must be doubt before there can be conflict.
And every doubt must be about one's self.
Christ has no doubt, and from his certainty
His quiet comes.
He will exchange his certainty for all your doubts,
If you agree that he is one with you
And that this oneness is formless, endless, timeless;
And within your grasp because your hands are his.
He is within you, yet he walks beside you and before
Leading the way that he must go to find himself complete.
His quietness becomes your certainty.
And where is doubt when certainty has come?[31]

On her "Mutant Message" walkabout, the Aboriginal people frequently asked Marlo Morgan if she knew how long forever was. When she answered affirmatively, indicating to them that she could focus on such issues, they replied that this allowed them to answer her questions. Consider the spirit of awareness that would be evoked if we were asked that same question. Just how long is forever, or is forever even a question of length?

As recorded in "Message From Forever" (page 251), she also learned from her aboriginal tribe a means to keep relationships in perspective. The dialog states,

"(Aboriginal teacher): Human life is a spiral, we come from forever and we return there, we hope at a higher level. Time is a circle, and our relationships are also circles. As aboriginal children, we learned early in life the importance of closing each circle, each relationship. If there is a disagreement we will stay awake until it is resolved. We wouldn't go to sleep hoping to find a solution tomorrow or at some future date. That would be leaving a circle open, with frayed ends...

(Beatrice): So you are saying that if I close the circle on a spiritual high, that's the end of that for me! If the other person accepts, then the circle is closed for him too. If he doesn't accept what I say, it doesn't matter because any circle left with frayed edges is strictly his circle, his spiritual challenge. He is keeping it open...

(Aboriginal teacher): Exactly. You don't have to like everybody. Not everyone is likable. What you did agree to do before you were born was to love everyone. *It is easy to do. Love the forever in all people, and put your*

---

[31] A Course in Miracles: Text—page 511

energy into those who are of like consciousness (*emphasis mine*). The only way you can influence anyone else is by example. They aren't going to change until they are ready. And remember, it is okay. In the scheme of forever, it really is okay. You come into this world on one level of spiritual awareness and have the opportunity to leave on a broadened plain."

The childlike mind is able to ask, "How far is up?" or, "How long is forever?" or, "What is the biggest number that exists?" Children's minds are also able to admit when they don't know. It is only later as adults that we feel obligated to produce answers to these questions. We think we understand terms like infinity or eternity, but just because we have invented them as labels for non-definable concepts does not mean that our homemade symbols have become adequate to contain what is impossible. We may even believe we have answered these childlike questions with our childish labels. The label 'God' is perhaps our most childish attempt. Perhaps this is why Jesus said that we must become as little children in order to enter the kingdom. Children are typically *childlike*; it takes an adult to be *childish*.

There is an immense difference between childlike and childish. Our religious rituals and theological concepts may try to convince us otherwise, but their forms are only labels and not reality. Neither theology nor ritual is adequate to express the true nature of god and god's relationship to the world. One exception I may note is that a story or exercise may for some, convey feelings that words cannot and these feelings may bear a silent witness to the Real. When word and ritual are understood to be form, it may be that seeing beyond the illusion is accomplished, allowing us to feel the reality of Spirit in our experience. Our awareness may be opened to the energy of Spirit. Words and forms when understood as symbols, can allow, in the silence of our Spirit, an awareness of the Real.

It was the genius of Jesus to be able to use stories and parables to point toward spiritual reality. When Jesus said, "The kingdom of heaven is like..." he was not referring to an outer, phenomenal, objective god who resides in a place called heaven sitting on a great white throne within a golden city foursquare. The kingdom of god is within us, as a treasure hidden in a field, or a pearl of great price, so valuable that we must be willing to sell our entire materialistic outlook in order to allow ourselves to achieve an awareness of it. The "Pearl of Great Price" is already within us.

We may believe we are born of the flesh, live in the flesh, die in the flesh, and ultimately return to the material earth from which we have sprung; 'ashes to ashes and dust to dust'. If so, we will come to believe that the only immortality we attain, are the memories that are left behind. If this is all there is, we have no hope.

We have been taught that we are part of a world of separated things. But, this is not our reality! It is not the truth of our being! Perceiving ourselves as temporal beings without any eternal dimension, we have not yet understood that our sense of space/time separation in our temporal world has prevented us from realizing our unity with this eternal principle.

Modern science teaches that matter, energy, and time all have a common source, as yet unnamed. In this name that cannot be named, there is a principle of coherence and non-object reality, that underlies our space/time universe. This name that cannot be named, is the immanent; yet, transcendent, invisible foundation of all that we experience. The Nameless extends Itself as eternal principle and enables us to realize who we really are, and what our Real world truly is.

This unseen foundation underlying our apparent world, though intrinsic to space/time is also transcendent, and along with Jesus, was referred to by the sages of the world, as Spirit and Truth.

God and love, instead of being labels, need to be understood as symbols of value, instead of objective nouns. We need to see god, as the heart of everything we experience or perceive, and love as the intrinsic worth of all that is Real.

The healing mind is the unified mind, wholeness and holiness, not the split mind of the separated. There must be a decision to heal the separation by letting it go; dissolving the unreal by undoing it. From the position of the split-mind one can make a choice for entry into the realm of the whole mind. Within the whole mind there is nothing to be healed. One moves beyond the need to be healed into the sphere where, in oneness, healing is no longer needed. However, this oneness can not be experienced as the separated mind of a distinct entity, it can be known only as we are known. One can bring illness to the healing, but healing can not be brought to the illness. An individual can not bring healing, while in the belief of its own separation.

Love and Joy are the context of Unity. To have love is to demonstrate that fact by giving it away. Giving and receiving are the same. To have healing one must give it away. To love god, to love our brother, and to love our self, is the same. Love, Joy, and Healing are reciprocal. To know the Love of god is to know that at the level of the real; we also know the love that is the source of our neighbor, and the source of us.

There are a lot of things we need to move beyond, not just Christianity: provincialism, parochialism, nationalism, racism, and other debilitating factors, including any 'us against them' mentality. Consider the adversarial nature of a relationship, when we say, "We are the best!" emphasizing to others that they and theirs are second-class. We are an extremely litigious society with lawsuits at the drop of a hat. The denial that we are one is never so concrete as in our judgments on one another.

Paul Woodruff suggests, "We are most irreverent when we believe we act as god." We need to move beyond arrogance to reverence.

Jesus' expression of the Law of One was in the terms of the Golden Rule. Do as you would be done to, for you are one. If we believe this law, then its corollary is also true. *When it seems to be done to us, we are the cause.* We are always doing *it* to ourselves, whether good or ill.

Our conflicts can be endless. They describe the nature of the world as we have determined to judge it. Judgment results in polarities such as: Jews vs. Arabs, *YHWH* vs. Allah and the Irish orange vs. the Irish green. Our continuous war cry is, let's take sides on an issue and let's fight. This is not the Way and this is not Tao. Tao is unitive and universally neutral.

In our materialistic experience of childhood we could believe that we really were the center of the universe and that everything in it was related to us and us alone. As we grew older, we developed a sense of individuation and separation, sometimes to the extreme belief that ours is a dog-eat-dog world, and sometimes extending so far as the paranoid belief that everyone and everything is out to get us. The paradox of healing is that if we seek to save this separated life we will lose reality itself. But if we let go and lose the separated life we will gain the whole sea of reality, which will become god's reign in our consciousness. We will know the unity of god expressing Itself as everything and everyone.

A further statement we need to make about the Tao is in regard to the unfolding process of the Universe. As Pierre Teilhard de Chardin argued in "The Phenomenon of Man", the Omega Point toward which the universe strives is present within the process from the beginning. Part of the mystical and spiritual journey is the realization of our own experience of god extending Itself *as us* from within eternal being. Our awareness is usually only on the cusp of this expression. Inasmuch as god as Spirit is timeless, god's expression *as us* is a metaphor seemingly trapped and limited within the concept and movement of time. But not only is god extending Itself *as us* in time, god is also pulling us upward from the beyond of timelessness. The Omega point of Teilhard de Chardin exists like a divine feedback loop guiding our experience. As in a high fidelity sound system feedback loop, part of the speaker transformer output is transferred back to the input amplifier in order to clarify the sound fidelity of the system, so too, the Omega point is an inherent function of the inner kingdom. Consider Teilhard de Chardin's:

Discovering Fire

Someday, after mastering The Winds, The Waves,
The Tides and Gravity,
We shall harness for God The energies of Love,
And then, For the second time In the history of the World,
Man will discover Fire.

The English poet Francis Thompson speaks of god who is:

The Hound of Heaven

Pursuing us down the labyrinthine ways
Of our minds and lives whose
Strong feet that followed, followed after
But with unhurrying chase,
And unperturbed pace,
Deliberate speed, majestic instancy,
They beat – and a Voice beat
More instant than the feet...

He beautifully states the unity of the universe in his poem:

Mistress of Vision

All things by immortal power, Near and Far
Hiddenly To each other linked are,
That thou canst not stir a flower
Without troubling of a star.

Chapter Two—Personal Journey
Spirit and Religion

The Journey

If we fill our lives with things, and yet more things –
If we feel that we must fill every moment we have with activity.
When will we have time to make the long slow journey,
Across the burning desert, as did the wise men?
Or sit and watch the stars, as did the shepherds?
Or brood over the coming of the child, as did Mary?
For each of us, there is a desert to cross,
A star to discover and follow,
And a being within ourselves to bring to life.

Lillian N. Fandt

Phillips Brooks, a master preacher of Boston in the late 19th century, made the statement that in preaching, truth must be conveyed through personality. His analogy was that truth is pure light and personality is like a stained glass window. Light filtered by the colors of that glass is experienced depending upon the colors of the glass and the perceptions of the observer. The observer is the source for the meaning given to the colors.

That the reader might have an understanding of the workings of Spirit in my life it is necessary to share my own spiritual journey. To clarify the journey, I will seek to present the personal filters that color the story.

Setting down established theology is a relatively simple process, but perceptions of god must be clarified by the lessons of life. The difficulty is that a spiritual journey is for most a lengthy process; one's adopted vision of god is constantly redefined by the guidance of experience.

A spiritual journey is about inner personal development garnered on the path of life. The 'Aha!' of Experience doesn't happen by itself, but in the context of continually being brought by spirit to a point where we will become able to recognize the inner Reality that has always been.

In the past I hesitated to put in writing concepts about god, because my ideas about god changed, sometimes radically. If my god today is larger than ten years ago, it is safe to assume that the smaller god was not a god fully realized, and my concept of god will yet expand to greater horizons.

God must be at least as great as I am able to conceive it. There is a vast difference between knowledge of god and knowledge about god. Knowledge *of,* implies experience, knowledge *about* does not; rather, it implies the secondhand formulations of religious dogma. We must make a choice between firsthand experience and the secondhand tradition of imparted theory. Tradition may be thought of as faith of the head or I *believe* in god, contrasted with knowledge of the heart or I *trust* in god.

This pilgrimage encompasses both a religious and a spiritual journey. Some think that these are identical or synonymous, and indeed the religious journey itself often starts out accompanied by that kind of assumption. Only when we find our religious journey in conflict with spirit, will we begin to question the difference. We need to comprehend that the words spiritual and religious encompass different qualitative levels of belief and experience.

From the standpoint of simple observation, it is not always easy to delineate that which is truly spiritual from that which is merely religious. Courses are offered in systematic theology on the assumption that creeds and dogma can be categorized, but I do not believe that it is possible to approach the spiritual path within or anywhere near that kind of system. The Spirit works, in 'ways past finding out'[32]. Spiritual awareness may sometimes come because of our involvement in religion, but more often arrives in spite of it. Often it comes as a reaction to religion.

I was born into a home nominally Protestant and into a culture permeated by traditional Hebrew/Christian values. My mother was a very social person who was caught up in a whirlwind of activity in various organizations, with offices, duties, and responsibilities. These included, but were not limited to, Grange, Three Links, Eastern Star and the Altar Guild of the Episcopal Church. She had a formal religious faith in the Episcopal Church whereas my father had a healthy skepticism about religion and preachers. He had no formal religion and did not attend church. He did like the personable United Brethren pastor Curtis Gould, who had married my brother and his wife in our home. But he was turned off religion by such events as listening to a conversation between a local pastor and a visiting evangelist regarding the best ways to squeeze more money from the flock.

---

[32] Romans 11:3

As a child, I was exposed to my mother's 'high church' Episcopal setting. My early experience in her church was basically one of playing in the sandbox and learning to socialize with other children. My major recollection of that religious path was being taught to genuflect when crossing the center of the church if the red candle was lit. I wondered if some people always sat on the entrance side just to avoid crossing the center. I also remember the kneeling benches and a rudimentary explanation of the trinity symbolized by three interlocking rings, to me reminiscent of an old Ballantine beer advertisement.

When I was in second grade, because of lack of work during the depression of the 30's, we moved to my mother's family farm in a small hamlet in upstate New York called Pleasant Valley or Kabob. We lived in relative poverty but I was not much aware of that fact, because almost everyone in our community was in the same circumstance.

At that time, I attended a one-room church of the United Brethren in Christ with a small Sunday school of six or eight children in my age group. It was the smaller of a two church, single minister charge and over time was supplied by a variety of appointed supply ministers. I was nurtured on the declaration that Jesus Christ had shed his blood for me and if I accepted this gift, his blood would wash my sins away and I would go to heaven when I died. I continued in this small church and in my junior high school years participated in the youth fellowship, which at the time was led by a very conservative Baptist minister. With this exposure, I became thoroughly indoctrinated and molded by fundamentalist Protestant religion and its forms. My religious outlook was a simple absorption of the way things were and was not in any way the result of a particular conversion.

Accepting this theological structure did not seem to me to be a big deal, for I had always been exposed to the cultural norm of these beliefs and there had been no need for a personal behavior shift in order to become involved. I did have some difficulty with pronouncements that I needed to be saved, because I know I had absolutely no feelings that god had lost me. There were many deprivations in my life because of the poverty of the depression years but the lack of a religious outlook was not one of them.

As an adolescent, the Biblical library was available to me, and my earliest readings centered on the book of Proverbs and other Wisdom Literature. I thought a great deal about the nature of true wisdom and the distinction between wisdom and knowledge. I concluded that wisdom was the proper application of knowledge and have had no reason since to change my mind. The religious teachings of the time conditioned my mind to accept the Bible as some kind of authority that I was obliged to follow; so I particularly determined to undertake a path of wisdom and virtue as outlined in the biblical material. I was already part of an environment that told me that Jesus was the 'Son of God' and that he had died on the cross for my sins. Along with reference to the Ten Commandments, assumed to have been written on stone by the finger of god, these ideas were part of the prevailing culture and were a basis for religious dogma that one accepted along with all the other social do's and don'ts of the time.

I was saddened by the realization that in olden times god supposedly spoke directly to people but for some reason or other did not seem to be doing so any longer, most especially to me or to anyone else I knew. Why did the Bible constantly refer to god as speaking audibly to the patriarchs and yet god no longer seemed to be talking with anyone now alive? God spoke to Abraham, why not to me? The answer of the institutional church was that, with the authority of the Bible and church, god no longer needed to do so. The simplistic conclusion was that god had already said everything that needed to be said and god's words had been written down in the Bible.

Any sense of contact with a vital, living god presently active in the world, was for all practical purposes, no longer available. God was now confined within the pages of the 'Book'. The Bible, convention, tradition, and the church stipulated proper behavior. The Commandments and proscriptions of the biblical record became substitutes for the Living Word that Abraham and Moses seemed to have experienced and enjoyed. The several forms of religion along with the Bible were now believed to contain the only god that could be known by us today.

"Seek and you shall find – Knock and it shall be opened unto you."[33] Years ago I began to seek and to knock. I bear witness to the fact that over the years I have found much, and much has been opened to me. Perhaps one of the greatest difficulties in listening for the voice for god is that the inner kingdom of Spirit often gives a different witness than that of institutional religion. Institutional teachings have become stumbling blocks, perhaps unintentionally, and it has been difficult to turn these teachings into stepping-stones. The process has more often become one of removing the stumbling blocks in order to find the stepping-stones.

Idolatry of the Bible or biblical library stands in the way of the awareness that god is truly the same "Yesterday, today and forever"[34]. The idolatry of the Bible thwarts the realization that as Jesus taught, the living god is alive within us today. The Bible has become for many an *object* god, constraining people to belief in a thing instead of challenging them to discover the Living Spirit. The 'Voice for god' did not cease with the

---

[33] Luke 11:9
[34] Hebrews 13:8

canonization of the biblical library. We must also realize that not all statements in those books come from the same level of spiritual experience. Unfortunately, these formalizations of belief systems based on sacred scriptures are demonstrated not just in the Hebrew/Christian tradition, but seem to cause a dilemma in other institutionalized religions as well.

Perhaps the chief error that I have experienced with the institutional church is its attempt to worship god as an objective, outside personality, rather than to seek union with the Impersonal God that is central to the Impersonal Self.

The question that needs to be addressed is, "What is the nature of god in timeless, spaceless reality?" Most people think of god as *other*. We are not separated but are one with god. Just because we choose to think that we are separate and make an illusion of god as *other*, does not change god's reality. To quote Walt Kelly's Pogo, "We have met the enemy and he is us."

Religions have constructed a god of material objectivity, a god of time and space perceived as *other*. Jesus, however, taught that god is Spirit and is to be worshiped in the union of Spirit and Truth. To affirm the existence of an object god is to deny the Unity of Spirit. We need a different paradigm or model for god than that of the traditional, objective, *other*.

One can view less than whole numbers from the point of view of fractions or decimals, and both are used in simple arithmetic. With fractions one may divide ten by three, with the result of three and one third. If we try the same exercise with the decimal system we end up with an infinite progression of threes (3.333333...). Using the decimal system, one could conclude that it is impossible to divide ten into three parts. We must change our paradigm to fractional reasoning if we are to be successful. On my personal name card I have a motto, *"Pas de Lieu Rhone que Nous."*[35]

The same paradigm confusion extends to other logical puzzles. Assume a dog chasing a rabbit and running exactly twice as fast as the rabbit. The dog runs ten feet and the rabbit runs but five. The dog runs the remaining distance but the rabbit continues another half. From a linear (space) point of view the rabbit always moves ahead of the dog, staying ahead half the distance gained by the dog, and from this paradigm alone, logically, because of progression into the infinitesimal, the dog will never catch the rabbit.

From an interval (time) point of view, the rabbit's escape is always by a lesser amount of time, and the time needed by the dog to catch the rabbit is soon used up. The puzzle, impossible to solve from a paradigm of space, is easily solved with a paradigm based on time. Paradigm shift is simply another way of looking at things. We have held a paradigm in our culture

---

[35] The paradigm is not French but English! (Speak French, and listen in English.)

for a god that is object, personality, and thing. In order to move forward on our spiritual journey, we must now begin to see god as an inner principle central to the whole of the universe and to our own lives in particular.

Worship of god in many if not most instances follows a form. The communion service, as it is practiced in most churches, is itself a construct derived from an ancient system of sacrifice; worse yet, the form of sacrifice was human sacrifice. For many, the death of Jesus is assumed to placate an angry, vindictive, and very judgmental personality called 'God'.

True communion needs no outer form; it is union with the inner Spirit and the realization of oneness with All-That-Is. True communion is union. The fallacy is, that in giving such great status to an institutional formal exercise we think that in acting out the ritual we have accomplished the goal and no longer have need to experience the unity of being.

I believe we have missed Jesus' teaching that we are to love god as our transcendent Self, love others as the same Self and love our Impersonal Self; for there is only one Self, All-That-Is. Instead we formalize this spiritual reality into a command to try to love an external objectified deity and our neighbors also externalized as outside and *other*.

In adolescence I moved from parental and formal external authority to the beginnings of my own inner authority and to a different set of outside authorities that included peer pressure and enlarged exterior religious and social concepts. This was before any awareness that one could experience Self-actualization and deep-seated inner authority.

Reflection upon my past seventy plus years, reveals how very much belief systems are dominated by the pervading social and religious outlook of the adversarial culture in which we live. When real growth occurs, both spiritual and intellectual, it is not by any external revelation but by an inner journey, which discovers Self as the source of revelation and insight.

The fact remains that most adults are still dependent upon the external authority of religion or a cultural tradition and have not yet found an inner core of identity and strength. Witness the soap opera consciousness of "You did it to me." This is the idea that power, people, and things outside us determine our state of being; thus we can only be happy if they fulfill our expectations. Jesus said, "Peace I leave with you; my peace I give to you. I do not give to you as the world gives. Do not let your hearts be troubled, and do not let them be afraid."[36] Even the peace of god, though not a gift of the world, is often perceived as coming from outside rather than inside.

---

[36] John 14:27

There is a saying that I have found helpful, "There are things that happen around you, there are things that happen to you, but the only things that really count are the things that happen in you."

From high school biology I remember the lesson that Ontogeny recapitulates Phylogeny. More simply put, the development of the human fetus follows a pattern that was established during the process of evolution. The embryo in the womb copies stages of development patterned after those of human evolution. Holding a view that we are eternal beings, I suspect a possibility that as we proceed through the process of physical, intellectual, and spiritual growth in each lifetime, we repeat lessons learned in prior conscious experience. We do not come into this present journey of life as a blank slate. In watching the growth of our children and grandchildren, I have come to believe that each newborn comes complete with an agenda, and is 'loaded for bear'.

I owe special thanks to my father who was in his sixties when I was in High School. He retired to our farm after working as a millwright and a cabinetmaker. Dad had only a second grade education, but was a genius in his own right; he could watch the unloading of a truck carrying lumber and determine within a very close margin the amount of board feet it contained.

Starting from scratch, with material and hand tools, Dad constructed a table saw using a second-hand mandrel he had acquired. Then with the aid of the table saw he constructed a wood lathe, a jigsaw, a cider mill and cider press. I helped him hand pour the Babbitt bearings for the lathe and jigsaw.

When I worked with him remodeling some of our farm buildings, he would get a big kick arguing with me about the best way to do things. For instance, we were building an addition on our barn and putting siding on the outside wall studs; the boards we were using were of various lengths and we were finishing up between a window frame and a corner of the new addition. A lengthy and involved discussion took place about the question, "Should we start at the window and work to the corner or start at the corner and work to the window?" As I recall, it involved among other issues, whether it would be easier to mark and cut the final length of board when we got to the window or when we got to the corner. It took what seemed like twenty minutes to come to a mutual conclusion. Years later, I realized this activity was not only for my education but was a game for my dad, who got a great deal of enjoyment from the process.

These confrontations, with his wry way of testing me, could go on at length until we both agreed on the best approach to a solution. Once when I came home from school and announced the distance from earth to sun, dad wanted to know who had a ninety-three-million-mile tape and had measured it. It was years later that I discovered the means had been simple geometric triangulation from two distant points on the earth's surface. The consequences of simply not accepting external authority alone as a basis for assumptions and beliefs was not apparent to me at the time, or for that matter, to anyone else I knew. I was learning to ask the questions, 'Why?' and 'How?' My father was the one who honed the rough edges of my verbal and reasoning skills; he did not teach me what to think but rather how to think. It's no wonder that I didn't hesitate to take on College and Seminary professors if I thought they were wrong or their logic was weak; some of them were not quite up to having their authority questioned.

In my junior and senior years of high school I wrestled with the choice of my life's work. Our family could not afford the expense of a college education. My dad had an acquaintance with our local congressman and wanted me to seek an appointment to the Military Academy at West Point. However, this was not possible because I was so near-sighted I could not have passed the entrance physical. As an alternative, I registered and was accepted at The New York State Institute of Science and Technology at Buffalo, NY in order to study Optical Technology.

At that same time, in my church experience there were mounting demands to consider the role of god in my life. The directive from our preacher was to 'get saved'. He also challenged the congregation with the fact that no one from the church had ever entered the ministry. This pastor had a good affinity for youth and dominated my high school years in the area of religion. My attendance at services was faithful. I am not sure whether my prevailing motive was my spiritual quest for wisdom, which is to say an understanding of the nature of god, or simply the fact that I had a teenage crush on a pretty girl whose family attended the local church. This minister was very much interested that we all be saved and baptized. In a seasonal evangelistic meeting, I bowed to the pressure to publicly acknowledge what I had always accepted as the given system of salvation, which was to say that I was saved because Jesus shed his blood for me. This was an intense religious event in my life, but certainly had nothing to do with increasing my spiritual awareness. I now know that blood atonement is not relevant when considering a god imminently involved in our lives and intrinsic to the whole universe.

It is very difficult to find a religious institution in the Christian tradition that has moved beyond the concept of sacrifice. The old way of blood atonement is no longer practiced, but god is still conceived with a need to require it. Blood atonement has been somewhat cleaned up by the substitute of Jesus dying once for all. But at heart, god still is conceived with a need for human sacrifice that Jesus is supposed to have fulfilled. Why do we believe that god had a need to see Jesus killed in order to be able to forgive us? Will religion ever learn that there is no awareness of sin in god's mind? There never has been a debt to be paid. Which is easier to say, take up your bed and walk, or your sins be forgiven? Sins are not real, needing to be forgiven; they are mistakes needing to be corrected, an illusion of judgment and guilt, and an artificial condemnation needing to be lifted.

Jesus is no more god than we are, and we are no less god than Jesus was. Things of space/time are by nature limited, but Spirit is not constricted for Spirit has no boundary. Fear is the natural result of trying to find or make security in a materialistic, illusory universe. The security of the spiritual universe is produce by Love, which is the absence of fear. So much stress placed on being saved results directly from the fear of hell and damnation. Unfortunately, it is easier in our culture to image the fearful flames of hell, than to feel the Love of god. It seems easier to purchase cheap salvation than to have true vision of the mystery of Love. When we learn to take up our bed and walk we move beyond a concept of judgment into a paradigm of healing. We let go of past notions of sin and guilt and learn to trust the experience of Love's Presence.

The other powerful religious event of those years was my acceptance of a call to the ministry. This call ended up actually being a bargain with god. Inasmuch as my father was not a churchgoer, some doubts were cast in my mind about his being saved. The fact that I had just conformed to that religious standard of my culture, elevated the issue of my father's non-conformity. At the same time, I was wrestling with pressure by the local pastor who was continually saying that our local church had never produced a minister. This culminated in a mental contest as to whether or not I was willing to serve god by going to Africa as a missionary. My picture of Africa was a teenage view of that Dark Continent dominated by the fearful scenes found in a dozen Tarzan movies. I did not have the simple awareness that Love never fails in our process of being healed. The bargain referred to earlier was the exchange of my willingness to go to Africa and be a missionary if, in turn, god would do everything possible to 'save' my father.

Not a very profound theology, I admit, but an accurate picture of my religious mindset at that time. I had just graduated from high school (1947) and was already registered to study Optical Technology. When I spoke about entering the ministry instead, the local pastor directed me to Houghton College in New York State, a fundamentalist college that I later learned had a misguided passion for what it termed 'high academic' standards.

Soon after my decision to become a minister and with no ministerial training, I was asked to speak to a youth group in the church of a relative. I was convicted by a gospel quotation that I interpreted to mean, one should not worry about what to say but to trust god and I would be given the words for any such occasion. As a result I attempted not to prepare anything and when asked what I was to speak about before the service, avoided answering. When the time finally arrived, after much prayer (pious worry) and no preparation, it was undoubtedly a horrible experience for the local youth group. I trusted my interpretation of the biblical phrase that I would be given the words to say. It was a pitiable experience but a powerful lesson about biblical literalism. I was learning the difference between religion and the real, and beginning to discover the Christ of inner experience.

My post high school summer job involved working with my brother at a nearby furniture parts factory. Because I was not yet eighteen, I was not allowed to use any of the saws or other dangerous equipment. This meant a very minimal wage, which was not a great help toward my savings for college. It was at this time that my brother crushed part of his hand in the high-pressure rollers of a re-saw, a device like a large band saw used to cut thick boards into thinner ones. My brother was the main support of his wife, my father, and me, as we were all living together. With the injured hand, my brother could not work so we had no money coming in. I had not saved up much for school, perhaps about two or three hundred dollars. Tuition was only ten dollars a credit hour at the time, but now the funds were needed to meet family expenses. It was a crisis of faith for me, but I became convinced that if god wanted me to be in school, a way would be opened. In the late fall of that year, my mother received an insurance settlement from injuries in an auto accident and she provided me with a start to pay the Spring Semester bills. I had delayed the start of college until January 1948, because I could not afford to start in the prior Fall Semester.

My mother worked away from home, in a TB (tuberculosis) sanitarium, first as a night nurse and later as a cook. She faithfully sent what money she could for school expenses, did my laundry by mail because postage was very low, and carried me as a dependent on her Blue Cross hospitalization policy. Hospital rooms were only fifteen dollars a day at that time. I am much indebted to my mother for financial aid in meeting my college needs.

The basic wage for student labor at that time was forty-five cents per hour. Because of my good experience with high School Physics I was able to get a job with the college as an electrician for the sum of sixty cents an hour and later formed a crew that wired local homes for the better scale of one dollar an hour. Wages and costs were much less in the late '40s. By working summers and during the school year, and with my mother's help, I kept just a little more than even with the costs of tuition, room, and board.

When I entered study for the ministry, I did not understand that academic preparation for professional ministry was not about learning and teaching spirituality, nor was it designed to enable one to follow a spiritual path. As I progressed at college I realized more and more the distinction between religion and spirit. Rather than through formal training in the classroom, my insights into spiritual awareness came through informal discussions or 'bull sessions', and in later years in the form of growth groups.

Although Houghton was a 'Holiness' school, with a great deal of emphasis on sanctification, the experience was taught as if it came from an outside source and, like salvation, was perceived as a gift from an exterior god. I do not remember one statement in my entire theological education that dealt with enlightenment, or any inner mystical experience. It may have been that the concept of Second Blessing Holiness had some connection with the mystical aspects of the spiritual journey but the practice of silence and an understanding of meditation were not part of the curriculum.

The ministerial course I took was designed to maximize knowledge of biblical content. Most extra-curricular discussions centered on the differences between the many brands of fundamentalism, with 'proof texts' from scripture supporting each particular theology. I learned that there are many self-contradictions in Christian fundamentalism. Fundamentalism holds the Bible to be literally true. But fundamentalist belief is only directed toward the parts of the Bible which support a particular group's doctrine. The Baptists, who believe in eternal security, and the Wesleyans, who believe in holiness as sanctification separate from salvation, tended to ignore those editors of biblical literature who did not support their own belief systems. The Church of Latter Day Saints believes in the doctrine of baptism for the dead. They also hold that a wife is saved by means of her husband. (Both ideas are briefly mentioned in the Bible) The Roman Catholic Church teaches that Peter was literally given the keys to the kingdom and is succeeded by a lineage of popes who receive them by succession. These doctrines and practices are followed only in their own respective communities.

Because to Fundamentalists it is obvious that god wrote the Bible in Greek and Hebrew, there was in my ministerial course a great deal of emphasis on the Greek language. Hebrew was not offered as a course.

Fundamentalism often has all the right labels for all the wrong reasons. One can speak of being one with the Father, which is true, and do so as if it were some kind of mechanistic arrangement limited only to Jesus of Nazareth. One can preach salvation by grace, which is true, and still believe that salvation is a result of meeting the legalistic requirement of a particularly worded confession of faith. The witness is correct, the rationale is wrong. It's reasonable to say that in Christian fundamentalism there is a 'Heinz 57' variety of how different groups perceive their Truth. It is also reasonable to suggest that in the Bible there also may be fifty-seven perceptions of Truth; but it is not rational to assume that all perceptions of truth are actually true.

College was a learning experience in more ways than just in the classroom. The so-called high academic standards were to me a kind of false pride resulting from the self-righteousness of a rigidly religious institution, but there were redeeming factors. I should have failed my first mid-semester Greek exam but the teacher was a beautiful soul who loved his students. I got a dismal twenty-six on the exam and he still gave me a D rather than an F. I was frightened enough to really try to make an effort, and finally learned the forty-eight ways to say 'who' in Greek. Many years later, when he was dying of cancer, I thanked F. Gordon Stockin for the kindness of his D, and his reply was that *he had long ago realized that students were more important than grades.* He was a man who believed that real education is the teaching of students, not subject matter. I am very grateful for his witness. By contrast, on one occasion I even lost my ministerial scholarship because of a failed question on a final exam in a pre-med Zoology course. I had correctly identified all the parts of the honeybee's legs but had labeled them first walking leg, second etc., as one would the legs of a grasshopper. Rigid grading dismissed all credit for the question even though all of my labels on the parts of the legs were correct. I should have labeled the legs as pro-thoracic, meso-thoracic and meta-thoracic. This was not the only case where it was demonstrated that grades were held in higher esteem than education.

In the same sense of rigidity, the college physician, who was a retired missionary, taught an adult Sunday school class in the local Wesleyan church. One morning he lectured on the evils of divorce according to Matthew's gospel and insisted that the only acceptable solution for those who were divorced and remarried, as far as god was concerned, was to divorce the present partner and re-marry the original partner. The former marriage was a yoke that god had made for life and to continue with the second marriage was obviously adulterous. To their credit many of the class disagreed with his stringent view, including my house-parents.

On the very positive side, I am still deeply indebted to the family in whose home I stayed. The wife and mother Dorothy taught me much about the reality of a loving family relationship. I worked with her husband E. Everett Gilbert on the college maintenance crew and they both became substitute parents for me. For their gift of love I honor the memory of Ev and Dorothy to this day.

I was one day playing catch with Edward D. Angell, a college pastor with whom I had become friends. I did not know he had once played professional ball. He had a windup so complicated that I could not tell where the ball was going and was embarrassed often by failing even to catch his throw. I would have looked even sillier if I had been trying to use a bat. On the other hand, he asked me to work on his broken tape recorder because he had not figured out how to take it apart. A mechanical genius he was not; but he was one of the best preachers I ever heard; his delivery was from a clear mind and an open heart. He challenged me to realize some of my own abilities in that undertaking. I remember his waggish statement to the effect that "Even Balaam's Ass could preach, when it had something to say!"[37]

The open-heartedness of some persons and the closed-mindedness of others are among the most vivid impressions of my college venture. I still am troubled when I see the proximity of open hearts alongside a closed mind. Can these two aspects of awareness actually be contained in watertight compartments to such a degree that they have no effect on each other? Perhaps the more one's heart opens, the more the closure of the mind is undone. On the other hand, it is absolute tyranny when a closed mind prevents one's heart from opening. I would opt for open hearts and open minds. My spiritual journey at school continued to be pushed by interactions with students and the religious community.

I had made a decision for god, but the religious community immediately began to stipulate its expectations of what that entailed. This took the form of external religious authority mandating obligations and guidelines for my behavior. The amount of nit picking was amazing. For instance, I wanted to see my first television set but when I visited a local bar, the only place TV existed at the time, I was severely criticized. It was suggested to me that purchasing a Sunday paper was immoral, even though I tried to point out that it was Monday's paper that was printed on Sunday.

Two incidents on my religious and spiritual journey that perhaps best delineate the struggle between religion and spirit occurred at this time in my college life:

On the occasion of one of the scheduled bi-annual revival meetings that are so much a part of conservative Protestant religion, I determined to do my best to bring revival to the campus. Some of us were involved in a student fast and prayer hour on Thursday noon, where we gave up our lunch in order to fit more religious activity into our schedules. At the time of the revival I pledged myself to the discipline of forgoing all meals except breakfast for that week in order to pray for revival. At the end of the week two things were happening in the situation: First, I was eating ravenous breakfasts and second, I was becoming disappointed in god because no great revival was

---

[37] Numbers 22

happening. My belief that god should answer my prayers, especially since I was giving up meals, was severely challenging to my inner peace.

But as Spirit will instruct if given a chance, even in those circumstances, I was shaken into wakefulness when in some literature I found a reference to fasting in a Bible passage I had never noticed before. "Is this such a fast that I have chosen, in order to make your voice to be heard on high, a day for a man to afflict his soul? Is not this the fast that I have chosen, to deal your bread to the hungry? You shall not fast as you do this day."[38] These words spoke to my condition and I learned from Second-Isaiah (Scholars believe that the book of Isaiah had two major authors.) that giving up bread for the hungry was meaningful, but trying to bribe god by that approach, was not. It is obvious that I am not the first to ever deal with this issue.

The second incident in my experience also took place at one of those same revival meetings. Several times during the week, under the emotional pressure of the Evangelist and the repeated pleas of Hymns such as "Just as I am", I went reluctantly forward to the altar. I had the feeling that in spite of some public humiliation, if god had a greater experience for me, I wanted to have it. Each time while listening to the plea to go forward I felt the need again to trade my discomfort in a bargain with god for sanctity. I was wrenched with the belief that I ought to be willing to suffer the embarrassment of 'going forward' in order to receive as much as god would exchange for this act of devotion. Finally, after several nights of repetition my roommate asked me what I was trying to prove. When I tried to explain, he simply asked if I didn't think god would already understand and accept both my evident desire and my sincerity. This was one more step in learning to trust the inner authority of Spirit rather than depend upon the outer authority of religion. From a religious point of view, I lost ground; but from the standpoint of Spirit I believe I had made a giant leap forward.

As I look back on this narrative, I see several explicit times when I have tried to bargain with god. The lesson I was being taught is seen in the understanding that god is not an outer power demanding negotiation, but rather an inner mindfulness of the implicit order of the universe.

The very attempt to make a bargain with god suggests that god has a mindset that can be changed by outside influence. A god who can be so influenced is perceived at best as equivocal, and at worst as capricious. Such an external, objective god is anthropomorphized, i.e. god is discerned in the same way that we perceive other humans. Spirit is not a separated other. The inner resource of Spirit is the same yesterday, today and forever

---

[38] (Edited) Isaiah 58:4-7

– time-less. There is no external god needing to be changed. There is no eternal to be found within the temporal!

This same lesson has been replicated in my quest to understand the nature of effective prayer. I cannot see any sense in the practice of using prayer to inform god. Some of us at the college church saw humor in one of the pastors who used prayer as a means of informing the congregation. He would often pray for god to bless the Ladies Aid that was meeting on Thursday evening at 7:30 P.M., and continue to note in his pastoral prayer the time and place for other events that he wished to promote. I have come to believe in a god immersed in the very structure of Life, and thus do not feel any need to plead for Spirit's involvement. I believe that even invocations at religious services are misleading and should be affirmations of the Presence of god rather than requests for its attendance. In the same sense that we need not seek to become what we really are, we need not seek to move god beyond what god really is. Traditional prayer seems to try to inform god about what god already knows and seeks to involve god in events in which god is already at the center.

Prayer is conscious participation in the flow of god's creativity. The direction of the energy of prayer is not from us to god but from god through us, to the concern voiced. Effective prayer is affirmative of the energy of god flowing through us to the concern. We are not causing god to do work, we are allowing god to be, extending through us. Doing the will of god is not using the energy of an externalized god; it is allowing god's energy within us to accomplish its good purpose. Prayer without ceasing is *being* prayer not *doing* prayer.

A friend once told me the story of a son who had heard his father at the regular mid-week prayer meeting pray for a poor family who was suffering hunger because of lack of funds. After the meeting was over and the family returned home the son said, "Dad, if you will give me the keys to our root cellar, I will answer your prayers."

Most people are trapped by the power of external authority, and for many, religion is one of the most powerful impediments to discovering the power of god within us. We learn that the Tao is the discovery of the kingdom within. I have learned much about what religions say that god is, but I have learned more slowly what the genuine inner experience of god actually is. I had not yet learned that "A universal theology is impossible but a universal experience is not only possible but necessary."[39] There is no need to argue about experience, for as Louis Armstrong said about Jazz, if you have to ask you don't know. If you know, you don't need to ask.

---

[39] A Course in Miracles: Manual for Teachers: Clarification of Terms, Introduction

My wife Lillian and I were married in my senior year at Houghton. Well before our marriage Lillian knew that the odds of her bearing children were slim indeed. As a teenager she had contracted undulant fever (Brucellosis) by drinking raw milk from cows infected with Bangs Disease, which causes calves to be aborted. We entered marriage knowing that our children would be chosen in the process of adoption. Indeed, after the adoption of our first child, our daughter Kara, Lillian underwent a complete hysterectomy in her early 20s. To suggest to those of us that have adopted our children that the sexual relationship is primarily for the purpose of reproduction is silly and shortsighted. There is in some conservative theology the idea that the pleasure of human sexual union must be paid for by the conception of children: hence, strict proscriptions against contraception. The conjecture that sexual union functions only for the reproduction of the species in the union of sperm and egg is another ludicrous assumption of folklore given high status in some religious circles. Even Parmahansa in his "Autobiography of a Yoga" seems to believe that the only time his parents experienced sexual union was when he and his siblings were conceived. We acquire many strange assumptions in our early years.

Biologically we know for fact that the germinal cells of reproduction have made a continuous replication of living DNA for countless thousands of generations. The half chromosome of living sperm and egg cells un-united die away naturally and their potential ceases to exist by the millions. They are gradually replaced in body chemistry by millions more. The unsustainable statement, made by countless supporters of 'Right to Life', i.e. that human life begins at conception is supported only by the conjectures of their tradition.

After college I attended both seminaries of what was then the Evangelical United Brethren Church, now merged in the United Methodist denomination. These were theologically described as middle of the road schools, and presented a somewhat more critical approach to biblical literature and tradition than my college background.

As a first year student in Evangelical Theological Seminary in Naperville, Illinois, my student church all but forced me to consider leaving the pastoral ministry, until a young couple from the church took my wife and me aside and told us not to be upset. They informed us that that particular congregation had put every student minister they had ever had through hell. After that kindness, I felt that maybe we could stick it out, at least until the end of that year's appointment. It was also the beginning of my insight into the different expectations congregations have with regard to ritual and doctrine. The organist of the church felt I was using too many

'Eastern' hymns, as he perceived Martin Luther's, "A Mighty Fortress is Our God". According to his own statement, I did not realize that the reason people were coming to church was to hear him play the organ. After that first year we moved to Ohio where we worked as house parents in a children's home and I continued my education at United Theological Seminary in Dayton, Ohio.

After graduation from United and ordination by the Erie Conference of the Evangelical United Brethren church, I accepted appointment in the New York Conference of that denomination. The president of the Seminary, Dr. Roberts, called me in for a word of counsel just before my graduation. He advised me that he usually did not get involved in the placement process, but because of my urge for theological growth and the changes I had already experienced in my spiritual perspective, I would have much more elbowroom in the New York Conference of the former Evangelical Church than in the Erie Conference of the former United Brethren Church. The Erie Conference was a very conservative group with few Seminary trained clergy.

Before assigning me to our first full-time church in Binghamton, N.Y., Bishop Gregory said not to worry, because in all the troubles the congregation had faced with the mental illness of the former pastor I could do the church no harm. After two years there, where I developed the reputation of being a good teacher in the field of adult education, I accepted appointment as a Minister of Education in a much larger church on Grand Island also in the New York Conference of the EUB church.

It didn't take long to become aware that in a church with such a large church school, my job consisted more in replacing teachers who needed pregnancy leave, than in having anything to do with teaching adults. I did enjoy working with two large Youth Fellowship groups and counseling with them in summer church camp experiences. My next assignment, in conference mid-year, was to a small congregation in Wayland, N.Y., where the bishop had removed the pastor because of ethical problems. The congregation made it easy for me because they felt it must have been very difficult to work in the circumstances caused by their situation.

After reading the book "The Three Faces of Eve", I could not help but ask myself the question: which one of her personalities should be 'saved'? Because the congregation had some very open-minded people, we could approach such concepts as multiple personality.

The re-incarnation story of Bridey Murphy raised more questions about the traditional concepts of salvation. It became more and more clear to me that children have already gained some kind of awareness before they are born. This was certainly true in our children and I see it clearly in the identical twins of our daughter. Their differences are simply not entirely genetic or hereditary.

When reading the book "The Diary of Anne Frank", it was clear that Anne was not a Christian. How then, according to fundamentalist doctrine and dogma, could she be saved? It was apparent from her life and testimony that she was Jewish and a child of god.

I remember the questions the Wayland Youth Group wrestled with after studying Anne Frank's diary. I pointed out that Anne was a Jew and not a Christian and asked them if they thought she would be saved and get to heaven without belief in Jesus. This question was a key point in bringing home to them the issue of religious doctrine that insisted that only belief in Jesus as a personal savior was valid for redemption. My own belief is that god has faith in the universal and infinite worth of individuals no matter what their religious background, or lack thereof. God does not extend itself as something other; we are all begotten of god.

There is a considerable difference between Christianity and the teachings of Jesus. Christianity seems to be more concerned with a religion about Jesus than what he actually taught. God at the heart of everything is the reality of Love that is within us. We need to see this reality in order to know who we really are. We need to be about the task of rescuing Jesus from the church and religion, in order to experience the teachings of Jesus as affirmed by personal spiritual knowledge.

We question, "What is the Christ of god, anointed military, political Messiah or spiritual logos?" Sacrifice is taught as a means to influence god, but god does not need to be influenced. If it was god's Love that sent Jesus to earth, then sacrifice had nothing to do with it. How long will it take society to move beyond the archetypes of blood atonement and a vengeful god? The Son of Man shall be lifted up, but not as a military commander or a blood sacrifice. Jesus is simply a demonstration of the Way!

Theoretical science has abandoned the material world for a reality without dimension and boundaries. Reality is boundary-less, which gives rise to understanding a spirituality that comes from within. Religion comes from without. Things are by nature limited, Spirit is not. It has no boundary.

Does god really love the sinners he supposedly sends to hell? Being saved is a cheap salvation if it only allows us to be on the inside looking out. What about the hundreds or thousands of loved ones and acquaintances on the outside looking in? When we fail to convert them to our worldview of being saved, do we actually believe they spend an eternity in hellfire and brimstone?

People of all Religions can experience the truth. The key is inner experience and not the outer theology of their faith. Roman Catholic,

Fundamentalist, Unitarian, Buddhist, Hindu, Jewish or whatever the form, it is the content and quality of life that reflects the energy of Spirit.

Because of belief in a democratic church polity, my next large step in moving away from religious form was a denominational change. It was political, from an episcopal government in which ministers are appointed by a bishop, to a congregational system where ministers are called by the local church. The reasons for my doing so are apparent in the story below.

Because I had an interest in further work in graduate school, I accepted appointment as a Student Pastor in the Methodist Church at Seneca Castle, NY, with intention of taking some work at Syracuse University. The school program didn't work out so after serving the church for some time, we began conversations with the congregation about their future. After many meetings and much discussion, the Seneca Castle Church voted to merge with two smaller neighboring Methodist Churches at Flint and Aloquin. The decision was based on the belief that as a combined parish the congregations could afford a Seminary trained full-time pastor, who could choose which of the two parsonages he would live in.

A short time after the congregational votes, the Methodist District Superintendent called me to confirm that I was planning on leaving. I expressed to him, I had agreed that if they voted to combine I would plan on leaving to make room for the new full-time pastor. He reaffirmed that he understood I was leaving.

After I left, he informed the churches that the Central New York Conference of the Methodist Church had too many student pastors needing assignment and he would not allow them to merge. I could not believe that a Conference would put its needs ahead of the local churches. Ironically, several years later, the Conference established that three-point charge.

I investigated the Congregational Christian Church, The Society of Friends (Quakers), and The Unitarian-Universalist Church. I accepted a call to a Unitarian-Universalist church in the community where my aging parents resided. In that Unitarian-Universalist Church, a member quipped after my first Service, that the last time Jesus Christ had been mentioned in the building was when the janitor fell down the stairs. I learned from this congregation that the need for intellectual prowess could be a trap in itself and that it was more important to be child-like than childish.

Later on, in a Congregational Christian Church of the United Church of Christ in Seneca Falls, N.Y., a member became very upset when I made the observation that Jesus was a Jew and not a Christian. But in that congregation, we had a delightful time with a very small church school, where the teachers were able to accept the idea that teaching children was more important than teaching the dogmas of religion and legalistic salvation.

It was at this time that I became exposed to the works of the psychic, Edgar Cayce. He was a man of great integrity who demonstrated the reality of clairvoyance, or distant seeing. His readings often carried an accurate description of events occurring thousands of miles away. Along with the Aborigines of Marlo Morgan's "Mutant Message", he also demonstrated telepathy, which is mind-to-mind communication without words. Because literacy generates literalism, Marlo Morgan's aboriginal 'real people' did not intend that their children learn to read and write. To do so would be to diminish their facilities for telepathy, memory and recall.

Cayce's story was my first real exposure to the possibility of transpersonal psychology and gave contemporary evidence that mind was a force much beyond the limits of the physical brain. The concept that the mind has produced the brain, rather than the brain producing the mind, was another giant leap in the awareness that Spirit, not matter, is our Source. Because of this encounter, I also pursued extensive reading in the field of parapsychology and psychic phenomena. In spite of the fact that there is a lot of substandard material floating around, these fields produce quality evidence that the material world is not the reality we think it is. There are many breaks in the space/time continuum, or as Joseph Chilton Pearce called them, "Cracks in the Cosmic Egg."

Louisa Rhine, whose husband J.B. was famous for research in parapsychology, illustrated the ability to experience the future as a displacement of time when she told the story of a young mother, awakened from her sleep by a very clear and strong dream that a collapsed ceiling had injured her child in another bedroom. The first time the mother had the dream she chose to ignore it. The second time she dreamed, she became aware that the time of the crash of the ceiling was registered on a clock in her dream. As it was not yet that late, she chose to take the dream as a warning and brought the child to her own bedroom and put the child down to sleep. At the time the dream foretold, she was awakened by a loud noise as the ceiling in her child's bedroom came crashing down. This clear dream of what we perceive as the future had apparently saved her child's life.

Another area of mind that intrigued me was psychologist Carl Jung's demonstration of several polarities inherent in personality. The pairing of Introvert – Extrovert, Sensing – Intuitive, Thinking – Feeling, and Judging – Perceiving, as shown in the Meyers-Briggs test, was very helpful to me in understanding some of the concerns and conflicts I was feeling with religion and the institutional church. I became aware as an intuitive of the different attitude I had about observing religious ritual from those who were more sensory in their approach. The other difference between myself and perhaps most other clergy was that I was heavily a perceiver and had little interest in judging or changing the world. My basic motivation was to understand it.

Many years of service in relatively small congregations have taught me most of the dynamics of ingrown religion. I have chewed my way through the lessons taught by fundamentalist, conservative, and avowedly more liberal congregations, as concerning their religious and political structures. Interspersed with pastoral service as pastor-teacher and theologian in residence was business experience: as a systems engineer with International Business Machine Corp., as a computer programmer with Welch Foods, and as an optical dispenser with Sterling Optical. It is a sign of the times that I was always accorded more status when I told people I worked for IBM, than when they found out that I was a minister. The ministerial role always seemed to provoke distance and suspicion in reference to the implied question, "What *kind* of a minister?" One of the advantages of secular employment was more free time in our evenings. With the children now in their teens, my wife and I took advantage of several growth groups, which focused on developing greater psychological maturity. They provided great opportunities in learning to trust one's inner voice.

During this period out of the pastorate, and with opportunities to explore larger horizons, I became motivated to study more in the areas of spiritual healing, and positive thinking religion. William James' book, "The Varieties of Religious Experience" explains the differences between positive and negative religion: whether one's energy is focused on feeling the love and grace of god or is directed toward avoiding the fear of punishment and damnation at god's hand.

Having had ample exposure to negative religion, we decided to see what the positive side had to offer. Our family moved to Lee's Summit, Missouri, enabling me to study at the Unity School of Practical Christianity. I have many positive feelings about our two years in the Unity environment. Unity has an emphasis on divine order, which was evident in our lives, beginning with the very day we moved in. We had secured an apartment in Lee's Summit and my son and a friend were helping me unload the rental trailer, crammed with our possessions. My wife and daughter had stayed behind to clean up our house, now on the market for sale. As we were unloading and carrying boxes up the flight of stairs, a young man who was visiting a resident in our building, asked if we would like something cold to drink. As it turned out, he was with a group, most of whom were Unity School students. When they found out our purpose for moving to Missouri, they organized a box brigade and in no time our goods were piled neatly in our apartment. When I called my wife to report on our progress, she informed me that our house had already been sold.

Because I had no formal exposure to the Unity movement, other than reading, I was not accepted immediately into the ministerial program. I worked on the School maintenance crew and got well acquainted with a work partner, Rick Grace, who was one of the founder's grandsons. While working days, I was able to take advantage of the many layperson courses available. The next year I was accepted into the ministerial school full time and worked part time with maintenance. I enjoyed most of the faculty immensely as their essential approach was based more on the experiential than the academic. I enjoyed the student body even more: they had a very diverse background and for the most part were pursuing a spiritual rather than a religious journey. There were exceptions of course, but my wife and family felt very much at home. I still have good friends from that group, nearly thirty years later. There was also an emphasis on the psychological development of sensitivity and awareness. Many of the students were skillful leaders and practically all were enthusiastic participants. The political structure of the movement was my chief disappointment. The school itself was run as a family dynasty with a self-perpetuating board of trustees. The churches in the field were very individualistic depending upon the founding ministers, many, who owned the church buildings, lock, stock, and barrel. It was too much for me as a firm supporter of congregational democratic polity. There were also those, as in any administration, who were devotees of the letter rather than the spirit. I faced the simple fact that my prior ministerial credentials in the United Church of Christ were still valid and believed firmly that if the principles of positive faith worked, they would work in a traditional church as well as they would in a specialty New Thought atmosphere.

After two years in the Unity environment, we returned to the pastorate, with ministerial standing in the United Church of Christ, and full time ministry with a small congregation, First United Church of Christ in Dayton, Ohio. I had found a denominational home within a group that accepted me as a cooperative maverick. While in that pastorate, we were able to develop a much more person-centered ministry. My theological 'call' had shifted away from fear, and my intellectual need to learn more about god, to an awareness of god expressing Itself through me in healing outreach.

Early in that ministry one or two traditionalists discovered that I was not using the phrases they expected with regard to personal salvation and biblical inerrancy. When a heresy hunt was attempted, a majority of the congregation declared that they could see no problem and the few disgruntled ones left. In my funeral services, because of my extensive reading in the field of human survival after bodily death and a strong faith in that survival, I had a very fulfilling ministry with families when death occurred.   In the years of experience that followed, I also moved emotionally from burying members to burying friends.

On one occasion the secretary of a nearby church, whose minister was on vacation, called me. A very distraught lady was requesting a pastoral call. I called to find a widow who told me she was facing a choice, very concerned about her late husband's approval. I suggested she visualize him sitting next to her on the couch and ask him what he thought about her questions. After a short time of silence she laughed and stated that he had told her not to worry, he didn't really care and told her to follow her own sense of the matter. The next day the church secretary called me to express the lady's gratitude for my help in the matter.   The help I gave, was acceptance of her continuing relationship.

We became active in outside study groups; particularly a long time group focused on "A Course in Miracles". There is much more to be said about our involvement with that course in later chapters.

One of my challenges was overcoming some of the statements of traditional negative theology such as: god is testing us; the Lord never takes anyone before his or her time; the Lord took him home; and the Lord needed an angel (for a child). These pictures of god are tragic in that they place blame on Spirit, which is Absolute Love. Pain and grief are not the gifts of god, they are a consequence of our total immersion in the belief systems of our space/time dimension.

At times I still think of myself as a recovering fundamentalist.

We also learned with that congregation about problems associated with a large building debt. Because a building fund had been started during years of church school growth, a former minister had been excited about building a new educational unit. Unfortunately, attendance had already peaked and had started a steep decline by the time the building was actually constructed. We faced low attendance, and a huge mortgage on the new structure. It was a matter of real grace to experience the congregation struggling with refinancing the debt and coping with falling attendance.

Eventually the debt was paid in full and a mortgage burning was celebrated. Because of the openness of the congregation, we were able to stay with them almost ten years until their financial situation necessitated a change to part-time ministerial service.

My whole life has consisted of learning adventures; each situation has been an effective, if not always pleasant, teaching encounter. These lessons, along with a good wife and family, have been the major factors in my continuing spiritual and psychological growth.

This period of retirement that began in 1992 has become one of the most interesting and spiritually profitable in our lives. I have had time to work on this book and apply the principles outlined here.

Many find it impossible to believe that the higher Self may well use bodily affliction to teach the lessons we need to learn. Our attention needs to be on what our internal intentions are, not on the existing appearance of what seems to be. We are often influenced by tribal convention. In retirement Lillian and I have dealt with several surgeries and both of us are cancer survivors. True healing is by effortless accomplishment (*wei wu wei*) in our very being. We are healed, even without being cured.

God does not do anything external to its own being. God as Principle simply *is*. The energy of being is where all reality resides. The lesson has been to learn to trust the process and allow the flow of life to accomplish its own ends. We talk to bodily disease not in demand or argument but in terms of the blessing it brings and the lesson that it is here to teach.

This book is not an academic work, although I attempt to credit sources I can identify. My basic motive in this effort is to leave a record for our children and grandchildren. I also hope to give encouragement to those who face the struggle of change and growth on their own spiritual path. I write too, because I have been encouraged by some in churches and study groups to put my journey on record; for years I resisted, because as I reviewed my changing viewpoints over each decade, it was almost unbelievable how much many of my belief systems had changed. I was glad that some of my earlier stupidity had not been recorded. Now, in my reflective years, it is the time to record the pilgrimage.

My years on the journey have made me very aware of the problems of biblical literalism, as well as problems in the political struggles of organized religion. Successful ministers devote much of their energy to building and maintaining the institution; exactly what most parishioners want. I was not very successful as an organization man, in part, because I had opted instead for greater involvement as a contemplative. In spite of all its problems I am much indebted to institutional religion for providing me with subsistence while making it possible for me to spend time in study, thought, and reflection. The journey has taught me some basics of the spiritual life. Although I no longer view the 'Book' as infallible authority, and in spite of the many primitive beliefs it represents, the library of the Bible still contains powerful witness as a diary of the spiritual journey of many of its heroes, chief of whom is Jesus of Nazareth.

The logic of dogma pushed to extreme says that Jesus was sinless. But if Jesus was sinless and death is a result of sin, then Jesus would not die. If he could not die, then he could not supposedly die for our sins. I agree, this is logic reduced to absurdity; but then, religion is famous for that.

In spite of the attribution of contradictory and lesser ideas to Jesus, there is still a substantial collection of sayings that enable us by their example. We should at least begin to accomplish in our lives what Jesus was able to accomplish in his. "Greater works than I have done, you will do."[40] God is not a foreign object; it is our inner essence.

Jesus was transformed from *within* by the enlightened awareness of the Spirit of the Universal Christ. The concept of Messiah as an anointing from *without* is that of an external god commissioning a unique person to perform a military and political task involved in fixing the world. The anointing from the internal Spirit means healing and empowering persons from within. In regard to the Messiah's coming, Jesus warned us not to seek outwardly, for the internal anointed is here, there, and everywhere. If someone says, it is out there, don't go.[41]

Jesus spoke with power and taught that we have the same authority as he to become sons of god. This is the true meaning of being Christed. To be Christian for some today is no more than being given a name at baptism.

Jesus said, "My kingdom is not of this world" – the kingdom is within you – not as the world gives does the Spirit give. Peace is from within, not from without. The kingdom comes from heaven within to the world without. When we know the kingdom within, we will see the world through the forgiving and loving eyes of the internal Christ and perceive the spiritual reality underlying the kingdom supposed to be without.

---

[40] John 14:12
[41] Luke 17:23

The Imprisoned Splendour

Truth is within ourselves; it takes no rise from outward things,
What e'er you may believe.
There is an inmost center in us all,
Where truth abides in fullness; and around,
Wall upon wall, the gross flesh hems it in
This perfect clear perception – which is truth.
A baffling and perverting carnal mesh
Binds it and makes all error; and to know
Rather consists in opening out a way
Whence the imprisoned splendour may escape,
Than in effecting entry for a light
Supposed to be without.

Robert Browning

Chapter Three—The Quality of God
Prologue to the Gospel According to John

John 1:1

The Greek *logos* (translated word) is a philosophical term defined as divine wisdom acting as the ordering principle of the cosmos or universe; its equivalent *nous* (translated mind) is the principle of cosmic mind responsible for the rational order of all things. Both *logos* and *nous* can be understood as the commonsense sagacity (sage-like, discerning, farsighted, sound judgment), that is inherently the essence of the universe. Logos is the intelligence, skill, and wisdom of the mind of god. When logos is the agent for speaking the mind of god, it can be understood as Word, Mind/Voice, or Wisdom. Logos is the energy of the content of divine mind.

According to scholarship sources, the traditional translation of John 1:1 is not clear with regard to the author's intended relationship between the logos and god, for it is based primarily on conventional theology instead of the original Greek text. The traditional translation is:

> In the beginning was the Word,
>
> And the Word was with God,
>
> And the *Word was God.*

All nouns in the Greek language are accompanied by a definite article (our word *the*); there is no indefinite article (*a* or *an*) in the language. Scholars speak of the anatherous (no article) use of the noun in Greek. In Greek a noun with no article is the device used to convert the noun into a descriptive modifier, in our grammar an adjective or an adverb. In this setting the word without the article is the final noun *Theos* or god. Thus to say the word was god, is not the intent of the author, rather the intent was to say that the word was godlike. The quality of god, god without an article, equals Love. There are two inaccurate ways this noun without an article has been translated: the first, to follow traditional theology and ignore that the article was omitted, 'was god'; and the second, to assume the presence of a non-existent indefinite article, 'was a god'. A literal translation would be:

71

> In beginning was the logos,
>
> The logos was in the presence of the god,
>
> And the logos has *the quality of god.*

The Greek noun 'son' in Mark 15:39 is without an article; thus son of god without an article suggests the qualities of son of god. Translated in the Revised Version, *a* son of god and in the King James Version *the* son of god, neither is accurate. In English the same basic effect is accomplished by adding 'ly' (a derivative of the word like) to an English noun. Man plus (ly) equals manly or in this case because we can't express 'sonly' of god, son-like of god, or like a son of god.

To understand the distortion derived from the traditional translation of John 1:1, compare the mistaken sense of Logos, affixed as a footnote to John: 1:1-5 in The Living Bible: "Before anything else existed there was Christ with god. He has always been alive and *is himself God.*" The Word used synonymously with god is not only understood as meaning that the Christ is god, it also unfortunately infers that Jesus is considered by the gospel writer to be god as well.

This discussion might seem like hairsplitting, but a more precise interpretation of John's prologue opens a whole vista of meaning implied in the statement of the first verse. It also unlocks a far more accurate comprehension of the way in which Word or Logos is used in reference to Jesus of Nazareth, and to the rest of us as well.

It will be helpful to construct a simple parallel for the setting implied in John 1:1. There is first a Source, which is god as the speaker; next there is the action of expressing god's mind as voice speaking, and finally, the resulting combination of voice and listener. The last is more complex, for there may be the energy of voice but there is no voice heard until there is the function of a listener. The elements we are left with are these: god as speaker, logos as mind/voice, and what the listener hears. In this setting, a paraphrase of the meaning the author is trying to convey would be something like this:

> From before time, was the Wisdom of the Mind/Voice.
>
> The Mind/Voice was in the presence of the Source.
>
> And the Mind/Voice represents to the listener,
>
> All the qualities of the Source.

It is important to understand that both Mind and Voice are in the presence of Source and still retain all of its quality and integrity.

If a tree falls in the forest and there is no one present to hear, did its crashing to the ground make a sound? Air compression and waves were created but sound is a matter of interpretation by the ear. An ear, brain and mind, are needed to create sound. There will be vibration from the crashing tree, (sound energy) but there will be no crashing sound without the hearer. Sound is in the mind and experience of the listener.

We have Speaker and Mind/Voice in the presence of god, but not the sound of Mind/Voice. The sound is where we come in. The voice has only the meaning we give it, as the listener. Ah, there's the rub! Source – Mind/Voice – Listener/Message; the Source fully understands its intention, the Mind/Voice conveys the full intention of the meaning given, but the message depends on the meaning received. We, as listeners, are in a developmental state of deafness and must learn to hear clearly. The Universe attempts to speak to us in sign language or whatever else it takes. Some suggest it communicates by karmic equation; we reap as we sow. As poor listeners we bring upon ourselves an inferior message conveyed by pain and frustration. It is a mistake to perceive the Word of god as a physical phenomenon. The real Word of god is invisible and silent and is not within the appearance of space/time. Do we listen with the ears of the *eidolon* individuated self or with the heart of *daemon* the true Self?

Rivers of living water flow freely in reality. In the unreal illusion they are dammed up by judgment, condemnation, hatred, prejudice, fear and the like, and restricted from our awareness. We must engage in the task of removing the dam; i.e. the blocks to the awareness of love's presence. It appears to be work in the task of undoing the unreal because we have labored long and hard to build it. When we allow the father within to do the work, then for us work ceases, the burden is easy and we accomplish without doing. (effortless accomplishment – *wei wu wei*)

There is within us a reflection of god's glory, an imprint of god's nature; in Colossians Paul refers to Christ within us the hope of glory. The word in Greek *boka* translated glory or righteousness means an imprint of god's nature and a reflection of god's image within. This imprint is an accurate reflection that will transform us from within. The inner Christ is the engraved Word and our imprint of glory. To accomplish this change the Holy Spirit needs but a 'little willingness' on our part. Conscious activity will still be involved in the material needs of the world, but the spiritual mind is guided and corrected by the work of the Holy Spirit. We may seem to work to remove the dam that impedes the flow, but having done so, the flow will progress and accomplish by itself.

We used the lesson of optical illusions and most of us have experienced examples; we now face the problem of symbolic auditory illusion. In its spiritual meaning, we hear only what we are prepared to hear. Our pre-judgments distort our hearing of the voice from the presence of god. We must yet discover with the inner ear of Spirit what it means to hear clearly.

Genesis 1:3 proclaims "Let there be light"; in like character, the Gospel According to John states that all things came into being as a result of the Mind/Voice or Logos. The Logos was in the beginning with god: all things were made through logos, and without it was not anything made that was made.[42] God is expressed, or in other words god *presses out* and emerges as the essence of all things made.

Tradition maintains that god created the world. But, in that picture the created world is perceived as a thing, divorced from its creator. This position places god on one side of the equation and the created world on the other. We in effect are asking how does god *do* the world? The answer is god doesn't, god did not *do* the world, for the real world is god energy pressed out. *God being* is the essence and unseen reality of the perceived world. Language does not convey god *be'd* or *be's* the world. In this age of materialism with little understanding of the spiritual dimension, the physical world is perceived as source itself, instead of an effect of Spirit.

There may have been an original idea of the world as an extension of its creator, but this idea succumbed to the legend of the fall, the belief that the world is separated, inferior, cursed and a thing apart. Yet there has been no divorce or fall, for god has not created a thing apart. The Mind/Voice is the energy of the emergent world and we are enabled to see the reality of the world with the eyes and heart of Spirit. We can choose to see spiritual reality or we can be transfixed by the space/time illusion. From the base of our space/time mind we cannot accept both at the same time. When we do we create a dualism, source and expression separated and in conflict with one another. This is effectively perceived as a split mind; the spiritual mind separated from the physical or body mind. Some teach that we must choose between the two; I believe we need rather, to unite them. It is not a matter of having to choose either/or, for apprehension by the spiritual mind creates a unity that dissolves the split and integrates the dualism of spiritual and physical mind. We are enabled to live constructively in the reality of spirit and the illusion of space/time concurrently. Living in space/time while knowing the spirit, enables us to see the real world. Even though the real world may physically appear the same as the illusion, we have become aware that its reality is different. We now have an opportunity to live in and understand the wonders of both the world of spirit and the real world energy underlying space/time.

Tom Brown, Jr., who follows a shamanistic tradition, tells of learning the ways of spirit from his teacher Stalking Wolf, whom he called Grandfather. "I learned to communicate with the world of nature and the

---

[42] John 1:2,3

realms of spirit in a very real and dynamic way, so that I began to walk the duality of flesh and spirit as Grandfather had done."[43]

Source is Pure Being, god unmanifest. The Cause or Source and Mind/Voice are of the same aspect, quality and intent. The space/time universe inherently is of the same quality as the source, but because we observe it in its temporal and spatial dimension, it will only assume the correlation or meaning that we give to it. We have a choice to see the universe from either of two polarities: We can see it joined with the Spirit of god in wholeness, or we can see it through the eyes of personal ego, as separation and illusion. With a mind split from the whole, we experience a world separated. Unified mind knows the vision of the Real world.

The Real World is not something that god did but the result of something god is. In the same sense what *we do* is part of the illusion, what *we are* extends our reality. In our oneness with Source and Logos, we too, participate in creative activity with god. We too, extend our reality with unified mind as the builder. Our real creations are not things, but extensions of our Self as god's real creation is an extension of its Self. Love begets love. The Source as essence or Being conceives intent as Mind/Voice or Holy Spirit and extends itself as Sonship as an integral part of All-That-Is. As enlightened listeners our minds become the arena of god. (Realm within)

Each of these delineations of the process is a state of being and not an act of doing. Source is being, Logos is being, Sonship is being and the Real World is being, as in point of fact all Reality is being. The truth is, and does not do. We are the ones who have projected a mythology of god and ourselves as doing. This is not to say that what we are will not unfold in harmonious manifestation. The being of an acorn will unfold as the being of an oak tree; but it does not need to push the river in order to accomplish it. It is precisely at this point in understanding the Mind/Voice role in creative emergence that we see the connection of the Chinese concept of *wei wu wei*, doing through not doing (effortless accomplishment). The whole scenario of the Logos, is god expressing being, not doing. Religion deals with space/time illusion. Spirituality deals with invisible Reality!

Being that acts with the intention of oneness will remain One, but being that does, with a separated goal in mind, violates being and brings about a duality because the goal is not in unity with its being. The act of doing to achieve a goal seen apart from one's being is a doing that separates. Only in the act of being can oneness remain the same. In the unitive dualism of spirit and flesh, we set the stage in our choice to be *of* the world of spirit and

---

[43] Awakening Spirits, Tom Brown, Jr. – page 8

in the world of flesh. This means that any decisions we seem to make in the flesh are actually cooperative acts with our true spiritual being.

Zen Buddhism has a phrase that speaks to this point of being what we are; it is in Zen terms called 'original enlightenment' and is used of the place where we must start and also of the place where we must end. It is our true being and nothing can change that fact. It can not be attained, it is something we already are. The question is of course, have we become aware of its existence within us? What better words, to state Jesus' idea of god within us, than original enlightenment?

To illustrate, if I *am* helpful, I will *be* helpful in carrying a package for someone else; in short, I am *being* helpful. With the same outward appearance, if someone else coerces me, I may grudgingly carry a package but I am not *being* helpful. I am simply *doing* helpful. When we are faced with the false sense of doing helpful brought on by the demands of others, we need to develop the ability to be faithful to our Being and just say no! (or at least recognize our doing) In the same sense, many *do* their religion.

A human male may beget a child but it is a different quality to *be* a father. Because we are Love we can be Love in our actions, but no amount of doing as we think Love ought to do will help us to comprehend the Love that we are. We cannot do to be what we are; we can, and must, will to undo barriers to an awareness of being's presence. This undoing is not, as some metaphysical groups say, "Fake it till you make it." Undoing is the removal of unreal blocks and has no pretense attached. The Greek word (*hupocrites*) translates as pretense, pretend, actor and hypocrite. It is not spiritually helpful to fake an act of living by doing. What we are we need not fake, nor can we do to attain what we are. Yet there still remain the blocks we have erected and need to remove. In the illusion of space/time we need to dissolve what we are doing in order to see beyond space/time. We accomplish this most simply by changing our intention. Undo the unreal!

We face all kinds of choices in life: we can be someone, or we can play a role. I would rather eat a meal prepared by someone whose intention it is to be a cook, than by someone who does the food. We are more enlightened when we *are* Christmas Spirit, than when we *do* Christmas.

We say practice makes perfect, but it is the matter of intent that determines if we are extending creation or are simply doing the illusion. Do we practice the piano because we want to discover and implement the piano player we are, or are we simply fixed on the goal of performing before an audience? Practice can be a memory of being or a drudgery of doing.

Focusing on doing will not reveal what the Silence can demonstrate. It is far more expedient to focus in Silence on Being than to struggle in illusion with the objective of doing to become.

Focus on doing, in the materialism of religion, is clearly seen in a discussion of tithing. Historically there was a change in the concept of tithing. In Deuteronomy,[44] the tithe of the crops was to be brought to the temple center and eaten before god. If the distance was great then the tithe was converted into money and carried to the temple area. The tithe money was then exchanged for meat, wine, strong drink, or whatever one's heart desired, and these symbols were eaten as a celebration and feast before god.

It is hard to imagine a person eating ten percent of their crop at one sitting, so I assume the tithe had an original meaning of a token, rather than a materialistic percentage. By the time of Malachi, the people were being accused of robbing god for not bringing the tithe to the priests for their use.[45] Institutional religions derived from the Hebrew/Christian tradition almost always make the arrogant assumption that if you give funds to them, it is identical with making a gift to god. They tell you, if you obey god, you should give ten percent of your income to their cause. There is great arrogance when an institution says, what you do for us you do for god.

From a spiritual perspective the whole of life is involved in god, not just time and money contributed to religious institutions. Be unto others and share bread with the hungry. To be aware of the needs of our families is no less a gift to god. Religious needs and demands do not properly evaluate our responsibilities. It is amazing to me that some positive thinking groups, who embrace the concept of the inner kingdom, really get hung up in a legalistic view of tithing when their own institutional needs are at stake.

We need to acknowledge the sense of mystery as to what we are and what we shall become. "It does not yet appear what we shall be: but we know that, when He is revealed, we shall be like Him, for we shall see Him as He is."[46] It is this mystery that consistently and convincingly calls us to the awareness that although we may be fashioned in god's image, god is not limited to ours. We need to learn to live with the mysteries of our lives knowing that in our soul learning, they serve their purpose. To know as we are known is to affirm that the dewdrop can contain the ocean. Each segment of a laser plate contains the total laser image. It is not that the ego self is enlarged to contain the whole, rather it is dissolved to allow the Self, already containing the whole, to emerge. He who loses his life shall find it.

It is appropriate to understand the distinction between the theological terms pantheism (all is god) and panentheism (all is in god). Panentheism is defined as all things are in god, or that god underlies all things. Pantheism in its simplest form means all things are god. But things are never that

---

[44] Deuteronomy 14:22-27
[45] Malachi 3:8
[46] I John 3:2

simple.   There are two pantheistic views: acosmic (not the world) and cosmic. In the acosmic view one starts at the point of the Reality of god and considers the relationship of that which is considered non-god. For practical purposes panentheism and acosmic (not the world) pantheism are identical. In cosmic pantheism the changing world is in its totality defined as god.

In Eastern thought, the eighth century CE (Common Era) Indian philosopher and religious teacher, Shankara, developed the system in Hindu thought of Advaita (non-dualistic) Vedanta (fulfillment of the spiritual teachings of the Vedas [spiritual writings]). His central message was that the essence of the individual soul (atman) is fundamentally identical with universal being (Brahman). He believed that because Brahman is absolute and undifferentiated from the individual soul, the entire world of physical experience is *maya* or illusion and has no independent reality. Maya is the perceived appearance of the visible world which obscures the spiritual reality from which it originates. In order to avoid dualism, the invisible unmanifest is Reality and the visible manifest, illusion. This is the position of panentheism and acosmic pantheism, a non-dualism with which I concur.

In Western thought, the Dutch religious thinker and philosopher, Spinoza, took up the cause of acosmic pantheism. In 1674 he wrote that in regard to the metaphysical 'substance' of all reality,[47] both things and ideas were temporal modalities.   These modes have their existence in time whereas their underlying reality or essence is timeless.   God and its indestructible world exist as eternal essence, but not the visible temporal world of existent things. Spinoza explained that every existence (thought or thing) has a universal or essential character; but to realize this character the existent thing must free itself from the boundaries of its own structure. Only in nontemporal self-caused being is complete freedom possible; only by identification with god is immortality and, with it, peace obtained.   One thinks of Ken Wilber's position in his book "No Boundary", where he makes the profound and humorous statement, "There is nothing but present experience, and there is definitely no path to that which always is. There is no path to wetness if you're already standing shoulder deep in water."[48]

Panentheism means god is within all things. In the similar view of acosmic pantheism, material appearance is not god, but god is not divorced from things either. For god is the invisible underlying energy, intelligence, and intent behind the world of appearance.

Inherent in this dialogue is what theologians call the problem of evil. If the whole world is the result of god manifesting Itself, then what is the

---

[47] Ethics Demonstrated with Geometrical Order, Spinoza
[48] No Boundary, Ken Wilber: page 143

source of apparent chaos? It may be that what appears chaotic is not as meaningless as it seems. It is our interpretation that the world is in chaos or meaningless. It may be that we have not seen the farsighted commonsense harmony and order implied in the prologue's enhanced picture of cosmos.

We see in the universe the meaning we give it; if we come from a stance of fear then we will see the fearful all around us, because of that which we project outward. Although there is no power in darkness, as a result of fear we can experience an absence of light and an absence of love.

God is at the heart of what the world truly is. The world as we perceive it, is our own interpretation, depending on the beliefs we project. Have we rightly learned to hear the authentic sound of the Mind/Voice of god? Can we let "Thy Kingdom" come into our awareness here on earth as it is in heaven? The world's Reality is not in need of change. It is the misperception called illusion, which needs to be healed.

Comprehension comes in the act of recognition that the world we are judging is a world of space/time illusion. Again, illusion does not mean the world is not a fact, but rather, that our judgments of it are mistaken. There is an old adage that *seeing is believing,* but it is more accurate to understand that *believing is the basis of our seeing.* Or perhaps in this case, that one's beliefs are the foundation of which word we will choose to hear: our own or the Living Word. Prejudiced seeing and prejudiced hearing are the source of misguided vision and the cause of our inaccurate judgments and beliefs.

The best analogy I can suggest is the sense that god's Spirit is expressing us with freedom to learn and experiment in this sandbox of life, much as children. We are still left with the tremendous mystery that the reality of the divine is yet beyond the limitations of our concepts and theologies.

We can do no harm to spiritual reality rooted in god because we are learning in a kind of materialistic dream, even though we experience it as very real. The solution to our problem is not so much to change the dream, but to awaken from its hold over us. By now we have spent countless lifetimes in the dream and it is finally time to awaken to the mind/sphere of Pierre Teilhard De Chardin. All of our experiences are lessons to be learned; learned with the freedom to make mistakes and then relearned by correcting them. In short, what appears to be chaos is of our own collective making. We have not threatened god's reality or our own; the games by which we learn are only of temporal significance. For this reason god remains at Peace. There is a certain incongruity in the traditional religious position that on the one hand, god is angry over our sins and very upset with what we are doing in the world; yet, at the same time, it is maintained that god is at peace and remains so, yesterday, today, and forever.

Just as Gautama the Buddha taught, our mistakes in the world do cause us much pain and suffering. Our mistakes in the world of appearance are just that, *our* mistakes, mistakes that we must learn to correct. Learn we will, for with time as an illusion, we have all the time it takes. When we express the healing of the Impersonal Life we will shorten the time when with god, transcendent to time, we see no sin separating our reality from god's own. As mentioned previously, this is a more accurate interpretation of the biblical statement "God is of purer eyes than to behold evil".[49] Traditionalists have argued that the meaning of this verse is that god in disgust turns his back on repugnant sin rather than looking at it. At the level of space/time, mistakes exist and must inevitably be corrected. At the level of god's reality evil does not exist. God is imperturbable because god is not one of the things of space/time.

Our circumstances are intrinsically related to our own behavior. We ultimately learn the lessons that mistakes carry their own punishment and that virtue is its own reward. It is succinctly put in the biblical saying, "Don't kid yourself; god is no fool; whatever a man sows, he shall reap. Sow to the spirit and reap life. Sow to the flesh and reap destruction."[50] Rather than recriminating punishment from an external object god, with god recognized as principle, this text simply means that in space/time we inevitably harvest what we plant.

A major fault inherent in traditional Christianity is the idea that Jesus had to balance our spiritual checkbooks by divine intervention. This is a posture bypassing the function of god as Principle. It is an external righteousness replacing an internal one. Principle is like simple arithmetic; two plus two equals four. If we insist that two plus two in our judgment should equal five, no matter how much faith we place in our mistaken belief, our checkbooks will never balance. Our assessment of the value of this principle becomes a problem to us because we traditionally expect results to be immediate and apparent, or at least in one's own lifetime. "What goes around comes around", will come back to us as lessons to be learned at the appropriate time, no matter how much of illusory time it might seem to take.

Jesus' role is correctly stated in John's gospel; he did not come to condemn the world on behalf of god, he came to bring healing.[51] The world was already under its own condemnation and needed to be healed of this condition; it does not need to be rescued from god's supposed wrath.

In the traditional church it has become the official conjecture that Jesus died for our sins. This is substitutional atonement with emphasis on the

---

[49] Habakkuk 1:13
[50] Galatians 6:7,8
[51] John 3:17

substitution. It is simply an archaic theological system about a god who demands to be satisfied with blood sacrifice. A pivotal issue is the belief that something supernatural happened in the past in order to guarantee salvation – an action outside our own acquaintance, rather than personal transformational change. According to this belief, we are now saved or rescued, rather than healed. Most 'Born Again' Christians now perceive the new birth as a certification, a legalized and externalized occurrence. It is not pictured as spiritual awareness unfolding within us. When our name is written in the lamb's book of life it is seen as something that Jesus did. This is a clear example of religious teaching *about* Jesus overshadowing the teachings *of* Jesus, who spoke of new birth as an internal happening, a process of growth and awareness springing forth to new life.

We must become aware that not only is Jesus an expression of Logos; so also, is the whole universe, including ourselves. Because Logos is wisdom and mind, all things brought into being have innate intelligence and connective awareness. We live and move and have our being[52] within the context of the oneness of All-That-Is. If god be for us, who or what can be against us?[53] Fear is cast out by Love,[54] and alienation is dissipated within the oneness of Spirit. Jesus is elder brother and example, not our mediator.

Pure being is the Cause, which is god Unmanifest; all materialization is expressed from within the quality of that Source. The Logos is not god as *Source*; Logos is *means* to effect. God is not the demonstration. This materialistic culture would make the symptom appear to be cause, when it is instead an effect. Emergence as it is viewed from the outside is not reality. The reality of emergence is the inner intelligence and energy that holds form together. The reality within the outer shell is god as Spirit. God does not become flesh but does demonstrate Itself through flesh and external form. Only the Invisible is real, for all appearance is an illusion of form and duration. God as Spirit energizes cause, not the symptoms of the apparent object. The manifested in its spiritual reality is Unmanifest. In short, from the perspective of the One, all is One; there is no shadow and there is no other. Visible form reflects spiritual reality but is an effect and not causal. Analogous would be the argument of students of Physics that all matter and energy are an expression of a mysterious unnamed source. This mysterious source I would name Spirit. Spirit is cause; energy and matter are the effect. All matter is in actuality, an energy/space of temporal duration held in apparent form, with Divine Intelligence and Intention underlying both.

---

[52] Acts 17:28
[53] Romans 8:31
[54] I John 4:18

We need to learn to view the world differently, to have the ability to see differently, to look within, and beyond the manifest in order to behold the Unmanifest. This ability to see with new light is understandably referred to as enlightenment. Too often we hide this Inner Light, which is our own, under the proverbial bushel basket. Hiding our light under a bushel is not a parable about refusing to give our religious witness to the world. Rather, when we do not see ourselves as the light of the world or the salt of the earth the meaning is clearly that we have not yet become conversant with the idea of god expressing as us. If we are not enlightened we have hidden the light of the world from ourselves as well as the world, for we have not yet learned who we truly are. An understanding of enlightenment in this context gives us basis for an insight into another hard saying attributed to Jesus. "Be perfect, therefore, as your heavenly father is perfect".[55] Having learned that the kingdom we are to enter is not out there, but within us, we understand that perfection is not something which needs to be accomplished as a task outside, but is simply the sameness of the Real. God's reality and our reality are the same, already accomplished. Be perfect, by allowing the perfection of the Father to express in our awareness as Impersonal Self.

Only when we know god can we become godlike, and we must be godlike when we know god. In Paul's terms we must eventually know as we are known.[56] To know god as an exterior personality as we now think we know other personalities, would be to set for ourselves an impossible task, if for no other reason than that there is no god *out there* to know.

Knowing god within, as the Real Self, is a task we do not accomplish. The true identity of the Self is already accomplished. Our task is to remove the self-constructed barriers to the awareness of its presence.

The walls we have constructed which prevent us from awareness of the god Self, are the same boundaries we have erected between others and ourselves. The implied restraint of our personal self from other selves is the stumbling block to realization of oneness with god. To know the oneness of god, we must know that there are in reality, no *others* from which we are separated. This is the Sameness of the real! No wonder Jesus based his new covenant on Love. Love god, love your neighbor and love yourself. We are all the same, and any judgment or condemnation will erect a deterrent to seeing that Sameness. Love your neighbor as your *Self* (not as your *self*). This is why the Principle of god as Love has no need to judge its own, for judgement and condemnation are the causes of perceived separation.

---

[55] Matthew 5:48
[56] I Corinthians 13:12

We have fashioned these obstacles to our awareness of oneness over an immense period of time, at tremendous personal expense. For this reason we must divest ourselves of these fabrications, no matter how high the seeming cost. According to our erroneous perception, the more elaborate the defensive barrier we have erected the more expensive is the seeming sacrifice that is demanded to remove it. With these seeming investments it is hard for us to enter the kingdom of heaven. We think it is an extremely expensive price to pay for the field in which the priceless treasure resides. In fact, because of the spiritual rule of sameness, we are asked to pay absolutely nothing in order to possess everything. To accept god's realm is to recognize space/time as illusion. It is impossible to do this when attached to material possessions. A material 'rich' man cannot achieve freedom from space/time when he is attached to material riches. With God it is possible when nonattachment has been experienced. We undo the unreal in order to know the Real. We perceive a huge price, which has no existence in Reality. The Pearl of Great Price is already ours, but we will not receive light to know this until we have sold the entire *nothing* we think we possess. This pittance we would gladly pay if we only knew the great spiritual wealth that is ours. Like the jealous older brother of the prodigal son, we are ignorant of the fact that all the father possesses is ours, so caught up are we in separation from our brother. Would that we, too, could see that our brothers are *alive* and not deserving of the harsh judgment we so easily pronounce! What profit indeed, if we think we can possess the whole illusion but as a result lose the awareness of our own true worth (our souls).

We will learn to let go illusions of the outer world, which we have constructed. We built them and we must dismantle them; they are our responsibility, not god's. For god to intervene would be a denial of the Principle of the power of creation afforded to us. When we create within the rule of Principle our creations are real and eternal, and when we attempt to *do* something that does not obey the rules we only solidify our illusion. Where we have generated illusion we must learn to let it go back into the nothingness from which it came. The lesson we all must learn is to undo our unreal illusions by the means of forgiveness. We must learn to forgive the results of our judgments on the past, now carried over into our experience as a falsely perceived present.

Some of the best published materials relating to this sense of awareness are by philosophers speaking poetically, and conversely, by poets speaking philosophically. Such insight is impossible to present in the descriptive arguments and categories of science; we cannot possess them, they can only possess us. It is only when these insights apprehend us that we understand the revelation realized by the poets. We feel we move toward god but there is no distance to travel. When the dimness is lifted from our eyes it will reveal the enlightenment we already are. We at last will understand that we who have been born of the flesh have always been born of the Spirit.

What is the potential from which the world appears? Potentiality is resident in the non-being, unmanifest godhead from which the whole space/time continuum springs. The whole issue at hand is an attempt to understand how the ground of Being, which is transcendent and wholly unmanifest, can be the ultimate source of the universe that seems to be materially a matter of apparent fact. The concept of Logos as Mind/Voice is an attempt to bridge this gap. When we are in league with the Logos we are at one with the act of creative extension; thus linked with the mind of god we are able to extend the realm of creative Spirit.

We let go of the outer world by approaching the inner silence. Silent, because it does not judge and separate into categories; Silent, because it does not do. In silence we learn to let go of the past. Silence is unification; the still small voice is silent. Joel Goldsmith called it the "Thunder of the Silence". Silence is what sages of the past have called the fullness of the void; fullness learned only in the awareness of the voidness of the full. The voidness of the full seems to be one of the most common avenues of spiritual growth available to us. When we get fed up with the 'world' as we perceive it, we should rejoice that we have begun to experience the illusion for what it is. The path to enlightenment begins with the realization that there must be a better way.

The true *Word* of god is silent. A still small voice, within. Words separate the world by classification and judgment, but Mind/Voice joins all in the One. We must have true vision in order to see that the same is the same and that the different is different. This is the awareness that what is not real is in all aspects not real and always the same in its difference from the Real. It is also the recognition that what is Real is the only Reality and always the Same. When we have learned that the Real and the unreal are always different, we have attained the foundation stone of enlightenment. Ultimately we will all hear the Silence of the Spirit and understand its meaning.

Love is not 'other-centered'. Love comes from its own core. It extends its own resource as a gift to others no matter how unlovely the illusion of their appearance. As William Shakespeare wrote, "Love is not Love which alters when it alteration finds."[57] To be other-centered rather than Spirit centered is to do, rather than to be. It becomes a "do good" attitude that

---

[57] Sonnet 16, William Shakespeare

does not come from inside but rather seeks to fulfill a supposed self-need derived from outside 'service'.

In the silent unity of pure being there is no communication, only communion. There is nothing to communicate and there is no other to communicate with. There is only the isness of the One. It is evident that if god is One, then there is no other. We all, who appear apart, are in reality not only an expression of the One; we are of the One and are the One extended. In union with the One, we let loose the boundaries of perception in exchange for the wholeness of the Real. This is the reason why the One is void and silent. In unity there is no other. When we give our allegiance to the material world as separated, and apart from its Source, we experience disengagement from the Source. With space/time as our reality, we lose the unity of the Isness of the One, the Timeless/Spaceless quality of the Real.

Four times, the book of Revelation states of god, "I am the Alpha and the Omega, the beginning and the end". Be clear, the statements do not say I was the Alpha or that I will be the Omega. There is only Isness – not what seemed to be; only Isness – not what seems to be; only Isness – and not what will seem to be; only Isness. Pure Being is not subject to the illusion of space/time. Beginning and ending are one, beyond the paradigm of space and time. "When we arrive at our destination; we will discover that we have traveled a journey without distance."[58]

The true light has shone in darkness, and darkness has not overcome the light. All things in the outer world are expressed from the quality and context of Spirit. Judge not the quality of god.

The Chinese equivalent of the Logos is a combination of Tao as the way with the integrity of Te as its empowerment. Tao is understood as the Teaching or Way; and in conjunction with Te it is also understood as means and not just path. The Tao is the dynamic that connects to, or rather *is*, our life at source. Te is not a means *to other*; it is integrally means as *expression and awareness of the One.*

John continues with the argument that the Mind/voice is to be seen exemplified as god's Love. Love means to heal the world and not condemn it. God so loved the world that god sent the only/begotten son.[59] Begotten not made, not other, but an expression of the One.

The generic or masculine translations of an earlier day need not be stumbling blocks to the power of their statements. From my point of view, it doesn't pay to get stuck in gender arguments. From ancient times, the sky and heavens have been referred to as masculine and the world below,

---

[58] A Course in Miracles Text: – page 150, 9.7
[59] John 3:16

mother earth, as feminine. In ancient mythology there has always been a balance of yang and yin (masculine and feminine). There is no indication of superiority or inferiority in the respective roles. The masculine has power to beget and the feminine has power to birth. Begotten is an old English word meaning to sire. Sonship is another reference to the underlying reality much like the 'I am' statements discussed earlier.

Unfortunately in English the generic word 'child' does not carry the weight of the maturity of sonship although it does imply heir. In Greek the words only/begotten are one word made up of two roots *mono* and *genesis* and could be literally translated 'one/source'. Mono is to be seen as a reference to the fact that there is only one Expression. In reality our spiritual world and being are that expression. Genesis is the word for beginning or starting place, so one should understand only/begotten as the one/source of all. The only/begotten is Sonship as the whole creation, not just Jesus. Jesus was a person who demonstrated the shared humanness that is the common appearance of all of us who dwell in human form. Sonship is the one essence of us all. We are all in our essence an expression of One/Source. When we believe on (experience) and know that Sonship, we cannot help but be healed in spirit. God so loved the world that god sent us!

Jesus prayed "That we may be understood as one, I in them and thou in me."[60] Sonship and the 'I am' are one, and neither refers to the outward appearance of Jesus, but to the Tao, the means or being of all things that appear. Tao is taken to mean the source, the pathway, and energy of appearance, not the appearance. God did not make the world as another reality apart from Itself. God is expressing as the world, or birthing the world, in only-begotten (*monogenesis*) unilateral creative extension. Our essential being finds its source in the logos. The logos has expressed the whole energy of the world from the Unmanifest.

The essential energy of the logos is light and as Impersonal Self we are the light of the world. This statement is not to be taken from the narrow point of view of ego, personal self or body but is the point of view of Logos. God, in its energy and aim, is the intention of our total world by means of logos. The real Self is not actually separate from the Real World. We are the light that is overcoming the perceptible darkness of the apparent world.

The context of our understanding is found in a story of the Taoist Sage Chaung Tzu. While asleep he dreamed he was a butterfly and when he awoke questioned, "Was I dreaming the butterfly, or is the butterfly now dreaming me?" We only become a light *to* the world when we realize we are the light *of* the world. All that we seem to behold is an expression of the

---

[60] John 17:23, 26

one essential Source. God is light and light is being expressed. We are the light god continues to express.

> We are not *the* expression of god.
>
> We are not *an* expression by god.
>
> We are god expression.
>
> We are One/Source and One expression.

This stream of divine creativity is impossible to state with precision by the means of symbols that we call words. Even the words are symbols at a second level; the first level of symbolism is the level of our concepts or thoughts. We are dealing with symbols of symbols.

In the struggle to convey the subatomic nature of matter, the physicist has dealt with this problem as well. We are told that matter, as such, is a form or appearance of intelligent energy.   We begin at the level of appearances we call things or objects; then we are told that these things are composed mostly of empty space. The electrons, protons and neutrons that make the atoms, that make the molecules, that form the things, are in turn made of quarks, mesons, gluons, etc. The electrons spin in orbits not unlike the planets around various suns. At the heart is an invisible yet unnamed mystery, which is the source of both energy and matter. This allows energy to be converted both to matter and from matter. This underlying principle is confirmed in atomic energy. Could this mystery be what we have called Spirit or Mind? Jane Roberts in her Seth material suggests the term 'mind-unit', as the root of all matter. In Spirit, the mystery energy is Love.

If, as physicists tell us, all matter and pure energy have the same root, that time and space are apparently illusions; then it is not too much to assume that the mystics and sages of the past were correct. These Sages told us the same things in regard to the energy of the Unmanifest Source and the forming of the manifest material world. It seems that the physicists of our day are our mystics and sages, inasmuch as today's clergy and theologians for the most part, have abdicated the role.

We live in a four-dimensional world according to our ordinary senses: length, width, height, and duration. This is our material experience. What of the world of spirit? Spirit is invisible because it knows not dimension or duration. It is Spaceless/Timeless. When we mistakenly perceive the word Spirit as a thing or object in our material way of expression, Spirit is automatically allocated the concept of an object (space) with duration.

Our whole language based on subject and object is structured in a material way of looking at things. Our culture and language unwittingly conceive of god and Spirit as things in time and space. Language, in spite of its limitations, is still connected to our past and holds many clues to the thinking process and worldview of our ancestors. Many words in our language are relics from outworn paradigms. The paradigm shifts but the vocabulary lingers on. The opposite is also true. Some words and phrases still retain insights into the meaning of our world that we have all but forgotten: words such as insight, understanding, unspeakable, it has come to pass, etc. are words that carry more depth than a surface scan will show.

The concept of the satanic, like the idea of Satan itself as the father of lies, exists at the heart of illusion. The appearance of things as source is based on the lie of external forms that are unreal. A lie is the absence of truth. By strict definition a lie does not even exist; and at best, as a denial of truth a lie is an illusion. Appearance is never the reality for Spirit, the invisible essence of the real. Salvation, or more properly our healing, results from the undoing of this illusory unreality.

Some of our paradigms about god are quite limited while others have excellent meaning. When contrasted with the idea of god as personality, the idea of god as Law or Principle is much to be preferred. We can speak of the law of prayer, the law of love, laws of justice, or laws of karma. When our sense of divine being is out of balance it is helpful to think of the principle that we may have added incorrectly, or have entered the wrong numbers in our spiritual checkbook. On the other hand, when we deal with a personal crisis and in desperation cry out for help, we are coming from our feeling-sense and are more likely to envision a divine parent than impersonal Principle. Fortunately our Spiritual reality continues to look after us in spite of any apparent metaphysical lapse; for eternal impersonal Spirit is our divine and very personally experienced parent.

One can believe that there can be a presence of the absence of god, as in the death of god controversies of the 1960's. I have wondered about the absurdity of the question, "If god died, did god go to heaven?" Could it be that some of the proponents of the idea, such as William Hamilton, were trying to say that it was the concept of the object god that was no longer valid? There can be no absence of the presence of god, as there can be no absence of All-That-Is. The presence of the absence of god can only be argued in the illusion of a material dimension. The Unmanifest reality of god is always the Presence of Eternal Now.

To understand some questions we must ask, "Are we looking at a presence or the absence of a presence? Is cold a presence or an absence? Is darkness a presence or an absence?" A scientific view tells us that cold is not a reality but simply a subjective label for the absence of heat. Likewise, darkness is simply our label for the absence of light. Metaphysically, sin and fear result from belief in the absence of love.

It is somehow difficult to experience cold, darkness, sunrise, and sunset and then be told these things do not exist. Standing outside shivering in below zero temperatures arguing that there is no such thing as cold appears to border on insanity. The choice is in the manner in which the incident is described. One can describe the situation as being very cold out, when in fact the explanation of the experience is more accurately stated as an absence of the energy of heat or that it's not very warm out. Lower temperatures simply absorb more body heat.

Consider the flashdark – A small cylindrical object containing negative energy that can pierce the light with a beam of darkness – but nobody ever made a flashdark! One does not click a switch to turn on the darkness, only to turn off the light. In a similar manner, the experience of darkness is really awareness of the absence of the presence of light. Darkness is not energy; that is why darkness cannot overcome light. In the same sense, evil is not a form of energy and in the words of the prologue cannot overcome good. In the realm of metaphysics we can, by negative belief, think that we have succeeded in turning off the light of god. "Darkness is a lack of light as sin is a lack of love."[61]

It is a major shift of paradigm to realize that the sun does not rise or set but rather the earth's horizon is doing the movement. Sunrise is actually earthset and sunset is as a matter of fact earthrise. It is a similar shift to recognize that cold and dark are not real and have no causal energy and are only experienced as an effect.

Very few, if any, philosophical or theological issues can be classified concretely as right or wrong. Mathematicians can say unequivocally that two plus two is four; but with most concepts and ideas there is always another side to the equation. In these areas acceptability is always on a sliding scale. Legalists tend to see issues as black or white; religious legalists in particular seem unable to cut anybody slack.

In the conflict between legalism and the need for non-judgment, Jesus espoused the spirit of liberty. It is the distinction between the letter of the law and the spirit of the law. Principle must be upheld but not at all costs. When principle is violated, the act is a mistake, not a sin against principle. A proper response is one of correction, not judgment and condemnation.

On this basis, one can look at some of the judgmental statements attributed to Jesus in the gospel accounts and question their authenticity. The biblical record contains many statements Jesus never said. Some sources have argued that statements attributed to Jesus may have had their source in at least three different teachers of that time.

---

[61] A Course in Miracles, Text: – page 9

Contrast Matthew's gospel, which has Jesus argue that divorce forces people into adultery, with the story in John's Gospel of the woman taken in the very act and brought before him. The words "Neither do I condemn you" are much more in the spirit of the law than the intention of those who in their purpose to stone her demanded the letter of the law.

Unfortunately, because of scriptural texts on both sides of the issue, many churches and their people are very uncomfortable with the issue of divorce. The Roman Catholic Church is famous for its sophistry in arguing that certain marriages in fact did not really take place. Hence, the annulment of something which is supposed to have never really happened.

Where does one find the correct paradigm for understanding the relationship between Unmanifest Eternal Spirit and the apparent world of substance and duration?

The laws of physics demonstrate that space/time must be thought of as concepts and ideas, points of choice and intention, rather than the apparent facts of life. When light is observed from the paradigm of wave theory it appears to the observer as wave; when observed as particle it appears as particle. Our view of spirit is no less influenced by the paradigm of the observer. Our decisions are always based upon our beliefs. Too many times we try to change our behavior when, in fact, the one thing we are able to do is change our belief system.

Many seem to believe that personal value is based upon things possessed or controlled. The story of Jesus and the rich young ruler concerns beliefs regarding the supposed value of things. The young man wanted to enter the kingdom but was asked to give up attachment. There is no worth in attachment and there is no merit in detachment. The value is in non-attachment, a place where things or lack thereof are given no value whatever. Neither riches nor poverty are a problem, but attachment or detachment in regard to either is. It is the love of money (attachment) that is called the root of all evil.[62] Edgar Cayce put forward that the young man came back the next day, having followed Jesus' suggestion.

The gospel records that the Son of Man had no place to lay his head. We might respond to this as many have with the attitude, "My, ain't it awful". However, this is not a statement of loss but a statement of choice. Trust in the flow of life allowed Jesus not to be concerned about what he would wear or where he should stay; he knew that he did not need to possess a place to lay his head. Paul said he died daily and that in the flesh he had

---

[62] I Timothy 6:10

learned both to be abased and to abound. He had learned that in whatever state he found himself therewith to be content.[63]

To possess a thing is a trick of time. One has the anticipation of getting, coupled with the fear of losing. Even when believed to be possessed in the now, the thing is always other. When the thing is gone, one has the memory of possession. We can think we possess a thing but to do so is instead to accept that the thing has possessed us. As Henry David Thoreau pointed out in his adventure at Walden Pond, we do not own a house, the house owns us.

Again, a tree falling in the forest makes no sound. Sound is the product of a tuned receptor. The electromagnetic spectrum is very broad. The universe is filled with energies that are not perceivable to our bodily senses: X-rays, Cosmic rays, radio waves, atomic radiation, and magnetism. We speak of the absence of visible light as darkness, but we must include the question "If there is no sound without the ear, is there no light without the eye?" Is light the product of a tuned receptor tuned to presence or absence? We are surrounded with Light the body's eyes will never see.

Every understanding is from an inner meaning given to outer observation. Suffering and depression have their source in our mistaken and judgmental inner meanings, projected outward. Innocence makes no judgment on experience. Forgiveness is the way we bring about release of judgment. Things and circumstances have only the meaning we give them.

The material world has a 'factual' existence as form, and form does have a relationship to Spirit. The material world, however, is not cause, it is effect; and effect is perception by the personal self and is not spiritual reality. Change can only truly be brought about in our perceptions of the material world through the vision of the reality of Spirit. The effect of perception is in our mind; we must choose differently in order to see differently.

A vital issue of the relationship of Spirit and material world is the problem of evil and the nature of the material world; it is the question of dualism against monotheism, and understanding panentheism or acosmic pantheism. For most people, the major difficulty with the central theme of this book would probably be its position that the material world is an illusion. Historically, theologians have been wrestling with this issue under many different guises. In general, the question has been called the problem of evil; stated in its simplest terms, "How can there be one god all powerful and good that coexists with evil?" The theological and philosophical attempts to solve this question are varied. One of the more direct answers to

---

[63] Philippians 4:11,12

this question is to accept the dualistic idea that there are two powers in the universe, one good and the other evil. There is also the position that god is source of both good and evil; one might call this a radical monotheism.

Traditional Christianity has accepted a modified dualism. According to its position, there are at present two powers, god and the satanic; but the satanic's power is subservient. God permits the satanic to operate in the world, and after the world is tested, in the fullness of time, the devil will be put into chains. In some inexplicable way the satanic is serving god's purpose, at least temporarily.

The nature of the material world is at the heart of this question. The question of evil is derived from our experience or perception of evil in this world. The question asked is, "Does evil exist and if not, what is the meaning of what we must call 'apparent evil'?" Others begin with the unqualified statement that evil exists: "Evil exists, but where does it come from?" Some argue that the source of evil is the material world; but this approach raises the next question, "Did a good god create this material world, that we now suppose to be the source of evil?" "Did god create this material world with a free potential to separate from god?" (The fall)

The theological solution to these questions presented by the bulk of traditional churches in our country is based on the hierarchical system of theology that was accepted in the early centuries of the church when it became dominated by the political beliefs of the Roman Empire. This system begins with the monotheistic assumption that god is the ruler and source of the world. The created world was separate from its creator and had the potential freedom of rebellion just like any other political subject. This was, after all, the experience of the Roman Emperor and the Roman Empire. To understand the connection of the politics of Rome and the theology of the early church, it is necessary to recall that for generations the emperor had been considered divine, having received his powers directly from the god or gods who had created the world.

As might be expected according to this theory, in god's newly created world a rebellion took place. This theory did not find its source initially in the Roman Empire, as it was also a reflection of the Jewish political theology of the day. Jewish theology of evil had also been based on rebellion against authority. The Hebrew people developed a complex system of fallen angels whose chief was Lucifer, a fallen angel of light. The Jewish legend of the fall combined the rebellion of newly created humankind with the prior rebellion of one-third of heaven's angels.

The result of this mythological background was that the early church had a built-in system to explain the nature of evil. Evil found its source in the god-given freedom to rebel. The story of the fall, at this point, tells of god's angry reaction to the rebellion and his curse upon the earth and humankind. There results a mythology about The Garden of Eden where everything was perfect; but now humankind as a result of god's angry action is forced outward into a world of sweat, toil, tears and pain. The existence of evil is a result of god's curse. Evil is explained and monotheism as a modified dualism has been preserved.

Confronted with the evident fact that god had cursed humankind, the priests of god needed to develop a theory of reconciliation. In earliest form, burnt offerings wafted their pleasing smoke into god's nostrils so that god would overlook the transgressions. When priests took over, this then shifted to blood offerings so that the priests could consume the meat. Finally offerings became monetary gifts, much more convenient for institutional religion. From the beginning, these were substitutionary offerings; in simplest terms the death of one in place of another. At times, even human sacrifices were offered, but these extremes were gradually modified to the place where eventually monetary gifts or tithes were also acceptable.

Institutional religion has always seemed to be able to make people pay for their salvation. One of the crassest examples in history to my knowledge was the sale of indulgences by the Roman Catholic Church in the Middle Ages to enable the souls of the dead to escape from Purgatory; this action was so offensive that it led to the Protestant Reformation.

This composite theological theory, which could be classified as a modified dualism, is the basic theology of the traditional church to this day. Traditional theology in its theory of creation accepted an initial separation of the creation from god in the guise of freedom to choose. It accepted the material world as something other than god. This was the essential meaning of the ancient god Mammon, *the god of the material world*. This is a form of dualism unacceptable to me.

Because a dualistic theory is unacceptable, there are two basic alternatives available: The first suggests that god created the world and the world is simply an extension of god; all of materiality is to be considered a part of god. The meaning of pantheism is, it's *all god*, both good and evil.

An alternate solution was the attempt to connect god directly to the world but not to actually be the world. This position was the argument that god was involved in the world but is not the world. The meaning of acosmic pantheism or panentheism is *in all things* god works. God, our true being, is involved *in* the world, but is not *of* the illusory substance of the world!

The problem with this position is that if god and the world are not the same thing and there is only one reality in the universe, what is the nature of the world? If the world is real we are back to the problem of dualism. If

93

god is the only reality in the universe, and the world and god are not the same thing, then in non-dual theology, the world cannot be real. It can appear real and we can accept the fact of its appearance; but ultimately we must understand that this appearance is an illusion.

Only in space/time can we experience the frequency of sound and light, which alone can form the beauty of a melody or the splendor of a master's painting. The vision of spirit is imparted into our vision of the 'real world' and underlies our experience of space/time. Since the genius of Albert Einstein, whole new vistas in regard to a non-dualistic understanding of the material world have opened. Physicists tell us, point blank, that the space/time universe is an illusion. Its underlying reality is a mysterious, unknown as yet, source of both energy and matter; current physical theory certainly supports the concept of panentheism or acosmic pantheism.

The theological basis of this book is twofold; on the one hand, to critique traditional theology; and on the other hand, to develop an understanding of the theology of non-dualism. Non-dualistic theology has ample witness among the sages of the world. I believe that Jesus taught non-dualistic theology when he emphasized the nature of the kingdom of god within us. Non-dualistic theology was the essential reasoning behind the prologue to the gospel according to John. It is at the heart of Buddhism and Vedanta and has been described as the perennial philosophy.

Jane Roberts, scribe for an entity called Seth, had some thoughts on going with the flow. "The whole thing about techniques is the idea that you need certain methods to make things work for you, when all you have to do is let them alone: Then they "work" automatically. If you forget that fact, then you'll always be looking for better methods which will never really work because Nature and your own nature work best when left alone. If you're going to study such issues at all, then look for what you do right, and you'll always find that in those areas you let yourself alone and do what comes naturally, because you are inclined in that direction. When you concentrate on what's wrong, you almost always try too hard. Look for methods that will work better than the ones you're using now. The truth is that the methods themselves stand in the way, whatever they are, because Nature doesn't use methods. It 'works' because it is what it is. Methods presuppose the opposite, in whatever area of your concern. They show your belief that nature doesn't work right on its own."

Paul testifies that his experience was not so much to apprehend as to be apprehended by.[64] We do not contain or express god, it is rather that god contains and expresses as us. The Timeless functions within our experience

---

[64] Philippians 3:12

of time, to will and to do of its own good purpose. This highlights the question of our own degree of involvement in the quest. Some speak of searching for god while others speak of god searching for us. Do we seek the Tao or does the Tao seek us? Our best way of search is to allow by active submission, "Be Thou in charge at my request"; the inner meaning of *wei wu wei* (effortless accomplishment).

Jesus said, in regard to the outer events we come to face in life, "What is that to thee? Follow thou me."[65] Seeing changes, the Seer remains the same. Events won't change our experience of reality, but our judgment of events will. It depends on what we choose to buy into. Buy into external temporal form or the only sensible alternative, Internal, Eternal, and Invisible Reality.

The peace of god is not peace from god. It is not peace received by god from external circumstance, or given by god to another; it is the peace of god Itself. Jesus said, "My peace I give unto you." We can know the identical peace we share with him; and as we allow ourselves to be perfected as god manifestation, we will have the peace of god Itself. It is likewise with love. It is not god's love for us; it is the love of god Itself we will feel and know within us, for we are as god is. Be perfect, for god has created you as Itself.[66]

---

[65] John 21:22, 23
[66] Matthew 5:48

Be Perfect

What God extends is perfect and complete.
If what we are experiencing is not,
Then we are not experiencing
What God extends.
What God extends is all there is.
If we are experiencing something
God has not expressed
Then, we are experiencing
Only a dream.
The choice is
To change our experiencing,
By allowing God to show us
Itself,
In Its Love and in
Its expression of Being.
All we need to do is,
Let go, the tight hold we have
On the experience of the unreal,
That God has not expressed.
God will find Its way to us.
We need not work to accomplish
God's Will,
But, to let loose,
And allow
God's reality to manifest.

George E. Fandt

Chapter Four—Being Born Again
Enlightenment

If You Love Me – Let Me Come (again) From Within Thee.

The western church and Paul still expected a literal physical Second Coming of Jesus as future sovereign and military, political savior. The Jewish prophets had referred to the coming 'Day of the Lord'. Many of the Jews of Jesus' day were eagerly expecting a Messiah, who would overthrow the tyranny of Rome and establish god's divine kingdom on earth. The conservative 'Bible believing' Christians of today are still expecting a 'Second Coming' of Jesus to do the same thing. What Jesus failed to do in the first coming, he is surely supposed to accomplish in his second.

The coming of the Son of Man is still awaited by those whose religious focus is on the outer world of appearances. The conservative religious view that the world is going to hell in a handbasket is amplified further by the belief that this terrible situation is the result of an external satanic force and therefore demands the outside intervention of god to set it straight.

Little credence is given to Jesus' own teaching about the coming of the Son of Man. The designation 'Son of Man' is one Jesus himself owned. It is similar if not identical to the '*I am*' statements he made referring to his own experience of the Christ of god as an inner reality.

When problems are viewed as the result of outside forces, upon which we can blame the situation, we rationalize with the notion that whatever the predicament, it is not our responsibility. When we understand effective prayer, we begin to get a handle on the difference between the inner world of reality and the outer world of appearance. Conversely, until we distinguish illusion and the Real we will not understand effective prayer.

Many prayers are directed toward god in an attempt to change exterior circumstances. One must wonder why we are so self-contradictory in our expression of prayer. We say we believe that god is all knowing and then pray in order to inform god of our circumstances and to let god know what is going on. We claim to believe that god is seeking to bring us to perfection in an all-loving concern for our well being and then pray as if it will take our persuasion to get god involved. We say that we believe that the will of god is in our best interest and then pray that god will help our own particular desires and plans to be carried out. We say that god watches over our loved ones and us and then pray as if god has forgotten that we exist.

All of the above statements about prayer reflect our belief in god as a Personality who exists objectively outside of us in a heaven located somewhere else in another dimension of space/time.

True prayer is not an exercise designed to change god. It should become an attitude in which change occurs in us in recognition that the heaven in which god resides is as Jesus said, within all things and us. Jesus experienced and taught the necessity of the experience of Christ within. This is the means by which we learn to trust and focus on our true Source. The Christ of god and its power is knowledge of the Father within.

I have made reference in preceding chapters to the difference between being born again and receiving a birth certificate. The new birth is not accomplished by an alteration to the supposed heavenly records of the saved and lost. It is not something that changes anything outside or elsewhere, and especially it does not change god or god's attitude toward us. Enlightenment does have a profound effect on our attitude toward god and on our understanding of the role Spirit plays in transforming our lives. This new birth or enlightenment cannot be achieved until one recognizes and connects the Universal Spirit and the individual. Every Sage of the major world religions has tried to communicate this abstraction. Each has faced the task of attempting to set forth in as concrete language as possible, what is impossible to concretize. Their approaches all seek to point to the means by which the Purely Unmanifest energizes the means of the manifest. It is certain that both the original Unmanifest and its Energy expression maintain original purity, for the Mind/Voice is after all in the presence of the Source. The Source and the Means do not lose their common identity with Spirit.

The Manifest world, however, being a construct of mind or thought form, retains its sense of spiritual reality for us only as we are able to hold the unity of its true identity. If known by the unified Mind connected to Source, the reality is maintained. If perceived by the ego as disconnected from its Source and as an end in itself, this split mind manifests a world that has become an illusion instead of reality to the perceiver. The problem of perceived separation is that in an encounter with suffering in the physical *effect* of manifestation, we have freedom to believe illusion. If that is our choice then for us the outer seems to have become material *cause*. The philosophical choice we all face in this dilemma is posed by the question,

"Which is real, Spirit or Matter?" If Spirit is real then matter is the illusion; if matter is real then Spirit is illusion, unless we accept that all is god, the concept of cosmic pantheism. To believe both the world and god are real is to hold the untenable dualistic position of having two gods and two powers.

Unfortunately, this was a position held by many at the time of Jesus, with god and the satanic acting as the power of good and the power of evil. We have not yet grasped the importance of the fact that Spirit and the physical, material world cannot both be ultimately real. We must learn that what is different is different; and what is the same is the same.

The fox in Antoine de Saint Exupery's "The Little Prince" shared with the Prince the secret, "It is only with the heart that one can see rightly; what is essential is invisible to the eye."[67]

The orthodox concept of the doctrine of the Trinity gets lost in an endless tangle of personality. When one understands that god is Spirit and not an object or person, the knot untangles. The Cause is god. The means is Word or expression, and the effect of god's expression is the Sonship. The Love that binds them as the Source to its Expression and welds them together is the Whole Spirit. These three are Source, Expression and Holistic oneness; or god, Love and Sonship, the Wholeness of All-That-Is. Jesus taught that the Source was god as Father; the means was the Holy Spirit; and the result was the Sonship. This is a proper logical sequence, but misunderstood when interpreted in the Trinitarian sense that sonship is unique to Jesus and not universal to the whole world. The Sonship of the world is misperceived when the manifest world is separated from its Source. This is a perception in need of healing that can be accomplished only by our own awareness of Sonship and its Unity. The birth of sonship always comes from within.

Most of us begin to see the potential of being born of Spirit. Few there are who have truly realized it. Being born again is not something we accomplish; its reality is already ours, and we must be found by *it*. We must remove walls of judgment and unforgiveness in order to prepare the way for the awareness of that Source, which has always been present.

Jesus expanded the Holy Spirit as the glory of the whole spirit to include everyone: "The glory (imprint) you have given me, I have given them, so that they may be one, even as we are one."[68] Thus, we too are the Son of Man risen with healing in its wings. We are the light of the world and the salt of the earth. It is by means of our own new birth that we will see our world born anew and know the Way, Truth, and Life because our minds are

---

[67] The Little Prince, Antoine de Saint Exupery:—Pg. 87
[68] John 17:22

one with All-That-Is. We need to understand Jesus as a teacher and Mystic who experienced the reality of the One. It makes no difference whether Jesus was the greatest or first to discover the real power of the One.

The prologue to John's Gospel presents the spiritual progression from god through logos to all things made, the whole universe, as born of god dwelling among us.[69] John used the term logos to refer to the means or energy by which all material phenomena are brought into being.

In a parallel of the same logic, the Pauline concept is that the universal Christ of god is found identically within Jesus and us. The Christ is god's Mind/Voice within us all. Paul taught that the Christ of god in us was the foretaste and hope of glory. In Paul's terms, this was the mystery hid from ages and generations and now revealed to us.[70]

"The glory you have given me, I have given them." "Christ in us the hope of glory." Glory is not a common word in use today. The word glory means honor and distinction, and a pinnacle of enjoyment and true prosperity; it is as before stated, the *imprint of god* within us. This Christ has been given to us and is god's imprint within us awaiting our discovery.

In the Buddha's teachings and the Hindu scriptures these same concepts are based on Sanskrit terms. Brahman is the Absolute transcendent Principle of all existence; Atman, the immanent eternal Self, is the inner reality fundamental to non-Atman, which is the world of things and the personal self. Thus the Unmanifest Brahman, by means of Atman, expresses the reality underlying the appearance of non-Atman, the outer world of self and things called Maya (illusion).

Lao-Tzu is credited with authorship of the 'Tao Te Ching' – 'Classic Way of Integrity or Virtue' which is the basis of Taoist teachings. Most scholars believe that Lao-Tzu was not historical but a composite of many teachers of the Tao. Tao is understood as the Way, or Means, by which the Unmanifest has given rise to the manifest.

Each of these approaches shares in some sense the same basic idea.

First, the source: The Godhead, Brahman, Cause, Tao, Source, Undifferentiated Unmanifest Potential, Energy, Mind, Love, Light, Reality and Pure Being. Transcendent, Pure being that does not exist in any form or objectivity whatever. Pure Being in the strictest sense is neither finite nor infinite, neither existent nor nonexistent, for even these polarities are perceived as differentiated things and objects.

Second, the means or way: Atman, Te, Logos, Mind/Voice, Christ, Holy Spirit or Whole Spirit, the Means, the Way, the Directive, the Emergence,

---

[69] John 1:13
[70] Colossians 1:26,27

the Unfolding, the Expression, the Imprint and the Living Word. The means is not the unmanifest Pure Being of the Father but a conveyance of god's quality, intent, intelligence and instrumentality; underlying a world still carrying the energy of the One, but operative in what appears to us as the outer world of space/time.

Third, the effect: expression of the Mind/Voice, outer phenomena, apparent things, solid tangible but illusory objects, personal selves, bodies, personalities and egos including thoughts and ideas. All of which are energized by impersonal Mind, but in the illusion of separation modified by the beliefs of personal minds seemingly split from the one mind.

In the simplest terms god is transcendent source or All-That-Is. The Holy Spirit is the immanence of the source energized and revealed when listening with the heart, and looking beyond the world of appearances (illusion). Individuated and separated persons not knowing the oneness of the Means and the Source believe the physical appearance of the world is its reality, and not knowing True Cause believe that effect is the cause. There remains a real metaphysical question: Did the separated forget their oneness, or in the process of unfolding have not yet uncovered it? Did we fall from perfection by forgetfulness, or are we still in the process of being expressed? I, for one, cannot conceive of losing an awareness of the Real once attained; but I can conceive that we are still involved in a dynamic process of Spiritual expansion and evolution.

Cause, means, and effect are a triunity of being, and at the spiritual level are all one. Jesus understood this relationship and could see beyond effect, to the means behind it as first cause. Jesus did not perceive his reality as a personal self, symbolized by his body. Rather, he accomplished and taught an enlightenment experience in the ability to know oneness. "The Father and I are one." Unfortunately, the church has taken this expression of oneness as unique to Jesus alone, and not applicable to everyone and everything. He becomes an idol to be worshiped rather than an example to be emulated. This concept of the uniqueness of Jesus as personal self elevated him in perception to a status *not* like other men. "Not like other men" was the unjustified prayer of Jesus' parable. What an irony, that one of Jesus' most potent stories should in its outplay of history be turned inadvertently against him! The parable of two men going up to the temple to pray, taught that the Pharisee was wrong and was after all like other men. In the current framework of traditional Christianity, Jesus is now superior to and unlike his brothers and sisters. The one thing Jesus wanted us to know was that with regard to potentiality, he was exactly like everyone else.

The text of John 14 specifies: "The Father works and I work, but greater works shall you do, than I have done." "I go to the Father and will send the comforter." *We also* will inevitably learn to say, "The Father and I are one." In these statements Jesus makes his connection with Source and so also must we. The basic fault with the church's traditional perception of Jesus as a unique member of the trinity, is the separation and gulf this dogma creates between Jesus and the rest of us. It is no wonder most of us look at Jesus' teaching and accomplishments and say, "Of course! He was god! What else are we to expect?"

Heaven and hell are based on the concept that there is a personal self or ego that is lost, needing to be saved. Salvation in terms of the ego can be looked upon either as a legal release from punishment or the healing of a debilitating condition. New birth is healing, not victory in a lawsuit. If we have not experienced inner reality we are living in hell (separation).

Again, religion in our culture talks about being born again as a legal document or birth certificate. The idea is, that by the act of an external savior this certificate is a reprieve or pardon from well-deserved punishment. As regards birth, there is in this approach little or no period of gestation. Travail is perceived not as a grand unfolding but as an escape from the punishment we deserve. Real birth is descriptive of a process of growth. It is also a kind of death to the pre-birth awareness. "Except a corn of wheat fall into the ground and die"[71] is an idea followed by a sense of resurrection. To be of the Spirit is to have undone the personal, separated sense of ego, and to have become alive to the realities of god (resurrection).

Only ego could want to *go* to heaven – the Spirit is already there! If you're born again, you don't go to heaven because you don't need to! The concept of going to heaven is not a reality – it is a functional illusion. We do not go any place; the reality we need to uncover is the fact that we are already there. The experience of being born again is recognized in one's ability to say, "The Father and I are one." The ego lives in the illusion of hell; Spirit lives in the reality of heaven.

So much of religion is dedicated to saving the personal ego. "I want to go to heaven when I die", translates, as "I want my personal self to survive bodily death". Actual salvation means being healed of this particular illusion. The dewdrop's identity is not separated when immersed in the whole ocean. To be truly healed is to discover that the so-called personal self is just a separated piece of debris that will dissolve when we discover that our oneness does not contain the device of separation. It is like ghostly energy that is left behind haunting the scene of a tragedy. It may well be, that as long as one believes in the personal self, this sense of separated self continues between physical lifetimes until the need for it dissolves.

---

[71] John 12:24

Jesus taught that we are a unity of energy or spirit, one with god and one with each other. He who seeks to preserve the personal self loses the wholeness of reality. One gains the world of separated illusion at the cost of losing recognition of one's own unified soul. We attain the true Self (soul) in the dissolution of personal self; enlightenment brings to us the joy and blessed awareness of this imprinted glory.

It is a difficult process to become aware that what we thought we are doesn't even exist. Our whole life in a physical body is caught up in the illusion that we are a distinct entity. We ultimately achieve release from this confusion and begin to understand that we are not a body but are free, for we remain as god created us. The memory of our identity remains as we incorporate the whole. (Holiness)

At this point it is well to remember the Buddhist story of the dewdrop merging with the ocean. The point being, that the dewdrop is not absorbed by the ocean but rather absorbs it. When we come to understand that we are not separated egos, we will also appreciate that we have not lost any of our creations of love even though created within the illusory limited consciousness of bodily existence. We retain everything that is real. Our memories of life experience will remain intact, and we will know from whence we have come. We will never lose what has true value to us. The world always has real meaning when we understand that it is not source.

The salvation which many of the peoples of the world pursue, defend, argue over, and fear to lose, is a sham. A charade not because they are not saved but because they are not lost. The salvation pursued in this charade is always outside and dependent upon some other – an external god or realm. This is the realm sought by the soap operas, and it is always dependent upon the behavior of others; those we believe make us feel bad or happy about ourselves. We think if only *they* would meet our perceived needs, then *we* would be OK. This is what I call 'soap opera consciousness'. Jesus said, "My kingdom is not of this world." and, "The kingdom of god is within you." This realm within is a state of being, not an external state of doing.

When Jesus said, "No one shall pluck them out of my hand."[72], which is to say, from god consciousness, he was not saying that the lost, once saved, could never be lost again, i.e. Calvinistic eternal security. He was simply saying that god has never lost anyone in the first place. It is an arrogant religious view to believe that we in our ego state have successfully destroyed what god has expressed; or to believe that we can destroy the life god is manifesting through us. Our sense of being lost is not that some sin has separated god from us, but that we are mistaken in who we think we are.

---

[72] John 10:28

This mistake can be corrected. To repeat: god has never lost anyone. The journey is without distance and when we have arrived at the end we will discover we have never been anywhere but *here*. Conversely, when we discover we are always *here,* we will have arrived at the end of the journey.

A PBS television program about Albert Einstein quoted him as saying at the graveside of a friend, "Time and space are illusions, albeit, very stubborn ones." A major problem with most religious institutions of today lies in their inability to translate this scientific realization of physics into a modern presentation of faith. If time and space are truly illusion, then questions arise as to all the apparent events and situations that seem to occur within the space/time event. All the judgments of traditional right and wrong, based upon appearance, come into question if the context in which they have occurred is found to be in question, which is to say, an illusion.

Religious institutions are not the only ones lagging behind in this context. The medical model that the physical brain has produced the mind raises the question as to the source of mind. The concept of material brain producing the mind is subject to questions raised by the space/time illusion. On the possibility that it is Mind or Spirit, that has produced the brain, Carl Sagan in his PBS series, "Cosmos", declared that there is not one smidgen of evidence for this theory. Sagan apparently had little exposure to parapsychology or the perennial philosophy.

The non-canonical "Gospel of Thomas" has a statement (logia 29, paraphrased) ascribed to Jesus – If spirit has brought forth matter – this is hard to accept (difficult), but if, on the other hand, matter has brought forth spirit – this is too much to accept (ridiculous).

The ability to see beyond the illusion of appearance is found in the spiritual root of forgiveness. Forgiveness is based on learning to hold the present experience of apparent perspective lightly, to see beyond the meaningless appearance and let go our judgment of what we now understand as an event in time. In appearances, we see only the past, we are not seeing the *is*-ness of reality but the *was*-ness of memory. The filter of memory/judgment forms the apparent world of space/time experience. The god of this world is illusion (the satanic), and this illusion needs to be released and overcome. Thus, the apostle Peter's assessment of the situation prior to Jesus' arrest was labeled satanic in Jesus' words, "Get thee behind me, Satan". This was a perception based upon Peter's fear for his lord's safety. His judgment, based on remembrance of past experience and prejudice, overshadowed his hope with a foreboding sense of the future.

We do not intellectually understand the timeless nature of spirit. Spirit experiences no *was*-ness of its is, and no *is*-ness of its was. The timeless has no awareness of either past or future. We can point to the meaning of time-

less-ness; but inevitably must fail to comprehend it. Such is the way of the Tao. Because our reality is Spirit, we must also come to understand that the personal ego self, too, is a construct of space/time.

Buddha taught that our perception of a separated self is the source of all suffering (unsatisfactoriness). Buddhahood, as Christhood, is the innermost spirit of us all and is recognition that there is no separated self and that the cause of all our trouble is but a mirage. This presents the problem of a self, trying to recognize that there is no self. In these circumstances one can only allow the sense of self to dissolve. It obviously can not be a choice of self to dissolve itself. One can only choose a willingness to allow the unfolding process of Spirit to occur. Once we give permission, Spirit will do the work; the only thing required is a little willingness on our part. We consent to the demise of personal self and in so doing let go of the unreal.

We must be actively involved in undoing our own constructs, our own attachments to the space/time world of illusion. At the same time, it is not our job to construct an inner kingdom that is already there. The kingdom will assert itself in what appears to be the fullness of time as a disclosure of time-less-ness. Ours is the task of letting go the outer, which has no real value, and accepting the gift of the inner, which is the only value that truly exists. By removing the barrier of externals we open ourselves and become willing to allow the inner to express that which it has always been.

At this point, most spiritual teachers lift up our need to experience a greater or higher Self. This higher Self is not individuated but universal Spirit and common to all. In Christian context it would be called the Christ. The universal Christ was the realm within, which Jesus discovered; so too, must we. It is an experience we all must learn as he learned "The Father and I are one." Paul expressed in Colossians, "The mystery hid for generations, now made manifest, Christ in you, the hope of glory."[73] The self cannot try to be enlightened! The self cannot be enlightened! The self is not enlightened; rather, the enlightened Self replaces it. When the sense of personal self dissolves, enlightenment is born. We are born again!

In this present Christian culture, where Jesus is separated from humankind into a person of the trinity, we are blinded to the view that he was a man who discovered these truths within him. We can, perhaps somewhat more comfortably, hear the teaching of Buddha as a man, discovering the same insights in terms of psychology and philosophy without the separating religious overtones of our Christian culture; because we can more objectively observe the Buddha's culture.

---

[73] Colossians 1:27

Meditation as an act of the self in order to attain enlightenment is an oxymoron (self-contradiction). Letting spirit do its work; allowing the logos to express itself; and knowing that our reality is in fact logos expression and not an isolated detached sense of discrete individual identity, is to allow union with the One. Enlightenment is not something that we do. It is the Silence that is within that which we already are. We may indicate our intention and willingness by letting go our judgments, but god energizes the experience. Meditation needs to be an experience beyond the restrictions of the personal self. In effect, one learns not so much to meditate as to be meditated. In meditation, we are answering the prayer of god and it is in answering god's prayer that our own prayers are truly answered. Certainly, prayer is not informing, motivating, or directing god to meet our needs and wants. Prayer is the Intention of god and the energy of All-That-Is flowing through us to refresh and restore us, inadvertently refreshing others. Prayer is not our using god; it is god exercising us.

Although one cannot define the meaning of the words, 'timeless' or 'spaceless', we need at least to point toward their meaning. Without time, there can be no was and no will be. Without space there can be no other, no where, and no subject/object. Language is rooted in subject/object, is, was, and will be. To suggest timeless and spaceless results only in an approximation; without duration and space, no object exists – only Spirit.

If time and space are illusions, as Einstein stated, then all space/time objects in and of themselves are appearance/illusion. Illusion, as we understand the craft of magic, does not mean that the appearance is only imagination, but simply that things, are not as they appear. In our material experience, appearance is accepted as a fact. The illusion is not the product or fault of the appearance; rather it is a fault of our perception and interpretation. In short, illusion is a product of our own belief systems. When we perceive illusion, we do not become sinful before god and thus in need of punishment by Principle. We are mistaken in interpreting what the body sees, and need to have our mistaken outlook corrected. The nature of spirit is beyond time and space. Spirit simply *is,* and cannot be objectified. Hence the Buddhist phrase, "God is, but there is no god." To repeat again, god as object does not exist – god as subject exists but the nonobjective existence of god remains a mystery. This same understanding applies to the perception of self. Self is, but there is no self. Self, objectified, is not the spiritual Self but the illusory personal self. *I am but there is no me.* The subjective, eternal *I,* is in unity with All-That-Is; *self* is an illusion.

The church has taught us that the gift of god is eternal life. It has also held the position that the gift can be withheld and will not be received until we are legally saved. It is a self-contradiction to say that at a point in time we are given eternal life. After all, what is eternal must go both forward and backward in its relationship to time. It may be that salvation/healing appears to occur at a seeming point in time; but we only have become aware that we already are in possession of life eternal. A personal experience may be thought of as having a beginning and ending in time, but Spirit is eternal and timeless in its nature.

The Chinese Taoist phrase *wei wu wei* (literally, do not do) means to accomplish without overt effort; allow, don't strive. The idea in modern thought is akin to, "Do not push the river, but go with the flow." The sense is that higher Spirit will direct and empower, if the personal ego will give permission. In reference to the inner process of the Spirit, Jesus on several occasions made statements expressing the belief that, "The Father works and I work." "The spirit blows where it wills", means that the ego or personal *self* is not in control of the workings of the Spirit or inner *Self.* "Judge not, lest you in the same manner be judged", suggests that when we do not integrate a peaceful communion between our inner and outer selves, our exterior behavior toward others will instigate such a cause/effect relationship that it will be impossible for us to experience inner peace. In other words, when our egos hold grievances we will not know grace.

The same principle is experienced in the Buddhist concept of mindfulness and is at work in the statement, "Forgive to be forgiven". Integrated harmony with the Father is also implied by Jesus' promise, "My peace I give unto you, not as the world gives, give I unto you."[74] This statement is evidence that real peace comes from inner cohesiveness, not outer power or possession.

The *Shema* of ancient Israel, "*Hear O! Israel*, The Lord your god is One.", instead of being a reference to one external god instead of many, may have carried the more basic significance that the inner god is one; When Jesus said that his yoke was easy and his burden light, he indicated something beyond religion; something that religion with all its ritual and behavioral restrictions has never understood. When you take his yoke upon you there is no burden, for 'god is good'. When Jesus suggests that we symbolically take his yoke, he is referring to a human yoke and not a yoke for oxen. The beam across the shoulders is cut out for one's neck and hollowed out to fit one's shoulders with comfort; it is an easy yoke. Ropes tied to the ends of the beam allow buckets of water or other burdens, to be carried with much less effort than by hand. I grew up in maple syrup country where the sap was carried from the Sugar Bush with human yokes.

---

[74] John 14:27

The central value of enlightenment or spiritual transformation is not only that it makes life more meaningful; it makes life easier. *We learn to trust the universe and discover that the universe has always trusted us.* When the story is told of Jesus and the little children, we understand that he said, "Allow them to come unto me for of such is the kingdom."[75] There is no doubt that he was responding to the desire and the trust of the children. They wanted to come to him but the disciples did not understand their need.

The picture is not only of the children who wanted to come; it is of a loving presence with unconditional positive regard that desired them to do so. We may see ourselves like trusting children but we can only do so in the presence of a god we can trust. When he said that the children were the ones to whom the kingdom belongs, he was also making it clear that the kingdom welcomed them as it will welcome us.

Intimations of Immortality

Our birth is but a sleep and a forgetting:
The soul that rises with us, our life's star,
Hath had elsewhere its setting,
And cometh from afar.
Not in entire forgetfulness,
And not in utter nakedness,
But trailing clouds of glory do we come –
From God, who is our home.

William Wordsworth

---

[75] Mark 10:13-15

Chapter Five—The Biblical Library
Spirit and Law

It is common in our culture to refer to the Hebrew/Christian library or Bible as if it were a single book. The more conservative Christians (Evangelical and Fundamentalist) traditionally refer to this book as the 'Word of god'. This common assumption causes a great deal of misunderstanding when one is attempting to listen accurately to the biblical witness. The contention that the Bible is a single book masks the fact that the reader is dealing with a library of books and a multitude of authors, most representing varied concepts of god, and differing points of worldview. The assertion that the Bible is the literal Word of god is in fact a clear-cut form of idolatry. A tangible object in the static form of words, a book, has taken the place of god, which cannot be contained.

Religion as practiced may demand concrete forms, but the idea of the Word of god materialized as a book destroys one's ability to understand the spiritual actuality of the real and inner Living Word. The bible as an idol, structures a paradigm for god, and that paradigm as an old-wineskin, forbids entry to a changed view of the bible as new wine; a vicious circle. Rather than Word of god, a simpler and more direct understanding of the biblical heritage would be to refer to the Bible as stories and traditions about god.

The Bible is best defined as a diary of the writings of the history and religion of the Hebrew/Christian tradition. These words about god reflect the religious and spiritual outlook of the people who recorded it. Relieved of its magical overtones, the Bible becomes an excellent source for understanding the spiritual journeys or faith stories of its heroes. Most of the biblical writings survived for long periods of time as unwritten oral tradition, passed down around nomadic campfires as a peculiar tribe or clan's explanation of its life situation, and their understanding of their relationship with their personal tribal god. The order in which records are listed in the biblical narrative is not chronological; the earlier tradition of the stories of Genesis was not the first biblical material to come into written form, nor was the book of Revelation the last.

The story of the Bible starts before Abraham, in ancient times with ancient peoples, much as the theme of the primordial well in James Michener's book, "The Source". Michener develops the story of the importance of this well to its community in Palestine, from primitive man up through the establishment of the City of Jerusalem.

The bands of desert nomads who later became the Hebrew people were mostly illiterate, innumerate, pre-scientific, scattered groups tied together by similar language roots, common desert codes, and generally overlapping territories. These territorial tribes had different dialects of a common language and used an assortment of names for their different gods. Their religious practices were full of superstition and often included human sacrifice as a part of their ritual.

Their pre-scientific views of the world often differed from tribe to tribe, and especially stand in stark contrast to those of the present day. They saw in the building of river deltas and the flow of volcanic lava, the miraculous creation of land. These experiences gave rise to the belief in four basic elements: earth, air, fire and water. The earth was the center of the universe, a geometric plane with four corners and four directions.

Two great celestial lights traveled across the sky and somehow found their way back to their starting point by traveling under the earth. The sun ruled the day and the moon ruled the night, except of course, when it stayed around in the daytime to be obscured by the sun. The cycles of the moon as it waxed and waned in a regular pattern were the source for a twenty-eight day month. The four-quarter phases of the moon gave rise to our present seven-day week. Eclipses of the moon and sun as well as planetary conjunctions were seen as divine signs and portents. The movement of the stars and constellations followed regular patterns from which a complex astrology was developed.

Over a year's time, sunrise and sunset moved on the horizon from a point far to the south to a point far to the north. At these extremes the sun stopped briefly, a solstice, before reversing its direction back. The ancients believed that twice a year the sun stopped. Supposing a battle took place during the summer solstice and the astrologers referred to it as occurring on the day the sun stood still. How long would it take in an oral tradition for common storytellers to credit the hero of the battle with commanding the sun to stop? Consider the account of Joshua's battle against the Amorites at Gibeon as recorded in chapter ten of the Book of Joshua. Biblical inerrancy is one of the greatest pitfalls faced when breaking free from religious orthodoxy.

I've seen at least one Jewish place of worship in the ancient settled areas of Palestine that used astrological symbols patterned into the mosaic tiles of a synagogue floor. This happened in spite of the supposed Deuteronomic prohibition against the making of graven images. We, who dwell today in the haze of urban sprawl, witness a dim nightly scene and have little awareness of the significant part the brilliant night sky of the desert must have played in the mythology of these people.

These were a people of tribes and clans to whom families gave fierce loyalty. Blood feuds were not uncommon. The scarce water supply was for drinking, as bathing was usually ceremonial only, normally reserved for religious ritual and the cleansing of the newborn and the dead. Even wounds were most often cleaned with the sterile sand of the desert. Territorial claims were bitterly defended, especially with regard to wells and other sources of water. War with outside groups in dispute over territorial claims was common. If the survival of one's own family, clan, or tribe was at stake, there was no compunction prohibiting the use of deadly force against any opponent in order to take what was required for survival.

People with psychic gifts were not unknown. There is ample indication of the existence of shamans, prophets, and oracles. Sometimes these gifts were respected and honored, as was the case with Joseph, and at other times sensitives were feared, outlawed and persecuted, as in the story of the Witch of Endor[76]. There were very few who had skill in writing, and most of the stories recorded in the Bible were passed down, amplified and edited by oral tradition, sometimes for centuries, before coming into written form. Storytellers often sang their stories, for the poetry and meter of the songs helped facilitate their prodigious memories. There is evidence that some present day Australian aboriginal minstrels can sing oral history going back for thousands of years. We are apt to forget the long oral development of gods, heroes, and legends in the mythology of the biblical peoples. We have been conditioned with a pious, non-critical, stereotypical appreciation to view the Bible as written by god.

In southern Europe, as was also the case in the British Isles and later in Latin America, Christian missionaries became quite adept at wiping out controversial and competitive religions and their traditions. Because of this intolerance, we have been exposed by a significantly lesser extent to the gods of Germans and Norsemen. When Christian missionaries came upon the scene, their acts of atrocity sadly depleted the oral traditions and written history of many indigenous people. If the biblical tribes had been urbanized with a written language they would undoubtedly have produced a panoply of heroes and gods, as did the Greeks and Romans.

---

[76] I Samuel 28:7

According to the biblical mythologies, there were giants in the earth in those days; men who angered god by constructing the Tower of Babel. Also heroes like Enoch who did not see death, Methuselah who lived hundreds of years, and Noah who, with his Ark, saved the continuity of humankind from destruction. Abraham became the father of Isaac and 'the chosen' people as well as the father of Ishmael whose descendents are still considered by the 'chosen' to be adversaries. Moses was the hero responsible for the union of the disparate tribes of the desert. He is the leader credited with the authorship of Torah (Law), the Pentateuch, or first five books of the Bible, notwithstanding they contain an account of his death. In addition, there were non-Jewish heroes like Melchizedek, to whom Abraham paid tithes, and Moses' father-in-law Jethro or Reuel, a priest of Midian.

The stories of the heroes and Patriarchs of the Hebrews and about Jesus and the birth of Christianity, are divided into two different covenants or sections; in Christianity they are called the Old and New Testaments. As we look at the Bible with understanding, we become aware of several general principles, ideas, and concepts. We have already spoken of both a religious and a spiritual journey. Both these themes are evident in biblical literature.

Early editors working with the stories about the dispersion of various Semitic tribes in Egypt at the time of Moses contrived to establish an account of their relationships, in stories told about the patriarchs. Some Semitic groups are left out of the coalition and only those whom the editors linked by lineage through the twelve sons of Jacob back to Abraham are included in the inheritance. Moses, in this editorial view, becomes the hero who consolidates the legend of the people of Israel.

The stories of Hebrew literature fall into various chronological categories. The time of Adam to the time of Noah is a legendary construct of later editors for there were no eyewitnesses and probably no written records from this ancient time. The stories from after the supposed worldwide flood center on the patriarchs, from Abraham to Jacob's sons, and the sojourn in Egypt. Later on, there was the conquest of Canaan, the establishment of the Kingdom and its division, and the dispersion of Israel into captivity with the resulting struggles to return.

The Pentateuch, the first five books of the Old Testament, basically contains an amalgam of oral traditions from several nomadic tribes. This viewpoint is supported by the several names for god used by the diverse groups, which probably represent specific dialects from various geographical districts. Most Bible scholars recognize the contribution of editors from these dissimilar cultural areas and also their special theological persuasions. Geographical source material is usually divided into at least three groups that used special names for god: *Adonia, Elohim* and *YHWH*

(Yahweh). Two other groups separated by theology were the priests and the prophets. Because of the many different editors and traditions; with much of the material, it is impossible to draw hard and fast lines for exact sources.

In the Pentateuch four groups are assigned initials relating to categories for the different names of god and ideology they represent. E represents *Elohim* and J was the German scholars' choice for *YHWH*. P stands for priestly and D for the book of Deuteronomy from the later prophetic group when they developed need for a written word. Thus, most Biblical scholars advocate a documentary concept based on J, E, P, & D. Added to the confusion about the sources is the fact that the priests edited the early J documents so the P represents an intermingling of J and P. Earlier stories are limited pretty much to J, E, and P, as the prophetic editors of D do not come into play until a later time.

In standard translations of the Bible, the names of god have been translated with a particular convention. Lord is a translation of *Adonia*; God rendered for *Elohim* and Lord God for *YHWH*. In the NRSV (New Revised Standard Version) *YHWH* is LORD or LORD GOD spelled in all capital letters. It should be noted that the name *Elohim* is a plural form.

This record of stories from diverse areas of the Near East is the explanation for the two separate creation stories in the book of Genesis; these two stories use different names for god. The first, a P (Priestly) account using the name *Elohim*, was probably a tradition written sometime after the Babylonian exile in the 500's BCE (Before the Common Era). The first story (1:1-2:4a) tells us of the seven days of creation and begins with darkness and void being overcome by light, linked neither to sun nor moon.

This story of the breath (*ruah*), wind or spirit of god brooding over the face of the primeval waters introduces a metaphysical dualism in its distinction between spirit and matter.

The primal world seems not to be formed by god, but exists already as a synchronistic potential. The primal dualism is then reinforced by the creation of light and its separation from darkness. Darkness is not yet considered negative, but rather seems to concur with the void representing potentiality.

There is a gathering together of the primeval waters and appearance of a firmament bubble in their midst. When dry land appears, the bubble is seen as a dome. The blue of the sky is perhaps understood to come from the color of the waters above the firmament dome. After plants and animals come into existence, generic mankind appears, male and female, whereupon god pronounces his creative work very good!

The account found in the second chapter of Genesis (2:4b–3:24), from the J (*YHWH*) document, tells the story of Adam and Eve, the serpent and the garden. In this story the god *YHWH* creates the primal couple in separate acts rather than creating generic mankind as a whole. Adam (the Hebrew word for earth) is formed from the dust of the earth and The Lord God breathes into Adam's nostrils the breath of Lives. This is the same breath of god, which blew upon the original deep in the first creation story. After that, the animals are created, brought to Adam, and named by him. There is no statement of sex in regard to the animals named by Adam, but sex seems to be presumed. Then Eve was produced from a vital part of Adam. A secondary dualism now exists; male and female. Apart from Michelangelo's artful rendition of this event on the ceiling of the Sistine Chapel, one could speculate that Adam had no need or use for sexual organs before the creation of Eve. So, did god modify Adam after the creation of Eve? Some Gnostics of the early church considered Adam as genderless; sexual organs appearing when he was split into two parts. Eve was one half of Adam; perhaps the better half?

This story of the garden continues with a metaphysical account of a fall from god's grace. Up to this time, the perfect couple was sustained by belief only in the good. They were here introduced to the dualism of good and evil by the shining serpent of appearance. Here we have the final and ultimate dualism, good and evil. Out of this split grew the concept of two gods, Yahweh and the satanic.

In their acceptance of this dualistic worldview, the primitive couple was expelled from the garden of perfection and the tree of life, to live all alone in the world. The concept of evil in contention with good was introduced, and the shining one (the serpent) becomes the symbol of the fallacy of illusion; or the mistake of judging only by appearance. The Genesis legend of the fall is a construct to explain why humankind is not perfect, as god certainly must have created them. The editors do not accept the evolutionary concept that there was no fall, and therefore fail to develop an argument that creation could be a continuing process.

In a primal sense of dualism, human perception structures an animal body and mind competing with the spiritual mind and body. The inner spiritual sense is now masked by the outer physical world and its concerns. The tension of good at war with evil preoccupies this history of humankind. The later teaching of Jesus with regard to the realm of god within is an attempt at healing this preoccupation.

Satan is here introduced as the symbolic god of appearance; the god Paul later refers to as 'the god of this world'.[77] Satan does not need to be considered a literal power in opposition to god, but is symbolic of the

---

[77] II Corinthians 4:4

illusion of display, i.e. the mistake of perceiving the appearance of form as real; rather than spirit. When talking about those who opposed Jesus, they are called children of their father, the Devil. Satan, as a concept, is of course a lie in itself, and is referred to as the Father of lies.[78]

This primitive pre-scientific worldview is further demonstrated by the story of the world's destruction through god's anger at mankind. God repented for what god had made, and caused great devastation in a worldwide flood. It is interesting to note that the floodwaters in the story are not as generally believed, the result of forty days and nights of rain. The real cause is that the firmament dome of the first creation story breaks, the windows of heaven are opened, waters above the firmament pour down, the fountains of the great deep are let loose, and the waters under the firmament gush forth. An angry god destroys the earth by bursting the bubble that was formed in creation.[79] One of several times this archaic god repents.

Again we are confronted by two accounts of Noah's story. Compare Genesis 6:18-21 with the record immediately following in 7:1-3. In the first story Noah is commanded to take into the Ark with his family two of every living thing: birds, animals, and creeping things. In the second, the numbering is altered. Of the animals designated clean by dietary law, seven pairs or a total of fourteen is the number to be rescued, whereas for the unclean animals, the number is still a single pair. The number of birds is also increased to seven pair. The increase undoubtedly was needed in order to conform to the priestly emphasis on sacrifice, for when they all disembark, Noah sacrifices from the extra clean animals and birds. (8:20)

The anger of this outdated warrior god unveils itself again in the destruction of Sodom and Gomorra. Aside from the picture of an angry god who apparently bargained with Lot to determine how many righteous people were needed to save the city, this story has another interesting facet. We are told that when Lot's wife looked back at the devastation, she was turned into a pillar of salt. According to George M. Lamsa, translator of the Peshitta, an Aramaic version of the Bible, this is an Aramaic idiom for someone who has a stroke, with resulting paralysis causing death.

The story picks up again with the story of the Jewish patriarchs: Abraham, Isaac, and Jacob. Abraham is moved by faith to journey in the direction of god's promised land. Abraham, by means of his two wives, becomes father to both Arabs and Jews. As would be expected in Jewish literature, Sarah is the wife and the other, Hagar, is but a concubine. The irony is that both groups are still fighting over who will inherit the same

---

[78] John 8:42
[79] Genesis 7:11

Promised Land. Of course, when the god of Abraham promised the land to Abraham, the gods of the indigenous people of those lands were not consulted in the matter. After Sarah's death, Abraham married again, and had several more children, but these according to the Jewish point of view were paid off and have no inheritance with Isaac, who remains, in the Jewish mind, the chosen son. To readily understand the Bible, when reading this Jewish book one must always be aware of a natural Jewish chauvinism.

Abraham came out from a land where human sacrifice was practiced. It is evident that human sacrifice continued to be practiced by the Hebrews as well. Support for this contention is seen in the last chapter of Leviticus, the story of Jephthah's rash vow and in Micah's comments about sacrifice.

Leviticus was material gathered by the priests to support their role in the forming of Jewish society. In the Leviticus account, every devoted thing (whether human or animal) was to be utterly consumed in sacrificial fire. Some things were allowed to be redeemed through cash payment, but devoted things, including humans, were not to be excepted from the fire.[80]

In Judges, the warrior Jephthah, in celebration of a military victory, makes an unbreakable vow to god in the presence of his troops. He vows that in payment for the victory, he will sacrifice to god whatever of his household should appear to him first on his arrival home. Unfortunately, the first thing he sees is his young daughter and, because he has vowed to devote her to god, she is therefore sacrificed.[81]

The story of the attempted sacrifice of Abraham's son Isaac[82] is not best understood, in the traditional interpretation of the story as a test; i.e. that god literally told Abraham to perform this act of human sacrifice and then after seeing Abraham's obedience, god's mind was changed. A clearer understanding would be, that coming from a culture that believed in the kind of primitive god who demanded the death of the first born, Abraham believed that his religious duty required this abomination. This is a belief that unfortunately persists even today, in the concept of the sacrificial death of Jesus. Fortunately, Abraham listened to his heart and not his religion.

Reflect on this scenario: Abraham grew up in a culture that practiced the human sacrifice of a first-born son by those who truly wished to prove their religious zeal and dedication. This was the outer voice of religion shouting to Abraham to prove to god his willingness to meet god's demands. On the other hand, consider that Abraham loved his wife Sarah and after a very long wait they were finally blessed with the child Isaac. Abraham loved his

---

[80] Leviticus 27:28,29
[81] Judges 11: 30-39
[82] Genesis 22:1-14

wife and he loved his child. He was now faced with the voice of a religious custom that required his son's death in order to meet god's demands. The question ordinarily posed by religion was, "Will Abraham obey the requirement of god?" The unspoken inner question Abraham faced was, "Does god really require this outrage?" The real question we all face in our spiritual growth is, will we follow the outer dictates of religious shoulds and oughts, or can we listen to our inner voice that speaks of coherence and love, the voice of the heart? The voice of the inner Christ is the proper guide. Abraham listened to his heart and not to his religion. At the point of Abraham's religious need to sacrifice Isaac, a spiritual insight enlightened his concept of god and shouted to him, 'No Way!' For listening to his inner awareness, Abraham, for this act alone, deserves to be considered a hero of faith. Would that Jephthah had been so insightful! This is a good lesson to learn, for many of our best spiritual insights are the result of an inner insistence to retreat from previously held untenable religious positions; with our own religious duty requiring us to perform abomination. When we face the untenable, remember Jesus said, "My yoke is easy, my burden is light."

It is a terrible misfortune that the basic premise of traditional Christianity is that Jesus died for our sins. In the acclaimed teaching of the prophet Micah, god does not require payment of rivers of oil or the sacrifice of ten thousand rams. Nor does god require the sacrifice of a first-born child.[83] The sacrifice of the first-born may still have been practiced by the extreme fundamentalists of Micah's day. The prophet makes a profound statement regarding the outer dimensions of sacrifice as over against the inner awareness of faith. Yet the tradition of the church especially, has been that god does require the blood sacrifice of Jesus. This traditional Christian view of god is regressive; would that the early church had listened to Micah!

This same mean-spirited picture of god is still held by those who are willing to sacrifice their children to religious systems that do not allow medical intervention for their health and safety.

One can only speculate as to what might have been the resulting ministry of the Christian church had the church been free from bondage to the belief that god needed the sacrifice of human blood in the death of Jesus. The church, instead of centering on Jesus' death, might well have chosen to emphasize the teachings of Jesus, as did the supposedly heretical Gnostics. Jesus tried to teach a Spirit filled approach to life, as over against the popular approach of form and convention, which is a way of 'doing' holiness. The ecclesiastical forces of the western church did not want such a change, for their social rank depended upon the status quo.

---

[83] Micah 6:7

Today, the institutional church does not want a Spirit of non-judgment, which would see all persons and creatures as extensions of god. The church desires only conformity to convention on the part of those called of god. This produces a conflict between lives based on a vocation in the material church and life grounded in Spirit.

The institution of the church is so ingrained in the acceptance of the early Jewish concept of blood sacrifice, it apparently no longer has the capacity to free itself from that mistaken concept. The celebration of the Mass in one form or another is the credible lie that has become the foundation of what most Christians call the worship of god.

One must remember that such stories as the sacrifice of Isaac were developed after the event. Pious storytellers have edited them to make them consistent with the acceptable theology of their time. In their primitive view, god was allowed to demand such a test and could change his mind at will. There is, as yet, in these rather archaic theological concepts, no consistency or eternal sameness in understanding the nature of the Unmanifest. God is still perceived in provincial and limiting materialistic terms. This primitive god is still conceptualized as a variable personality and an individualized being, rather than timeless and formless Spirit.

In language, an earlier aspect of more primitive culture is a different, more literal, magical deference and understanding of words and names. The name or identity symbol was granted an intrinsic power. Jacob wrestled with god's angel demanding to know its name. Moses, when confronted by the burning bush, wanted to be able to say the name of the one sending him on his mission. To name something was to have a form of control over it. To define and name with a symbolic word was to possess power over the thing named. This power was sought over persons, things, and especially gods. We have unmistakable potential when we can hold a Genie or Jinn in a bottle and control its power. We still believe, because we have labeled something we can claim to understand it. The original function of magic was control of the gods by special names, words or phrases. The word abracadabra (a b c d) was such a power term and is used even today by stage magicians.

Further complication arises from the lack of vowel symbols in the original Hebrew language. Only consonants were written, probably to save space, and the words were much like the form of shorthand used by our military. The reader must choose the correct meaning of the word, and this can be derived only from the context. Do the letters LV mean love or leave? Well into the Common Era a group called the Masorites added vowels in the form of small points placed under the consonantal text.

The sacred personal name of the god *YHWH* (Yahweh) was given the Masoretic vowel points of god's more generic name *Adonia* (Lord) in order to remind readers of written Hebrew not to pronounce *YHWH* but to say *Adonia* instead. No one was to have power over this god by being able to name him. This may have been simply fear of god's power or may have been recognition that no word could contain the reality of god. Perhaps *YHWH* was the unnamable name not because the word was too sacred but because naming god was believed impossible.

In the 1901 American Standard Version of the Bible, the vowels of *Adonia* having been linked with the consonants of Yahweh were used in the transliteration Jehovah, a word that on no account existed in the Hebrew language. This name Jehovah was never received with total acceptance although it had been occasionally used from the Middle Ages. Witness our reluctance to hear the words of the Twenty-third Psalm translated, as "Jehovah is my shepherd."

The very phrase 'Word of god' speaks of the link between Reality and language symbols. God speaks and the thing is accomplished. The New Testament concept of Logos derives from the same perspective. Even today we define science as the ability to describe, categorize, file, and name. Academic prowess is defined as the power, authority, or ability to state where something fits by naming it.

The opposite side to this rationale is of course the childish habit of 'name calling', such as the singsong chant "Liar, liar, pants on fire" and words like sissy, cheater, and dummy. These are attempts to put others into separate and negative categories and thus in effect wield power over them by giving them a spiteful name.

Adult epithets like the late Senator McCarthy's 'communist', or racist slang such as nigger, jap, gook, and hun are all attempts to dehumanize others by turning them into things, or worse yet, to deny them status as children of god. In war it is easier to kill an evil epithet than a human being.

It is Joseph, the great-grandson of Abraham, who next dominates the biblical narrative. His brothers sold Joseph, son of Jacob the grandson of Abraham, into Egypt as a slave. Development of this story of the twelve brothers later becomes the rationale for bringing together the disconnected tribes of Semitic people that found themselves in Egyptian bondage.

Joseph fell on hard times after the wife of Potiphar tried to seduce him. Joseph rebuffed her, and in humiliation and anger after being rejected, she accused him of sexual assault. As a result of her false accusation, he was imprisoned. The story may have been an acceptable explanation for the innocent presence of Joseph in prison, for that is where Pharaoh found him.

Joseph, because of his psychic abilities and his powers of divination, interpreted a dream of Pharaoh about seven fat cows and seven lean cows. He understood the cows as representing years of plenty and years of famine. As a reward, he was released from prison and attained high political rank. When the desert famine threatened his family he was able to bring his brothers to Egypt in order that they might survive. Joseph forgave his brothers for having sold him into slavery by saying simply, "You intended it for evil – god intended it for good".[84]

The story of Joseph's silver cup that was placed in his brother Benjamin's sack of grain will be understood much more clearly if we realize the value this cup held for Joseph as a tool of divination. The polished interior surface acted like a crystal ball, and enabled him to psychically dissociate his awareness for visionary purposes.[85]

Moses is the next hero to appear in the biblical story. According to the legend, he was born a Hebrew and later adopted into Egyptian royalty. He delivered the Children of Israel from bondage in Egypt and became most famous for his role in codifying the law and delivering the Ten Commandments to the people at Mount Sinai. Moses had lived for a time in the Sinai Peninsula and married Zipporah, a daughter of the land. His father-in law was Jethro, a priest of Midian. He returned to Egypt to weld together some of the loosely related Semitic tribes of the desert, and then lead them out of Egyptian bondage. It was at this time that the family connections of the story of the descendants of Abraham, Isaac, and Jacob were invented, in order to strengthen the alliance among the amalgam of Semitic tribes participating in the Exodus.

These stories were constructed along with those about Joseph and his brothers, with the intent to fashion a reason for the disparate Semitic tribes to form a political bond. There may have been Semitic people who did not join Moses in rebellion against Pharaoh. This may be a root cause of dissension between Israelis and Palestinians to this day. Ancient hatreds are not readily overcome if the present terrorism by ethnic groups is any indication.

Moses led his escaping people into the area of Mt. Sinai, which at that time was apparently an active volcano. They followed the volcanic display, believing it to be a sign from god. It was a pillar of cloud by day and a pillar of fire by night. According to the story, Moses went up onto the rumbling mountain to receive the Ten Commandments written on stone by the finger of god and delivered as codified law to the Children of Israel.

---

[84] Genesis 50:20
[85] Genesis 44:1-5

It is interesting that two versions of these Ten Commandments are preserved. We have a nomadic version[86] and one modified after the people had settled into the Promised Land.[87] The difference is that in the later version the people are enjoined not to covet a neighbor's field, a precept not needed by nomads who held land in common.

People who glibly state that they believe in the Ten Commandments are evidently not even aware that the very law they claim to accept prohibits the graven images carried around on their pocket money. It is interesting that Jesus, taking a coin with a forbidden image, said, "Render to Caesar the things that are Caesar's and to god the things that are god's."[88]

It was in the context of Sinai that the Hebrews, by virtue of being descendants of Abraham, began to identify themselves as the chosen people of god. This claim was a concept of tribal people with a nationalistic god; but the idea of being a chosen people was abhorrent when the concept of god became universalized. It may be, that no singular cause has resulted in as much Jewish persecution as this contention; for many perceive it as the ultimate form of religious arrogance. There is also a theological problem raised simply by the suggestion that god would distinguish or choose any particular group of people. As Principle, god is the same for all.

The term anti-Semitism applied to those who persecute Jews has an additional strange quirk of consequence. The people of modern Israel along with Arabs who are also a Semitic people could both be considered virulently anti-Semitic in their attitudes toward one another.

In the subsequent conquest of Canaan, the story of Achan of the tribe of Judah as told in the seventh and eighth chapters of Joshua, gives some further insight into factors involved in the development of the biblical narrative. After the fall of Jericho to Joshua's conquering army, the Israeli army launched a military assault against the relatively small city of Ai, and as a result the Israelis were soundly defeated. According to the narrative the cause of the defeat was 'sin in the camp'. Someone had taken personal loot in the destruction of Jericho instead of devoting (destroying) it as an offering to god as commanded.

In order to find the culprit, lots were drawn: first the tribe of Judah was chosen, and from Judah the clan of Zerah, and from the clan of Zerah the family of Zabdi, and finally Zabdi's grandson Achan and his family were indicated. Achan confessed to taking a beautiful robe, some silver and some gold. As a result Achan, his loot, his children, his livestock and all his

---

[86] Exodus 20:17
[87] Deuteronomy 5:21
[88] Mark 12:17

possessions were destroyed; stoned, burned, and covered with a great heap of stones. The place was then named the Valley of Calamity. Compare the concept of the god that caused this calamity with "God is Love".

Ai was then conquered using some thirty five thousand men rather than the original force of three thousand. The entire twelve thousand inhabitants of Ai were slaughtered at the command of god. Contrast this bloodthirsty concept of god with the loving heavenly Father of Jesus, or for that matter with the non-nationalistic god who rebuked the prophet Jonah when he sulked because the great city of Nineveh was not destroyed.[89] The lesson to be learned in the development of the narrative is simply that the rationale for the event is explained after the fact. Instead of recognizing that a misguided overconfidence, following the victory over Jericho, was the cause of their defeat, a theological/moral explanation was essential. A guilty party was needed and the belief that god would control the fall of the lot was all that was required to find one. The indefensible irony of the story is that in all probability almost everyone in the army was guilty of looting, and no matter where the lot fell there would have been someone to blame. If today a lot fell upon our clan and family, which of us would not have a skeleton in our closet? Jesus reiterated the same principle in the words, "He that is without sin among you, let him first cast a stone at her."[90]

Yet another clue to the way in which biblical traditions came about is the history of the common biblical phrase, 'from Dan to Beersheba.' Dan became the northernmost city in Israel, and Beersheba was at the extreme south of the land. The point of interest is that the tribe of Dan was originally assigned a place in the south. They had problems occupying the area because the local people offered too strong a resistance to the occupation. Was their tribal god stronger than *YHWH* the ancestral god of Israel? The tribe of Dan then picked up and moved to the extreme north and was successful in driving the people of that area out.

The clue that results is simply that many of the much earlier stories of Abraham and the patriarchs refer to the total country of Israel with the phrase, 'from Dan to Beersheba'; in a context long before the move of Dan or the division of the land by tribes. This indicates that later editors of these much earlier stories came from a period after the allocation and move had taken place, and working with much earlier material, were reading into it attitudes and theology from their own much later period.

The picture that emerges at this early time is that *YHWH*, the national god of this desert people, was very harsh, indeed. Coming from our own

---

[89] Jonah 4:11
[90] John 8:7

society, we little understand the political, religious, and geographical backgrounds that had such a major effect upon the behavior and attitudes of these biblical tribes. Compare the religion and gods of the well-watered and seasonally regulated country of Egypt. The Egyptian gods were considerably more reliable in controlling weather patterns and the ebb and flow of the Nile River. The food supply could be counted upon and living conditions were not at all like the insecurity experienced by the wandering nomads of the Sinai Desert. The gods of Egypt were dependable, whereas the gods of the Semites were unpredictable.

The Bible is not only a library, but many of its books are also diaries of the pilgrimages of its heroes. Three major types of heroic role stand out. They are prophet, priest, and warrior King. The priests are dedicated to what they interpret as the laws of god, which include ritual observance and behavioral prohibitions. The prophet is a visionary who seeks to challenge the status quo to rise or return to a greater sense of awareness. Sometimes their challenge is to the political structure and sometimes to the religious. The warrior King is patterned after Israel's war-like god Yahweh (*YHWH*).

According to the narrative, the first political power was invested in judges who were strongly associated with the priests and spoke for god in adjusting civil disputes. After a time the people demanded a king, anointed by god, so as to stand equal among the nations. Reluctantly it appears, god granted the coronation of Saul to fill that role. The prime function of the king beyond his ceremonial duty was to be a military leader. We are already beginning to see the setting for the concept of a militaristic Messiah. David follows Saul as king and is regarded as the greatest of Israel's kings. But the prophet Nathan rebukes him and calls even David to task in regard to his affair with Bathsheba and the contrived death of her husband.

At this point in Jewish history, a further lesson can be learned from the biblical library in a study of parallel accounts derived from separate traditions. Such an account is the story of David the king, numbering the people of Israel as recorded both in II Samuel 24 and I Chronicles 21.

In the Samuel account, the Lord moves David; but in Chronicles, the satanic moves him. The question becomes, was the numbering motivated by good or by evil? A larger census number is found in Chronicles. In both accounts, when god is angered David repents of the act and is offered the choice of three punishments. He chooses three days of plague at the hand of god and in both accounts 70,000 Israelites perish. God repents of the evil and stops the death angel before it reaches Jerusalem. What kind of god repents of evil? Certainly not a god, the same yesterday, today and forever.

The angel stopped at the threshing floor of a Jebusite named Araunah or Ornan. Araunah is paid 50 shekels of silver in one story and Ornan is paid six hundred shekels of gold in the other. The basic importance of the stories is that the threshing floor purchased by David was to become the site for the construction of King Solomon's temple. It appears the site later absorbed the tradition of the place where Abraham was willing to offer up his son Isaac. Still later, Moslems called it the Dome of the Rock, where Mohammed is supposed to have ascended to heaven on his favorite horse. When visiting the site I found the 'Rock' hollowed out and descended into the large room within it on stairs carved into the wall of the created grotto.

Solomon is regarded as the last heroic king and models the wisdom of the Judges. The Wisdom of Solomon was demonstrated in the settling of a dispute between two women both claiming to be a child's mother. The King's decision: cut the child in half! He perceived that the real mother was the one willing to give up the dispute in order to save the child's life. I'm not at all sure that logic would support the idea that the other woman would accept one/half a corpse and allow the child to die; but it makes a clever story. The priests also honor Solomon for the construction of the temple at Jerusalem. From that time on, the political power of Israel degenerates and with the division of the kingdom the monarchy falls into mediocrity.

The political history of the Jews shows strong dominance of the political power by the priestly faction. This is true at least in the records that have been preserved in the biblical books of history. Those Kings the priests approved were elevated in the record and those disapproved were recorded with scathing rebuke. For examples, see the listing of rulers in the books of Kings, Chronicles, and Samuel. The prophets more nearly follow an inner awareness. The word of the Lord comes to them. They have concern for justice (*misphat*) in the political arena. They stand for righteousness in the area of personal behavior as opposed to correct ritual procedure. Both prophet and priest seek to advise and to persuade the political structure. Sometimes they are in concert and sometimes they are adversarial.

In the later history of Israel, the differences in the biblical library continue to be reflected in priestly laws on one hand, and prophetic concerns on the other. The priests understandably emphasize religious ritual and the prophets speak out on ethical and political issues, namely from a sense of nomadic justice. The priests point to the written law as the Word of god, but not the prophets, for whom the Word of god was an inner voice.

It is astounding to realize that, as the priests were the ones who had no ability to hear the inner voice, they apparently needed to claim the authority of an external word. This was the reason they needed the written Law as an external source for their authority. Given the tradition of rivalry between the Law and the Prophets, it is evident in Judaism that eventually the Torah or Law gained the ascendancy. Jesus' interior authority places him in the tradition of the greatest prophets.

I am reminded of the true priests and false priests discussed in Joan Grant's fascinating posthumous autobiographical story of Egypt, "Winged Pharaoh". A winged Pharaoh was one who, in addition to being Pharaoh, had also qualified as a true priest. To be a true priest or true prophet, one must be able to say with regard to spiritual instruction, "I, of my own knowledge, tell thee that this is the Truth."[91] As a child of ten she learned to pray, "Master of thy wisdom, teach me to be a flame for the benighted ones, so that I may warm their hearts and light their darkness, until of their own knowledge they can kindle their own fire, and having kindled it can leave the darkness and dwell at last in the light of the sun."[92]

When the Pharaoh had grown and achieved priesthood, she traveled to Crete with her teacher. They witnessed the Minoan ceremonies of worship and the priestly rituals, which were done by rote. The Minoan priest asked how they liked the ceremony, and the Egyptian priest answered that he liked the music, damning with faint praise. On the way home the High Priest of Egypt comments, "Surely they are a strange people! I felt as unfamiliar as if I lived among beautiful monkeys and had forgotten how to swing by my tail. When I spoke the truth to them, they thought me a liar; and when I told them of wisdom, they thought me a fool; and when of my impatience I insulted them, they took it as a compliment."[93]

The wisdom literature, such as Psalms and Próverbs, abound in varying representations of the nature of god. Most contradictory to our idea of a loving, nurturing god are vengeful statements in the imprecatory (curse) psalms that speak of dashing the heads of an enemy's children against rocks.[94] These statements asking god to curse one's enemy and his children as well, came to be recorded as a result of the common practice of pagan people hiring wizards and soothsayers to pronounce curses upon one's enemy. In such a case it was deemed proper to ask god to return the enemy's curses upon their own heads. Unfortunately, this resulted in such spiritual oxymorons as, "In your steadfast love, cut off my enemies, and destroy all my adversaries."[95] A totally different and much greater ethical awareness is demonstrated in the spiritual discernment of Micah's statement, "What does the Lord require of you but to do justly, to love

---

[91] Winged Pharaoh, Joan Grant pg 125
[92] Winged Pharaoh, Joan Grant pg 75
[93] Winged Pharaoh, Joan Grant pg 326
[94] Psalm137: 9
[95] Psalm 143:12

mercy, and to walk humbly with your god?"[96]   Micah is called a Minor Prophet; but the terms Major and Minor in reference to the Prophets do not indicate their importance, simply the length of the book.

The prophet Elijah is also pictured as understanding god with an inner awareness.[97]   When the Lord passes by him on the mountain, he first encounters a terrible wind, next an earthquake, and then a fire. The Lord was not in the wind, earthquake, or fire. Elijah then experienced what he called a still, small voice. For Elijah, the Lord is in the awareness of that quiet silence; not in the calamitous preceding physical manifestations. This understanding of the experience of the still, small voice is an enormous step forward in understanding the nature of the spiritual kingdom.

Unfortunately, the story of the transfer of Elijah's authority to his successor Elisha comes from a greatly inferior tradition. In II Kings 2, the two men come to the Jordan River near Jericho, and Elijah, using his folded cloak or mantle, strikes the water. The river parts and both men cross on dry land to the other side. Elisha asks of Elijah a double portion of his spirit or power, and Elijah replies that if Elisha sees Elijah taken into heaven, the request will be granted. Elisha sees a chariot of fire drawn by horses of fire transport Elijah in a whirlwind into heaven. Elisha picks up the fallen mantle and when he strikes the Jordan, it parts for him as well.

Shortly thereafter, Elisha journeys toward Bethel, and the most fatal flaw in the story occurs. Small boys come out of the city and taunt Elisha for being baldheaded; then Elisha turns and curses the boys. Immediately two she-bears come out of the woods and maul forty-two of the boys. Without comment, the record continues that Elisha went on from there to Mt. Carmel. Contrast this vengeful god, with Jesus' attitude toward children and his teaching to love even one's enemies.

It is plausible that an actual event did occur where boys were mauled by two she-bears, when perhaps they came upon them with cubs, or conceivably may have been foolish enough to taunt the bears. To ascribe such an event as an act of god is to demonstrate the extremely limited theological perspective of the story's editors.

There were several periods of development in the biblical material. A great deal of editorial work was done during the exile under Babylonian captivity. No longer in their land, Jewish leaders emphasized dietary laws, the observance of Sabbath and circumcision of males in order to hold the identity of the people intact. They also gathered all the written records they held, began to write down their oral traditions and assemble these as a

---

[96] Micah 6:8
[97] I Kings 19:11,12

126

rallying point in order to remember their heritage. This was the beginning of the formulation of the Hebrew Scriptures.

Some would argue that the many different kinds of god depicted in the biblical library do not reflect the views of different men and varied belief systems, but rather purport to show ways in which god in its relationship to humankind has changed. Dispensationalism is a mechanistic theory that claims god, during varying time periods, found it necessary to change its manner of dealing with mankind. A scheme of dispensations is offered, such as Eden's innocence, an Old Testament period of law and a New Testament period of grace. This is in spite of the biblical premise that Christ is the same yesterday, today, and forever.[98] As some political strategists have argued, the bigger the lie the easier it is to swallow. God's sameness must be considered not simply as static sameness but as dynamic in the sense that Spirit, while maintaining an absolute core value, is able to express unvarying truth in spite of changing times.

The Jews of Jesus' day had already become a people of the book. The Law and the Prophets were considered to be authoritative writings. In addition, there was reverence for historical material such as the poetic books, Psalms, Proverbs, etc. The same dynamic of prophet, priest, and politician were also at play in the development of the early church and in the formation of the Christian record. At the time of Jesus the priests and Jewish politicians were in close accord, probably because they were united in their collaboration with Roman rule. The Zealots were a political force trying by revolution to bring about the overthrow of Caesar's legions and the end of oppression. The religion of Judaism was not a united front. The Scribes, Sadducees, Pharisees and the Essenes represented great diversity in Jewish beliefs, observances, and hopes for the future of Israel. In the immediate post Jesus period of the early church, there was a struggle to move the Jesus Movement as Followers of the Way, beyond the focus of a mere Jewish sect. Both Peter and Paul were eventually aligned in bringing the Gentile world into the formation of the church. There is evidence that inclusion of the Gentiles fostered traditions that may have come from the Greek mystery religions. After the early years, the eventual incorporation of the rules of the Roman Empire into the political and priestly aspects of Christianity as the official religion had profound effect. The priests and politicians were now aligned and firmly entrenched in Roman politics.

At the time of Jesus, there were more Greek speaking Jews in Alexandria, Egypt, than Aramaic-speaking Jews in Palestine. In the Third Century BCE the Greek-speaking Jews of the Diaspora (dispersion of Jews outside Palestine) brought about a Greek translation of Hebrew Scriptures

---

[98] Hebrews 13:8

called the Septuagint (Latin for seventy) or LXX, so called because tradition held that seventy scholars had translated it. The LXX was in the Greek language and was the standard translation of the Hebrew Scriptures used by the Greek-speaking Jewish communities throughout the Mediterranean world. It was in these Jewish centers that the early Jesus Movement flourished. The LXX also contained the books Protestants call the Apocrypha. The Jews accorded more authority to books originally written in Hebrew, than to those later books written originally in Greek, such as the Maccabees in the Apocrypha.

Aramaic, the conversational language of the first century Jews of Palestine, was a parallel language to Hebrew, developing from the same roots with many similarities. Aramaic, also called Syriac, was the language of the Fertile Crescent, and when the Babylonian and Persian empires ruled over Palestine, Aramaic became firmly rooted as its common language. At the time of Jesus, Hebrew was limited to religious use by the Jews. Because of the Roman occupation, the political language was Latin; the commercial language of the time was Greek.

Not only are the biblical languages different from our own, but also in addition, many local customs of biblical times are all but unknown to us. I puzzled for years over the story of the wedding guest,[99] who was kicked out for not wearing a wedding garment, even after he was conscripted to attend. It seemed ludicrous to go out into the highways and compel strangers to attend a wedding and then become angry because they weren't properly dressed. After hearing a lecture on wedding customs of some eastern cultures, the story began to make sense. Much as a host now provides silverware to guests, the host of that time provided a special wedding garment. By not wearing the appropriate garment provided, the guest involved had insulted the host.

The circumstances of the formation of the New Testament are somewhat different from those of the Old Testament. The basis for its construction is the idea of a new covenant (testament). This covenant centered on the person of Jesus. The New Covenant, in the words of Jesus was, "A new commandment I give, that you love one another."[100] Unfortunately, the New Testament was composed not only from the *religion of* Jesus but also from a *religion about* Jesus, and it is at times difficult to determine which one is being presented.

At this point we must understand that due to letters and arguments attributed to Paul, it is very difficult to discern which concepts and

---

[99] Matthew 22:2-14
[100] John 13:34

arguments were Paul's and which were written under the pseudonym of Paul. Church political structure had much to do with the fact that later anonymous letters were attributed to Paul. These attributions to Paul's writings result from two basic areas of concern. A major problem in the difference between the East and West was in regard to the gospel witness of Gnostic teachings over against western literalism, i.e. Gnostics saw the world as illusion; the Roman Church denied illusion. In addition, the western church concept of apostolic succession became a major difference in the enforcement of church authority.

It is evident, because of the controversy about the authorship of works attributed to Paul, that it is impossible to speak definitively about Paul's theology. The result is confusion as to what Paul actually believed. Scholars with computers using linguistic studies have tried to reach conclusions, but for the most part there is little consensus as to which is Paul and which are writers trying to support the orthodoxy of the western or Roman church. I am unable to speak authentically for whoever Paul really was and only seek to offer my impression of where he seems to be coming from. I suggest that when Paul's name appears, please read it as Paul [?].

The covenant, if *of* Jesus, should have been the new commandment he taught, i.e. to love one another. Instead, the covenant, later perceived by the church and Paul, was *about* Jesus, the notion that his 'last will and testament' was his death as blood atonement for sin. The theology of Paul [?] had a most profound effect on the religion *about* Jesus. Paul's main concern was to explain that Jesus came as the Messiah or Christ supposedly to accomplish complete atonement for sin, once and for all, fulfilling the Jewish sacrificial system. Paul's writings are the earliest and perhaps the largest part of what is preserved as the NT record. The final editions of the four canonized gospels came into written form in the years following Paul's letters and were heavily influenced by the Pauline [?] theology in which they were immersed. It is unfortunate that teachings *of* Jesus were from the very beginning shrouded by teachings *about* him in the letters of Paul [?].

In the letter to Colossians Paul speaks of the mystery formerly hidden and now made known, which is, Christ in you the hope of glory. Paul is also recorded as having ecstatic dreams and mystical visions. There is a strong case to be made that the real Paul may have been a Gnostic.

How was the western Jesus movement to control the beliefs of its converts? How were they to discredit the inner kingdom of the Gnostic tradition? The means used was to discredit any idea or conviction of those who disagreed with their authority. Pauline Gnosticism was attacked on two fronts. Letters were attributed to Paul that countered his Gnostic leanings, and his spiritual witness to the resurrection was challenged by insistence that the resurrection was a literal physical event.

One tangible illustration is found in the books of first and second Thessalonians. Scholars agree that First Thessalonians is indisputably Pauline in origin. Most scholars agree that the second letter was written basically to counteract the first letter and was not written by Paul.

The second attack on Pauline Gnosticism was the invention of stories such as those recorded in the book of Acts intending to limit authority to the original disciples and their successors. According to the stories, Jesus was in the flesh *bodily* with his eleven disciples up until the time of his supposed ascension into heaven. This of course meant that all later stories of contact with the Lord are an apparitional experience and not physical reality. *The Gnostics had argued that there never were any physical appearances of the risen Lord and that all appearances had been spiritual.*

Paul seems to be in great sympathy with the Gnostics and the tradition of inner witness. Paul did not use the teachings of Jesus in support of his viewpoint, which may reflect his own Gnostic heritage, for it was Gnostic tradition that a student should voice one's own inner awareness and not simply quote the thoughts of a teacher. Each student was to speak from personal experience and that certainly seemed to be Paul's witness.

Paul never quotes Jesus' teachings. It may be that Paul did not know the teaching stories of Jesus, or it may be that he preferred the power of the first-hand account of his own story. The New Testament writings with regard to Paul are subject to much scholarly dispute.

The bishops, priests and deacons of the Roman church claimed the authority of Apostolic succession as a result of the direct transmission of authority by ordination; from Peter [?], held by the Western Church to be the first pope, and the other apostles who had had direct physical contact with the risen Lord. They used literalism in the form of the bodily resurrection of Jesus to exercise the authority of clergy over the converts. This same literal interpretation of resurrection was also extended to all believers by the production of a so-called 'Apostles Creed'. Paul and others, including the Gnostics, who vouch for the spiritual awareness of resurrection, had small influence on the traditions of the Roman church.

One thing of pivotal importance in understanding the formation of the New Testament gospels is the interplay of historical incidents that took place during the time they were being formed. After the death of Jesus, the Jesus Movement began to spread as a sect of Judaism among the Greek speaking Jewish centers of Asia Minor. These centers collected many gospel accounts. The stories were oral traditions at first but began to be put into writing in the Greek language. The Jesus Movement was the forerunner of the Christian Church; identified in its earliest form with Judaism and later separated from Judaism as Christian.

About 60 CE (Common Era), tradition said both Paul and Peter were in Rome, Paul under house arrest and Peter perhaps in prison. In 64 CE, the city of Rome was destroyed by fire, probably because of the insanity of the Emperor Nero, who is thought to have set it ablaze. The fire possibly resulted in the deaths of both Paul and Peter. The destruction of Rome weakened the power of the Empire somewhat and may have led to the Jewish uprising in Palestine in 66 CE some thirty years after the death of Jesus. This was in the midst of the spread of the Jesus Movement within Judaism. The Jews of Palestine led an open rebellion against the Roman armies of occupation, and this revolt caused tension between the Jews in Jerusalem and those in the Diaspora.

Many of the Asia Minor Jews held Roman citizenship and were not eager to get involved in a war with the Roman Empire. The revolt began in 66 CE and culminated with the destruction of the Jerusalem temple in 70 CE. The last remnant of resistance was crushed at Masada in 73 CE. During this period there was a struggle between Gentile and Jewish followers of the Jesus movement. The argument concerned the question of Gentile observance of Jewish religious law, notably circumcision, in order to be authentic followers of Jesus, and is reflected in the epistles of Paul.

At the same time there was great tension existing between those who held that Jesus' message was at the heart of the gospel, and those following the lead of Paul that the core of the gospel was instead, Jesus' sacrificial death. As early Christianity came more and more under the political influence of the Roman Empire, the priestly philosophy of sacrifice began to win out. It is important to remember that at this point in time the four canonical gospels were still in a formative stage, and the disputed writings of Paul added confusion to the telling of the story. The political problem was that the emerging western church aligned with the Roman political scene and thus took a literalistic view of history and an authoritarian view of church government. They supported allegiance to the Roman system and discounted the witness of individual experience.

In the next two hundred years, the Christian Church became the official Religion of Rome. Some believe that the emperor Constantine was converted by the power of Christian witness, but the fact seems to be that the literate people on whom the government depended had become converted. These included slaves who were especially attracted to the freedom of the Christian gospel that was open to all. Constantine's basic motive for conversion may well have been that in his struggle to become

Emperor, he needed to develop greater support from the increasing numbers of Christians in the empire, which is to say, if you can't beat 'em, join 'em.

When the future emperor Constantine converted to Christianity, it actually resulted in the conversion of the Western Jesus Movement to the politics of the Roman Empire; thus Modern Christianity is more a product of the politics of the Roman Empire than the teachings of Jesus. The Roman form of Christianity became the survivor in the struggle between the various sections of the Jesus movement. The Roman form of the church survived because it now had official status and support.

The Roman church was now a state church and the cost of construction and upkeep of church buildings along with the salaries and support of the clergy was now a responsibility of the Empire. Constantine was responsible for the construction of Basilicas over the Christian shrines of the Holy Land. By the end of the third century the creed had become, "We believe in one god and one Holy Roman Catholic Church and there is no salvation outside that one church." Other forms of the early Jesus movement were suppressed and in some cases totally obliterated.

It was not so much that the Romans were Christianized, but rather, that Christianity was Romanized. The Roman Western Church approached the story of Jesus with a literalized historical view and was unable to recognize the mythological teaching stories abounding in the gospel accounts. It was the Gnostic Eastern Church that attempted to keep the teachings of Jesus alive. Unfortunately the Roman literalists won the battle; I can only hope that the teachings of Jesus will ultimately win the war.

It was politically expedient to structure church rule like the Empire. The Emperor received his authority from god and was sometimes even considered divine himself. The relationship of Emperor and Empire also became a model for the institutional church with heritage passed on by birthright. Priests in this period were not required to be celibate, and many had children who were favored to replace their fathers in positions of privilege. Because priests and parishes were in position to accumulate a great deal of wealth, the church eventually imposed the rule of celibacy. In the case of a celibate clergy the birthright was passed on through the legacy of apostolic succession and the laying on of hands. The church saw itself as a stereotypical political structure. At the top was god, and then came the bishop of Rome (Pope), other bishops, followed by priests and deacons, and at the lowest level, the laity following like serfs in a feudal system. Within such a system, the concept of the kingdom of god within each soul became both political and religious heresy. By the fourth century, with the help of the Roman Empire all parts of the Jesus Movement not in sympathy with the 'official' church were now being labeled as heretics and either pushed out of the mainstream or physically eliminated.

The most notable casualty to the sounding prophetic voice in the ascendancy of 'officialdom' within the early Roman church was the suppression of Gnostic Christians. The meaning of the Greek word *gnosis* is to know. This name was applied to those who maintained that salvation was internal, individual, and accompanied by knowledge correctly applied (wisdom?). The position they adopted toward the outer world as an illusion was not treated favorably by the political/priestly alliance. As a result, Gnosticism was suppressed as heresy. Modern church historians were in the dark for centuries about Gnostic beliefs, for the only records available to them were condemnatory writings and judgments against the Gnostics and their movement. An accurate picture of one's religious and spiritual outlook does not come undistorted from an adversarial party.

In recent years Gnostic material discovered at Nag Hammadi in Upper Egypt has given us a clearer picture of this group. This library of Gnostic materials was hidden in the sands of Egypt at Nag Hammadi near the Nile River. It was thought by scholars to have been buried by someone from the nearby monastery of St. Pachominus. The scrolls were probably hidden in the middle of the third century to protect them from destruction by what had become the official Roman church.

A major distinction between the Roman church of the Empire and the Gnostics was in the nature of their political structures. The Roman church supported the division between clergy and the laity. It also had a political power structure inherent in the hierarchy of its clergy. The bishop of Rome had absolute authority over the priests, the deacons and the laity. In order to retain church membership and be assured of heaven, obedience was demanded. The hierarchy made the decisions as to who were on the inside, and who were excommunicate.

The Gnostics, on the other hand, were a much more democratic group, giving equal weight to any individual, including women, who by enlightenment experienced the inner *gnosis* (knowing). Emphasis was on the invisible kingdom within each person and this realm was accessible to all that would follow the Way. Theirs was the earliest version of the priesthood of all believers, later championed in the Protestant reformation.

It was not just different ideas which separated the major groups in the early church. Official Christianity basically became a question of submission to the political and religious authority of the Roman clergy. An individual who had experienced the inner kingdom of god was not about to submit to the authority of a priest or bishop robed in the assumed power of ordination and the supposed apostolic succession of the laying on of hands.

Many, if not most, of these Gnostics had knowledge of the inner Christ. For them this experience of Christ was an authority far greater than that of any ecclesiastical institution. When Christianity became Roman Christianity, it was politically expedient to structure the church authority along the guidelines of the political hierarchy. The hierarchical order of rank was bishop, priest, and the deaconate, all considered superior to lay persons.

The earlier church had given recognition to the many women who were leaders in the Jesus movement. Women were accorded equality of leadership in Gnostic churches and certainly were not forbidden to speak. The Roman structure now went so far as to forbid women to speak or teach in the churches, as supported by some statements attributed to Paul [?]. Even though many women in earlier times held teaching and leadership positions in local churches, this was now forbidden. It was not so in the Gnostic movement. The Gnostics implicitly understood that women were fully capable of discovering the inner kingdom for themselves; and those who had this inner knowing of the Christ were honored as equals in the general movement of the Gnostic Christians.

In addition to the political split between the two groups, there was also disagreement in several areas of their theology. The Roman church adopted almost completely the prevalent Jewish concept of god, along with the ideas regarding sacrifice and blood atonement. On the other hand, the Gnostics, in a much more egalitarian framework, began to wrestle with perceived differences between the vindictive and judgmental aspects of the Jewish god, as contrasted with the loving Heavenly Father portrayed by Jesus.

Today we would be freer to simply reject these early primitive pictures of god as erroneous. The Gnostics, however, did not seem capable of rejecting the existence of the Jewish god. Rather, they circumvented this vindictive kind of god, with the philosophical structure of godhead. The Gnostics believed that 'Depth of Being' was the nature of the true god.[101] It was also their interpretation that although the Old Testament god existed, he was only an archaic figure of god and was thought by Gnostics to be inferior to the god Jesus portrayed as a Loving Father.

This allocation of Yahweh to being a second-class Jewish god, contrasting with the superior god who was Father in Jesus' teaching, separated the Roman clergy from the Gnostic leaders. The separation was based on a belief of the Gnostics that Roman bishops and priests were representing this Jewish creator god or demiurge. The Greek term for creator was the word *demiurgos*; this term was applied to this subordinate

---

[101] See Chapter Six:—Spiritual Libraries, under, Gnosticism

Jewish god or demiurge and the godhead was perceived as the mystery beyond god. To the Gnostics there was a fullness of depth beyond the Jewish god, who was now viewed as creator only of this world.

In the same fashion that I have been arguing for a non-object god, so also did the Gnostics. The Gnostics believed in god as Pure Being, or Ground of Being. Their difference from my presented view was that they still felt a need to accept the temporal reality of the object personal god of the Jews. They saw the Jewish god as inferior to their own awareness of the Spiritual Ground of Being. We, today, can reject the idea that the vengeful war god of Israel ever existed. The first century Gnostics apparently could not.

Phrases attributed to the Jewish deity were used to argue its inferior position. The phrase, "I am a jealous god, you shall have no other gods before me"[102] was in particular used to develop the new concept of godhead. Instead of recognizing that this view of a jealous god simply represented a nationalistic god of the Hebrews as over and against the gods of other nations, the Gnostics began to develop the idea of a god beyond god. It was no longer fitting to accept the jealous god *YHWH* as Source, because there were other gods of whom *YHWH* was jealous.

The godhead was now seen as the god of the first creation story in Genesis. In the creation story chapter one, male and female were created equally. The demiurge, or god of the Jewish people, was seen in the creation story of Genesis chapter two, where Adam is created first with Eve being subordinate. Other Gnostic stories speculated that Adam was androgynous, containing both sexes. This androgynous single being was then split apart to form each sex in separate bodies. The formation of both Adam and Eve was from the single androgynous Adam and neither of the first couple was considered subordinate to the other. The godhead was seen as gender neutral with attributes or characteristics both male and female, and was often addressed by the Gnostics as Father-Mother. For some Gnostics, the trinity was seen as picturing a divine family. God was Father, the Holy Spirit was Mother and the Son was all that which proceeded from their creative union. The fact that the Hebrew word *ruah* meaning spirit was feminine in gender offered support for this view. The godhead was conceived as Great Depth, Unknown Mystery, and Silence, not unlike the Chinese concept of Tao.

Much of the gospel of John and the Q document of Matthew and Luke (see later pages) seem to be essentially teachings of the Gnostic community.

---

[102] Exodus 20:5, 34:14; Deuteronomy 4:24, 5:9, 6:15; Joshua 24:19

Without these witnesses in our New Testament canon, the Bible would certainly contain precious little of the teachings of Jesus.

The Roman church gave emphasis to the rituals surrounding baptism, communion, and ordination, elevating them to the level of sacrament. The power of the Roman church was demonstrated in the official sacramental dimensions of its political and religious rule of law. The church dictated who had authority to administer these sacraments, the observances of which were required in order to obtain salvation and the reward of heaven. Baptism, Confirmation, Communion, Penance, Marriage, Ordination and Last Rites, were all official sacraments of the church, and were restricted to ritual performance by male clergy.

The bureaucratic Church of Rome, with its political structure, won the battle for survival; and the Gnostics, who emphasized the teachings of Jesus, lost. Valentinus and other Gnostic teachers in the early church were stripped of their authority and declared heretics. Countless Gnostic Christians were put to death at the hands of the Roman church. The view of various Roman church leaders was that the flames of hell would be hotter for Gnostics than for pagans because pagans had not distorted the gospel.

The Gnostics did not accept the political rule of the Roman bishops and believed literally in priesthood for all. Nor did they support the Jewish god proclaimed by the Roman clergy. For these two reasons, they were condemned as heretics.

Some Gnostic texts refer to the Roman sector of the church as the heretical branch. In terms of the historic situation, it is intriguing to speculate about what might have happened had history been reversed. What if the magical rites of baptism and sacrifice had been declared the heresy? What if the religious political hierarchy had been abandoned? What if the teachings of Jesus had been emphasized? How then, would the Jesus Movement be viewed today?

Unfortunately, it would seem that the inheritance of the Roman political church is what we are stuck with, and it is probable that no reformation will ever succeed in changing that weight of history. It remains that if the message of Jesus about the inner reign of god is to be presented, it will never be accomplished under the auspices of today's institutional churches. Let us hope that this religion with its teaching *about* Jesus, will lose its life in order to find life more abundant in the teachings *of* Jesus.

Why did god stop speaking to mankind after his last words to Jesus and the apostles? If god spoke to Abraham, Isaac, Jacob, David, and the prophets, as well as Jesus, John, and Paul, then, according to the experience of the institutional church, god quit speaking and fell silent.

The death of Jesus for sin, the bodily resurrection, and claims to be the political successors of Peter are beliefs supported and maintained by the popes and the Roman hierarchy in their self-serving politics of orthodoxy.

For the most part, in the institutional church of today, if we want to know what god says, we don't turn to Spirit or heaven within our own reality; instead we must hear the words of the church and the Bible. God can no longer speak the Living Word to us; it must be filtered through the written word of the Bible and the traditions of the church. The living god is either dead or silent; or, perhaps more realistically, it is just that many of us have not yet learned how to hear.

The early Gnostic Christians did not believe that this was so. Each teacher expected students to listen to their own inner voice and not repeat even the teacher's words by rote. The Spirit within speaks afresh as the Voice for god. The Gnostics with their sense of knowing believed and demonstrated this awareness.

In the present day, such channeled works as "A Course in Miracles", "Conversations With God", the "Emmanuel" books, and others, demonstrate that the Voice for god is not silent. But even these writings bend to political and religious pressures within the channel and sometimes conform to orthodox tests, instead of opening out to the Way.

Roman Church leaders concluded that the number of acceptable gospels must be reduced to the mystical number four. In this tradition, the gospels were likened to the prophet Ezekiel's vision of the four living creatures with faces, of Ox, Lion, Eagle, and Human. Lost in this process of redaction were perhaps dozens of gospels and other books containing teachings of Jesus, including the Gospel of Thomas, the Gospel of Phillip, and other Gnostic writings. The content of some of this written heritage will be reviewed in a later chapter about other spiritual libraries.

Of the surviving four gospels, Mark's gospel was written first and is based traditionally on the association of a young man named John Mark with the apostle Peter. This same John Mark is referenced in the Book of Acts; tradition holds that Mark was in the Garden of Gethsemane with Peter at the time of the betrayal of Jesus. He was, by folklore, the young man who escaped by leaving his cloak in the grasp of the authorities and ran off naked.[103] Mark's gospel was written in a much cruder form of *Koine* (common) Greek than the other three. There were several dialects of the *Koine* language, ranging from the rough speech of dockworkers to the more literary style of the scribes. It is evident that the gospels of both Matthew and Luke copied Mark, with each making certain alterations. They

---

[103] Mark 14:51

corrected his grammar and brought his writing into more literary form. The editors of Matthew and the author of Luke also used a common reference alongside Mark named by German scholars *Quella* (source), and referred to as the Q document. The Q document is a collection of sayings that Jesus spoke originally in the Aramaic language of Palestine and which had been recorded in Greek. Scholars point out that if Luke and Matthew had been using an Aramaic written source, there would have been substantial differences in the way each would have translated an Aramaic Q into Greek. In addition, the gospels of Matthew and Luke each contain some material unique to themselves. Because of their common base in Mark, these three gospels are often referred to by the term synoptic (with the same eye). The gospels are not history but arguments – polemics.

Mark has the reputation for being the most straightforward account, despite the variety of its endings. Matthew is edited to present Jesus in the light of Jewish tradition and expectation with many attempts to link him to Old Testament stories and supposed prophetic statements. In Matthew, there is much more emphasis on the Jerusalem temple. At the time of the final edition of the Matthean editors, the Jerusalem temple had already been destroyed. It is important to realize that the actual disciples of Jesus did not write any of the gospel accounts and that the final editors of the written gospels were not eyewitnesses. Luke/Acts, supposedly both by the same author, who was traditionally believed to be a Greek physician, is directed toward the Gentile world. Although Acts is supposed to contain a history of the early church, it is at times in conflict with the accounts of Paul, concerning Paul's own story[104]. In the book of Acts, the Jesus Movement is referred to several times as the Followers of the Way.

Conventionally, the Greek New Testament introduces only one gospel with four authors, each referenced by the phrase 'according to', followed by the Gospel name. Of the four canonical gospels, the Gospel According to John stands by itself and is the most mystical of the four. It is thought by some to be indirectly based on the witness of John, the beloved disciple, and certainly gives emphasis to the inner circle of disciples, Peter, James, and John. These three men were often called apart by Jesus because they seemed to have a greater psychic sensitivity than the others did. Many scholars believe that John is the one gospel that survived with Gnostic influence although some believe that the Q document as a 'sayings gospel' may also have had roots from the same group.

The attempt to link Jesus to Jewish writings gives us insight into the mindset of some of the gospel editors. The editors of Matthew were so zealous in trying to tie Jesus to the Old Testament record that they assumed

---

[104] Compare Galatians 1:16,17 with Acts 9:26-30

that each memorable event in Jesus' life must have been the fulfillment of some prophecy. This, in spite of the fact that in some cases there may have been no factual historical event to record. This is to say, if in their minds there was a prophecy, there must have been a fulfillment event. When reading a story about the life of Jesus in the gospel record, one must question whether or not the event actually occurred or was simply a gloss based upon prophetic expectations.

An illustration of this is found in the story of the crucifixion. The words, "My god, my god, why have you forsaken me?" as part of suffering described in Psalm 22, may have been quoted by Jesus or simply have been transposed into the account as a prophecy fulfilling event. There are many such examples, usually identified with words indicating that prophecy should be fulfilled. In one instance the statement in Matthew, "He shall be called a Nazarene",[105] has no source in the canonical record and perhaps was totally invented or may have been drawn from some tradition other than then current biblical material.

The story of Jesus is also enhanced by attributions from many of the teaching stories of the Mediterranean mystery religions. Most of the constellation of cultures of the Mediterranean world had localized concepts of a god/man/savior. It is important to remember that many of these stories about the god/man heroes of the Mediterranean basin were held in common. In most of the mystery stories a virgin birth was part of the tradition. These teaching stories are recognized as mythological in form and are not history.

The common theme generally put forth in the mystery religions of the area was that an internal Spiritual Force, the inner kingdom of god, was being demonstrated in the mythology about their god/man. The mythology was articulated in the form of events and circumstances in the life of their hero. The common people often perceived these outer stories as historical or literal. However, those who were initiated into the mysteries were taught the inner metaphysical or allegorical meaning of the myths. After Jesus' death many of these mythological adventures, seen as teaching stories, were also attributed to the story of Jesus.

The central thrust of these teachings is that the reign of god comes from within. We are all the heroic god/man. It should be no surprise that mystics and initiates into the mystery religions such as Pythagoras, Socrates, Plato and others who pre-dated the life of Jesus understood this spiritual truth.

The story of the virgin birth in the New Testament literature is intended to be such a teaching story. The account needs no historical basis and is simply a metaphysical construct indicating that the Christ born into our

---

[105] Matthew 2:23

awareness always comes from within us. It is 'virgin born', a myth meaning that the Christ does not come from any outside source. The attempt to tie the teaching story to the assumed prophecy in Isaiah[106] fails in a literal sense, for Isaiah speaks of an *almah* or young girl who simply may have married in order to conceive her child. The LXX had translated the Hebrew word *almah* with the Greek word *parthenos*, which can be rendered as 'virgin'. This Greek word in the quote from Isaiah is further evidence of the influence of the Greek speaking Jews of the Diaspora and their exposure to the Greek Mystery Religions. Luke may have appropriated a simple teaching story common in the mythology of that day as an historic event.

The account of the parents of Jesus losing him in the temple is also a teaching story. They left him behind and when they discovered Jesus missing, eventually returned to the temple where they found him. It suggests that we can be so busy on our personal journeys that we may even fail to notice that the Christ Child is missing. Jesus rebukes them for searching anxiously, and explains that they should expect to find him in the temple about his Father's business. The point of the story is that when we can not find the Christ Child, we must feel trust and not anxiety, and thus, we will not fail to find him in our inner temple. Because we have been so conditioned to search in the outer, it is a mistake to believe that in the outer we will find our Christ nature.

The stories of the stilling of the tempest, the crucifixion and resurrection, are told throughout the Mediterranean basin in many of the mysteries and applied to man/gods of several names. The New Testament gospels are not historical records, they are mythological "good news".

Another common mystery story is the conversion of water into wine at a marriage feast. The marriage at Cana becomes symbolic of the new birth. Water symbolizes temporal bodily life and wine eternal spiritual life. Joined together in marriage are the little self (*eidolon*) and the Great Self (*Daemon*); as with Socrates' Daemon, an inward monitor; an inner genius.

The story of the cleansing of the temple is easily misunderstood if taken literally. As a teaching story, if one reflects on the location of the real temple of god even with limited awareness, the understanding is clear that that temple to be cleansed is within us. In our inner temple, what would the many moneychangers represent? Avarice, greed, profit and a preoccupation with the material world are the problem. Our inner temple is to be a house of prayer, but too often we have made it a den of thieves.

Other stories, such as the cursing of the fig tree, become far more understandable if we go beyond outer mythology and look for the inner

---

[106] Isaiah 7:14

meaning. We are the ones who are to bear fruit. A tree without fruit is like salt that has lost its saltiness. Jesus' baptism by John symbolizes being buried in the water and resurrected as the *daemon* or Grand Self.

A few have gone so far as to suggest that the historical Jesus does not even exist and that the Jesus story is entirely mythological from the beginning. To argue that Jesus didn't really exist makes no more sense to me, than to argue that Pythagoras, Socrates or Plato didn't exist. Jesus as a teacher unquestionably understood the deeper teachings and symbolism of the mystery religions. His teachings were the foundation for his Gnostic followers in the early church. After his death he became a hero to his followers, and legends attributed to other spiritual heroes were doubtlessly attributed to him. These legends are not historically related to Jesus but the truths they convey are part of the teaching heritage he imparted.

The mystery religions and the Zodiac affected the whole religious mix of the first century world. The Greek speaking Jews of the Diaspora were much involved in the Greek religious culture of their day. Jesus was born at the beginning of the age of Pisces the Fish; a symbol connected to Jesus in the Greek word *ICHTHUS*, (fish). The letters are made to stand for the Greek words (*I*) Jesus, (*CH*) Christ, (*TH*) god's, (*U*) son, (*S*) savior. In like spirit, today we sing of the dawning of the Age of Aquarius.

Much of the surviving record, especially the teaching of Paul [?], is about what Jesus was believed to have accomplished at some celestial level. The Roman part of the church, from its first century inception, has put its teaching energy behind what Jesus is supposed to have done at that cosmic level. He was supposed to have reconciled the world and god, and to have shed his blood for the remission of our sins. He was believed to have been the triumphant, militaristic Messiah governing this world, who will one day intervene to set it right by coming again. He is thought to be the one who sits at the right hand of god the father, making intercession for us; the one whose purpose was to fulfill Old Testament prophesy.

How can the church teach or truly practice forgiveness when it believes in a god who has only conditional forgiveness to offer? The structure of institutional religion presents guidelines that it believes must be followed if we are to avail ourselves of god's grace. Can we have unconditional love and conditional forgiveness at the same time, from the same source? Fortunately, our acceptance or rejection of the church's theology does not restrict god, it only restricts us.

Forgiveness is directed toward a person who is appropriately perceived as a child of god. We forgive the person, not the behavior. If someone does something wrong we forgive the person; one does not need to forgive the action, it simply falls away. One forgives the person and undoes the illusion; the illusion is not 'there' to forgive. We forgive others by seeing their reality in god and thus remove the block to experiencing our own.

The tragedy is that neither Paul nor the Roman church truly addressed what Jesus taught. They seem not even to have cared that he tried to teach those who followed him to love god, to love neighbor, to love even supposed enemies, and especially to love one's Self. We are enabled to love others only when we have learned to love ourselves, and we love ourselves only when we truly remember the oneness that they, and we, really are. Jesus tried to illustrate how to let go of the past, how to let go of our judgments on the world, our judgments upon our neighbors, our judgments on our enemies, and especially our judgment upon ourselves. He exhorted his followers to forgive, and in doing so, to recognize that god is not a god of judgment. He believed that god is Spirit, Love and Light, and that in god's image, so are we. As he was one with the Father – so are we. God is not an object, the Self is not an object, for all selves are One. This is the new commandment (covenant), to love one another! For, we are in reality One and the Same, and in the sight of god altogether lovely.

The only way to see the reality of the One is to move beyond the plurality seen by the body's eyes to the Unity found in the vision of Christ. We cannot love others until we are able to love ourselves. We cannot forgive others until we have forgiven ourselves. The oneness of other and self is seen in the reciprocity of the Golden Rule; "That, which you would that others do to you, do you also unto them".[107] There is only *one* son of god and *we* are it, doing it to ourselves.

A story circulated about Paul in the early church to the effect that his theology about Jesus was based on consultation with the original disciples, and that he had gone to Jerusalem to confer with them.

Luke, if he is the editor, for whatever reason, in Acts of the Apostles, concludes that Paul had early gone up to Jerusalem.[108] In contrast was Paul's explicit denial that this had happened. Rather he argues, "I went not up to Jerusalem. I went into Arabia (the desert) and was instructed by the Lord".[109] I do not understand how his experience in the desert gave rise to awareness in Paul the vitally important conclusion about Jesus, that as the Christ, he was the consummate Jew and the Messiah. He was the savior chosen of god to die as a blood sacrifice for sin, thus fulfilling Jewish law and this for Paul, along with Jesus' resurrection from the dead, made the heart of Paul's 'good news' or gospel. It is difficult to discern if this is

---

[107] Matthew 7:12
[108] Acts 11:30
[109] Galatians 1: 17-18

really Paul or the Roman church speaking. Letters attributed to Paul, taken as a whole, are inconsistent in their theological views.

There seemed to be three groups of thought in the first century church concerning Jesus as Christ or Messiah. The first, those who believed that Jesus failed in that role and who still continued to look for a celestial king to establish an earthly throne and elevate the Jewish people to his side. The second, those who accepted that this was a first coming of the Messiah in order to accomplish atonement for sin, which would then be followed in the last days by a second coming to establish the desired celestial kingdom. The third, those who seem to be a definite minority and who understood that the kingdom of god is within and have stopped looking with any expectations of intervention. "If they say he is here or there, don't go."[110]

The church has barely noticed and certainly has not been very concerned that the Pauline picture has no awareness of, and places little meaning on, what Jesus taught. For Paul, Jesus plays a simple and direct role in fulfillment of early messianic theology; Jesus assumes the Messiah's place in the arrangement of the cosmos; it doesn't seem to matter what he taught.

In his many letters, Paul demonstrates very little knowledge of the teaching of Jesus. Except for what he called a 'received account of the final supper', he never once quotes Jesus in all of his epistles. His time in the Arabian Desert and his experience on the Damascus road do seem to give him a strong sense of inner process. Paul clearly states the expression "Christ in you (is) the hope of glory."[111], but the church still confuses it with the mistaken idea that it is Jesus in you. Paul knew that it was the Spirit that does the work: "I seek not to apprehend, but to be apprehended by."[112]

It may be that Paul did not mention what Jesus taught, simply because (by the law of parsimony) he had never heard what Jesus taught. Paul experienced mystical awareness of the cosmic Christ and equated that experience with Jesus as well. Again, it may be that Paul, even with his great understanding of the inner Christ (a universal), failed to understand and appreciate the genius of the man Jesus.

The historical Jesus was destroyed by absorption into the Christian Trinity, when the church failed to see the fact that we are all one with god. When the church uniquely and incorrectly connected Jesus to god in his statement "The Father and I are one", tradition failed to understand the reality that this oneness is not unique but universal! If we are already stuck with the traditional concept of Jesus as god, then we cannot understand his

---

[110] Mark 13:21
[111] Colossians 1:27
[112] Philippians 3:12

journey to god, or more accurately his emerging openness and the coming awareness of the One. We need to experience a shift in belief from, Jesus is god and not like the rest of us, to a belief that Jesus is of god and just like the rest of us. The Father is one with all and the core reality of All-That-Is. It is Christ who is the universal and not Jesus. Otherwise, in identifying Jesus as one with the Christ we ultimately do disservice to the historical Jesus, who is after all our elder brother and perhaps the greatest of many way-showers.

Paul spoke of inner experience but his religious expression was still tied to the outer. His spiritual freedom never quite set him free from his world of sin and separation. For Paul, the second Adam (Jesus) came short of undoing the work of the first Adam. He never quite learned as Jesus did, to let the Father within do the work. "The things that I would, I do not…sinful man that I am."[113] He believed in the sacrifice of Jesus to make payment for his sin, but never seemed to achieve a sense of personal deliverance from the 'sinful' world as he saw it. Yet in Philippians in reference to the question of being openhearted or open-minded, Paul speaks of the need to be sun judged[114] (*heilikrines*). The Greek picture of being sun-judged is based on the practice of holding a clay pot up to the sun to see if any cracks have been filled with wax. Such wax filled cracks would be translucent and self-evident. This picture of being pure is also carried into the Latin meaning for our word sincere (*sin cere* – without wax).

Paul's primary creed seems to be his belief that the fundamental purpose for which Jesus was born was to die as a sacrifice. "I am determined not to know anything among you, save Jesus Christ, and him crucified."[115] For Paul, Jesus rose from the dead to prove that he had accomplished god's ordained task and was now to be judge of all things. Both Paul and the western part of the Jesus movement believed Jesus had accomplished these things in his function as god's Messiah. Paul seemed to be able to understand the inner Christ but at the same time, he was tied to the Jewish sacrificial system. He is an enigma to me. He states that we are neither bond nor free, male or female, and all one in Christ. But, contrast this with his statement instructing women to keep silent in the churches. Are both from the same source? It is undoubtedly, as with the case of Jesus, multiple sources claiming to speak as Paul. This theory would explain some grievous contradictions. We know that the Book of Acts does not speak for Paul.

It is unfortunate that the church today is based on the theology of Paul rather than the teachings of Jesus; even as it claims to be based on the rock

---

[113] Romans 8:15—17
[114] Philippians 1:10 (*sincere*)
[115] I Corinthians 2:2

of Peter's confession, "Thou art the Christ, the son of the living god."[116] This confession expanded to include us all, means that beyond the teaching of 'flesh and blood', spiritual insight will reveal that each one of us is an extension of the spirit of the living god. Sages from around the world refer to this experience of the Impersonal Self as new birth or enlightenment. Sadly, the institutional church seems only to perceive the Christ as external, limited to the historic Jesus, and not the universal presence within all things.

Paul's personality is reflected in his background as a Jewish religious zealot. As a devotee of the Law and Moses, rules, regulations, and legalisms, he subscribed to the traditional concepts of good and evil, seeing god in conflict with a literal satan. In this orthodox position, Paul seems unable to free himself from the idea of god as a discrete personality, an object or thing. Until his Damascus road experience, he was even a persecutor of the early Christians, and as the biblical tradition says, responsible for the death of Stephen, the first Christian martyr.

On the other hand, Jesus had a much greater parallel with eastern mysticism. There is a tradition that the meaning of the childhood flight to Egypt was that he learned much at the feet of eastern sages. He believed in worshiping god as Spirit, not as an objective form. John the baptizer, who had a more traditional religious and political outlook, said, in reference to their respective teachings, "He must increase, I must decrease."[117]

In order to understand the difference between the beliefs of Paul and Jesus, one must construct a paraphrase of Jesus' teachings and doings. In order to do so, it is necessary to discount the parts of the gospel narratives that are based on the earlier catalog of Pauline theology.

Jesus believed that god is Spirit, not a thing or a personality; that god is Love, and not separated from us when we appear to be of the world. He taught that all manifest form is connected by the dynamic of Spirit-Energy-Love. He demonstrated that Forgiveness is choosing to let go of judgments, which we direct toward the outer manifest world, including our own self-perception. In forgiving and letting go of the outer, we thus recognize an inner invisible world of reality governed by the spiritual laws of love.

Jesus understood and taught that when we falsely perceive a world lost and damned by judgment, if we let go of judgment, with the perception of Spirit we will see an invisible world of innocence. As a result we will not experience separation between the invisible world and visible world. With no spiritual separation between others and ourselves, we will find the experience of life altogether lovely and love will become an 'easy yoke'.

---

[116] Matthew 16:16
[117] John 3:30

The Christ reality is of god, and is the expression of our own true inner reality as well. The Christ of god is the same as the Word or Logos, the inner reality of us all and the inner reality which is expressed by All-That-Is. The sages of the world in their experience of enlightenment often refer to this as unitive knowledge of the spiritual inner and Impersonal Self. This coming of the Son of Man is simply the enlightenment we discover in union with the *Self* we really are.

The 'I am', which is of god, is the light of the world. This 'I am' experience is the way, the truth, and the life. No one comes to this awareness of the inner Christ without the ability to say, "I am one with the Father". No wonder Jesus taught that if any one says, "Behold the Son of Man is here or there", don't bother to go, for the coming will be as the experience of a lightning bolt. When enlightenment occurs, there will be no doubt left, and no need to go elsewhere to find it. Somehow, biblical literalists have either missed that point or refuse to accept it. It is said, "Jesus preached the inner kingdom, but we got stuck with the church!"

There is a fallacy in trying to state the boundless because our concepts of god are limited and could ultimately become our final barrier to enlightenment. We need to let go our rigid perceptions and allow the Logos energy to express the universe through us. Jesus understood the boundless and that no one could express with discursive thought and language, that which is essentially ineffable. Jesus taught these truths by means of lucid illustrations and parables, which address the feeling level of Limitless Truth.

Two men went up to the Temple to pray.[118] One prayed, "I am not like other men". The other prayed "God be merciful to me a sinner", (I am just like other men.) Jesus pointed out that the second man was in touch with reality. The term 'sinner' in this context is not a sin that severs god from us, but a mistaken condition that is healed when the Truth makes us free.

One story Jesus told relates to an experience of our own family. The story is usually referred to in our culture as "The Parable of the Prodigal Son"[119]; in Germany, 'The Lost Son', and in the Near East many call it 'The Story of the Broken Family". After requesting and receiving his inheritance, the younger of two sons squandered his fortune in a foreign land and was reduced to poverty. He 'came to himself' and returned to his father's house hoping at least to find a job as a hired servant. Jesus told of the father running to meet the prodigal son while he was yet a long way off. The son, who had been perceived as dead, was now seen to be alive and the father

---

[118] Luke 18:10-14
[119] Matthew 21:28, Luke 15:11

rejoiced exceedingly. I am in awe when I think of god running to meet us, and I rejoice in the belief that god has never really lost anyone!

Some years ago, when our children were small, we had opportunity to visit the New York World's Fair. Because there were thousands of people milling around we instructed them both, if lost, to contact a policeman, who would see that they would go to a place where lost parents could be found. When we stopped at the end of the long line waiting at the Johnson Wax pavilion, our son Kevin, in typical kid fashion, distracted and hopping along with one foot on the path and the other on a white stone border, did not notice that we had gotten in line. His mother immediately started after him but I restrained her, to see what would happen. He continued for several yards further until he noticed we were missing. Because of the mob of people he did not see us watching him. Presently he left the path and walked over to a large tree, put his head and arms against the tree, and in apparent frustration, began ferociously kicking it. Then, very much like the father in Jesus' story, I ran to him in reassurance that he was safe. The relevance of the story is found in the question "Was our son lost?" The answer depends on whose perspective is used, his, or ours as observing parents. He *believed* he was lost; we *knew* he wasn't. When I ran to his aid the practical result was that he stuck to us like glue the rest of the day.

The Father ran to meet him.

One time I ran.

I ran to my son when he thought he was lost.

His family found him and he found his family.

It is the Father's good pleasure to give us the kingdom.

For the kingdom is within us.

We may believe we have lost our way to god

But god has not lost the way to us.

For god has never lost anyone.

Jesus told several stories dealing with lost and found, The Lost Sheep and the Good Shepherd, the Lost Coin, the discovery of The Hidden Treasure and The Pearl of Great Price. These stories all convey the awareness that the Universe has not lost its purpose for us.

Religion does not accept the illusion of form and appearance. It is difficult in an established tradition to learn to see differently. We need to adjust our interpretation of what we see in order to understand the meaning behind appearance. I am reminded of the difficulty our son Kevin had in the second grade with reading. The school psychologist tested his vision and discovered that he was dyslexic. His brain had not yet learned to interpret the upside-down and reversed image of his eyes. He saw letters as inverted or reversed, confusing letters such as b, d and p, or E, m and 3.

After Kevin worked with his mother for some time with the Frostig program of re-orientation, the psychologist asked him to copy a grid of diamond forms and Kevin asked, "Do you want me to draw them the way I see them or the way they are?" This is a good question to keep in mind any time we view the world of space/time. Religion is committed to the illusion of form and appearance. With Spirit as reality, when we look at the space/time illusion, "Do we want to see the world the way it appears, or the way it is?"

In the early part of this century, Texas oil money published a booklet entitled "The Fundamentals" (1909), listing what were called the five fundamentals of the Christian faith. These were considered fundamental, because belief in all five was deemed necessary for salvation; and without these beliefs one could not be considered a Christian. The listed five fundamentals were: (1) Belief in the bodily resurrection of both Jesus and all believers. (2) Belief in verbal inspiration and the resultant inerrancy of both Old and New Testaments. (3) Belief in the virgin birth of Jesus along with belief that Jesus is God. (4) Belief in sacrificial blood atonement for sin by means of Jesus' shed blood and (5) Belief in a literal second coming of Jesus at the end time.

One of the five fundamentals is insistence on a bodily resurrection both for Jesus and for the rest of us at the return of the messiah. The story of the resurrection was central not only to Paul but to the early church as well. The major question raised in the biblical record is whether the resurrection of Jesus was a physical or a psychic event.

Paul's Damascus road conversion with his experience of the voice of Jesus is a resurrection appearance. On the road to Emmaus, two disciples did not recognize him, and this was true also of Mary at the tomb, who thought he was a gardener. The record seems to lean toward psychic events.

For me, the most intriguing of the post resurrection accounts is that of Jesus meeting the eleven disciples at a mountain in Galilee. After the story is completed, the editor in Matthew adds the phrase, "and some doubted".[120] What was the nature of their doubts? If it were a physical appearance would there have been any doubts?

There is no question in my mind that the reality of Jesus survived bodily death; the question to ask is why does one need a literal bodily resurrection? Because god is supposed to have required Jesus' bodily death, is bodily

---

[120] Matthew 28:17

resurrection needed as a balance to make compensation for the deed? Is it an event needed to prove Jesus' teachings? Is what the Buddha taught less significant because he, with the rest of humankind, died? Would what Jesus taught lose its value if in death his human body went the way of all flesh?

The most powerful argument against literal bodily resurrection was the concoction of the ascension: if there is a resurrected body, then ultimately there is a need to explain what happened to it. Someone has calculated that the ascended body of Jesus, traveling at the speed of light, would now two thousand years later still be traveling in our Milky Way galaxy. Were the stories of a bodily resurrection and the empty tomb likewise fabricated in order to provide meaning to Jesus' life? Would not the continuance of his Living Spirit be just as meaningful?

The sense of psychic appearance also is supported in the recognition of Jesus' own abilities. He identified the past of the woman at the well,[121] and spoke to Nathaniel of seeing him prior to their meeting under a tree.[122]

In the awareness gained by new birth or enlightenment, there is no doubt of Jesus' survival after bodily death. I believe this knowledge of survival beyond bodily death is true of all who experience an enlightened spiritual awareness. It may be that there were not enough in the early Jesus Movement with this enlightened awareness of resurrection to suffice, and as a result, as time passed, and as they came under the influence of the Roman Empire, it would follow that belief in spiritual reality and spiritual survival would inevitably succumb to claims of physical resurrection. In religion, spiritual insights seem inevitably to become buried in material observances.

I am reminded of the Williams translation of the New Testament book of Hebrews. Following chapter eleven on "Heroes of Faith", chapter twelve begins with the statement, "Therefore, since we are surrounded by so great a crowd of witnesses…let us run with perseverance the race that is set before us." Williams translates the word 'witnesses' in Hebrews 12:1 as if they were viewers in a grandstand. Witness in Greek is the word *marturon* from which we derive the English word martyr. The witnesses are not observers from a grandstand but are like legal witnesses in a court who are giving testimony. The *marturon* are not passive spectators but active participants. There are many excellent translations of the New Testament by individual biblical scholars such as J. B. Phillips, James Moffat, and Smith/Goodspeed, but it helps to reference them to work done by more ecumenical groups.

There is a very real problem with individual translators of biblical or religious material. In spite of the fact that the Hebrew word *Elohim* is

---

[121] John 4: 7-30
[122] John 1:45-51

plural, no one translates Genesis 1:1 "In the beginning gods created the heavens and the Earth". It is almost impossible for one to recognize one's own bias resulting from prejudged beliefs. It is not so much a problem of believing what we see, but rather a fixation that causes us to see what we already believe. This law has both positive and negative effect. If we are fixed on judgment, we will see a world in hell. If we fix on Love and Spirit, we will see the world transformed.

When reading the biblical library, it is important to read with a sense of one's own coherence. Coherence is a principle holding that for a statement to be true, it must agree with all other truths to which one gives credence, for truth must be one. The simplicity of Jesus' teaching is supported by its coherence with the teaching of the other great Sages of the world.

In order to become aware of the fact that god has not lost the world, we need to hear and understand what Jesus taught. Jesus has much more validity for our lives as a teacher of The Way than he will ever have when perceived as a sacrifice for our sin!

People experience separation, and thus may feel that god has lost them. They no longer have an awareness of a bond with reality and may believe that it is up to god to reestablish what they perceive as a broken connection. The teachings of Jesus demonstrate that kinship with god is not broken. Our awareness is diminished because of our own self-constructed barriers. Love is the connection; and the barriers to the awareness of love we construct are our own judgments and our own unforgiving attitudes. We built these barriers, and by choosing forgiveness we will succeed in taking them down!

If I could convince the world that this book had been discovered in the archives of Albert Einstein, and that he was the author, it would become an immediate best seller.

Many stories, whose source were teachers contemporary with Jesus, were undoubtedly brought into the gospel accounts and accredited to Jesus. This perhaps explains why some teachings assumed to be by Jesus are not compatible with his apparent perennial philosophy. It is also evident that editors of the gospel stories improvised some accounts in order to support their own theological bias. We need to be continually aware that we are not reading recorded history, but gospels, by definition 'good news', which is to say news evaluated according to the beliefs of the particular witness who is telling the story as to what is 'good' and correct.

This same process of attribution or 'reverse plagiarism', in a way, applies to the monks of the Middle Ages, who invented stories about the childhood of Jesus, simply because their pious convictions made them believe that their productions were the way it must have been. One of the many stories will suffice to paint the picture. Jesus is portrayed as a child playing with other children, and in order to demonstrate his superiority to them made birds of clay, then brought them to life, so that they flew away.

Perhaps the most painful and tragic of Jesus' supposed teachings are the words concerning divorce attributed to him by Matthew's gospel. Specifically, the teaching that one who marries after divorce commits adultery.[123] One cannot imagine the untold misery caused by this teaching in the lives of those who have experienced real growth in their struggle through multiple marriages. Not many congregations offer healing to divorced persons who have remarried. It is unimaginable to me that the same teacher who would not castigate a woman taken in adultery would condemn the marriage of a divorced man or woman. It is also of interest to be aware that, in Jewish law, a married man was not considered an adulterer, unless involved with a married woman. Only a woman could adulterate a home by bearing a child sired by someone other than her husband.

A word needs to be said about some of the theological controversies of church history. I believe a different paradigm regarding the nature of humankind will result in a more straightforward understanding of the record. It is needful to bring healing to some of the personal terror these unfortunate beliefs have caused. Jonathan Edwards, an early (1741) New England preacher, caused people in his congregation to faint when he preached a sermon titled "Sinners in the Hands of an Angry God." He pictured sinners suspended over the flames of hell by a spider's thread.

Paul speaks of both foreknowledge and predestination. Those whom god foreknew, he also predestined to be conformed to the image of his son.[124] In the terrible belief held by orthodoxy that all are sinners and deserving of hellfire and brimstone, it began to be preached by some that only those whom god had predestined to be saved would escape hell. "Who are the elect?" And how could one know if they were among the foreordained?

The terror is easily dissipated if we understand that god has not lost anyone! We are all of us foreknown and predestined to fulfill the image of god's Sonship. How long it may seem to take in space/time illusion is up to us. Our healing is inescapable and inevitable!

The same awareness of universal sonship needs also to be applied to such theological controversies as the doctrine of incarnation. We all are in fact incarnations of god's Spirit. Jesus may have been one of the first to understand this fact. When he demonstrated sonship in his life, there were those who thought that this was a one-time unique expression. They failed

---

[123] Matthew 5:32
[124] Romans 8:28-31

to see that Jesus was trying to teach that oneness was an experience for all of us to realize. Again, Jesus is not an exception, he is an example!

The ultimate sense of separation is in the notion that one can be saved and go to heaven, while 'unsaved' loved ones will end up in hell. In the universal sense of oneness, we all go into heaven together. No one enters heaven until we all get there, for we are all one. Anyone left in hell, in some fashion leaves all of the sonship in hell.

Again, we face the limitations of language. There is only one only/begotten of god. God and only/begotten son, both can be referred to with the pronoun it, a non-sexist term. In our language, where nouns do not have gender, 'it' is a pronoun used of things and not of persons. Because of the limitations of language a double bind is created; god is referred to as both having gender and as being an object. The need to refer to god as a person infers objective reality. Being tied to language, or, for that matter, our thoughts being tied to language, our intellects do not have the ability to picture another dimension beyond persons and things; namely Spirit. It is in the feelings understood in the communion of Silence that the One Spirit bears witness to the reality of unity.

Silence

We can not objectify experience of Presence or Silence.

We do not seek to go to the Presence.

We seek rather, to let go of any objective awareness of other.

We let go the void of fullness knowing the fullness of void.

We experience no thing, for there is no other.

We cannot experience a thing of Spirit, for Spirit is no thing.

We can, however, feel the Presence of no boundary.

In Spirit neither god nor our own realities experience gender, which is appropriate for bodies but not for Spirit. Further, to use the phrase sons and daughters of god is to imply a duplicity that does not exist in Spirit. The Lord, our god, is One and so are we. The generic terms 'man' and 'mankind' have their limits, but so does a compulsive need to be gender 'correct'. Both positions show the limits of language in trying to express the inexpressible. Unfortunately English has no common gender, third person singular, pronoun. We can say she or he but not it. I once tried to invent a pronoun, combining these three but ended up with a scatological result.

Jesus said, "He that has seen me has seen the father." He was not speaking of his human personality but of the divine Presence. The church has been unable to sense that when *anyone* is truly seen, the Father is seen

152

as well. The same cogency is demonstrated as well in the 'I am' statements of Jesus: I am the Way, the Truth, the Life, and the Light of the world. Again, these do not refer to the human personality of Jesus, for the personal self of Jesus was as illusory as the personal self of anyone else. The prophetic tradition, of which Jesus was a part, contains numerous incidents of prophets speaking in the first person as god. The Rabbi Hillel is quoted as saying, "If I am here, (speaking as Yahweh), everyone is here."

The most indefensible interpretation to grow out of Jesus' words is taken from the statement "No one comes to the father but by me". The concept that the personality of the individual called Jesus is the only means god has provided for the salvation of everyone else in the world is ludicrous. Clearly, the 'me' Jesus refers to is the spiritual, inner, universal Christ.

The son is in the father, the father is in the son; we (all of us) are the only/begotten son of god. Only the truly born of the Spirit demonstrate the oneness of the Sonship. Jesus taught that his Reality, not his *form*, was the Light of the world and the Way (Tao). This Way is the means by which we in our true Selves demonstrate in our lives what he demonstrated in his.

The Eastern teachings of enlightenment are at their core, in form and symbol, the same as the teaching of the new birth. The words and images vary according to the particular culture involved. The Buddha saw the world differently than those attached to the natural tradition of a materialistic reality. The attachment to things, both in possession and power of control, is the reason for personal suffering in the world. Detachment from things, as a religious recluse, is attachment in mirror image. Avoidance of things carries the same sense of detachment, resulting in the suffering of fear. The solution to the problem of attachment/detachment is the Buddhist paradigm of non-attachment. Paul's learning to be content in whatsoever state he found himself, whether abased or abounding, is in the spirit of non-attachment.

The heart of Tao is learning to go with the flow, or doing by not doing. In today's parlance it is not pushing the river; it is to act from being with effortless accomplishment; not by doing.

Some time ago in "A Course in Miracles" study group, we had a conversation in regard to choice and decisions. The main focus was on forgiving god and our brother. At the level of the *real*, god, our brother, and we are the same. If we haven't forgiven our brother, we haven't forgiven god – for god and our brother are the same, and we must forgive god for putting our brother in our life (as a teacher). It is obvious to me that some of these lessons must be learned at the feeling level, for that night I experienced a very vivid dream and awoke to this poetic expression.

Forgiving God – Beyond Religion to Transcendence

I dreamt that I was a child with a small brother,
We were about to do something delightful,
When our austere father appeared and denied us both.
He stood in opposition to our desires!
I had a long wand in my hand,
I approached him with trepidation,
My flail was limber and quite like a stiff whip.
I hesitated to approach the father figure with my whip,
He was unmoving, dark gray, mute and very tall,
I began to sob as I moved closer.
Finally I decided to go for broke and swung down on him,
I was shaking with release of tension as I beat at him,
Then I began to curse at him, a dirty bastard and a SOB.
How dare he stand in the way of our delight?
He fell before me without a word,
I continued to beat him until exhausted,
The dominating father figure collapsed,
Withered he was no longer threatening,
It no longer stood in our way.
I express my own anger,
The god of fear is undone,
Our delight is at hand!

I remember Joseph Campbell who said, "Follow your bliss."

Jesus promised the gift of his peace to us. God is at peace because god is without judgment. The lesson is to follow the perfection of that example. The enlightened have learned to live in the 'I am' consciousness. Jesus exhorted us to be perfect, even as our heavenly Father is perfect;[125] it is important when using the word heaven to look within, not outwards or upwards.

Perfection can only be an attribute within the reality of the inner daemon (Self) it is not a quality attributable to the space/time eidolon (self). Our perfection must come from the Father within which is the realm of Love.

Tradition says that the following words were found penned on the wall of a cell in a mental asylum. If the story is true, it illustrates the presence of the healing power of god, even in the midst of profound mental anguish.

---

[125] Matthew 5:48

The love of God is greater far than tongue or pen can ever tell.

It reaches from the highest star, and reaches to the lowest hell.

Could we with ink the ocean fill, and were the skies of parchment made.

Were every stalk on earth a quill, and every man a scribe by trade.

To write the love of God above would drain the ocean dry.

Nor could the scroll contain the whole,

Though stretched from sky to sky.

(From "The Love of God" by F.H. Lehman)

The book of the Acts of the Apostles is almost universally presumed to be the work of the editor of the book of Luke. This is primarily because they are both addressed to Theopholis (lover of god). Acts starts out by saying the former treatise, a reference to the gospel of Luke that was also directed to Theopholis. In the sense of attribution of one's works to others this statement must cause us to question whether the author of Acts and Luke are actually the same.

A recent documentary on PBS dealing with the development of the early Jesus Movement, "Peter and Paul", used the chronology of "The Acts of the Apostles" as if it were historically accurate. The attempt to follow the 'time line' of the writer of Acts was not successful in harmonizing statements attributed to Paul by the author of Acts with the words of Paul as found in his own authentic writings.

To reiterate the problem: Paul's authentic letters were written prior to Luke's gospel, and Acts attributed to Luke was obviously written later. The Gospel according to Luke was written after the destruction of the temple in Jerusalem, which occurred in 70 CE.

Jesus was crucified circa 33 CE, Paul's authentic letters were thought to have been written between 40 CE and 64 CE, when his death was believed to have occurred in Rome, in the fire set by Emperor Nero. Luke's gospel would be dated after 70 CE and the Book of Acts, attributed to Luke, sometime after that, perhaps several years latter than 95 CE. Acts, then, purports to record dialogues between the author and Paul fifty years after they could have occurred.

After the persecution of Christians, blamed by Nero for burning Rome, the Roman church needed to keep a low profile and learned to live without being a challenge to the Empire. Part of getting along with the political powers was accomplished by moving away from some of the more radical, Gnostic leaning, teachings of Paul. Letters were ascribed to him, which he did not write, and the "Book of Acts" was produced to discredit some of the same teachings.

It was obvious in Acts that Paul did not have Apostolic Succession and did not experience a physical resurrection of Jesus; beliefs fostered by the second century Roman Church. It is probable that the election of Matthias to replace Judas as recorded in Acts 1:15-26, was an invention to preclude any suggestion that Paul was the legitimate spiritual successor.

I have for some time questioned the accuracy of Acts as an historical report of the activities of the apostle Paul. I have previously mentioned a contradiction in the question, did Paul go up to Jerusalem? The book of Acts says that he did, but Paul's letter to Galatians says he did not. The problem with Acts as valid history stems from the fact that Acts talks about the early days of Paul's activities and ascribes words to Paul that were actually recorded fifty years after the fact. Scholars pretty much agree that the gospels were written after the bulk of Paul's letters to early churches and that Paul's thought had a profound effect on the theology set forth in the gospel accounts. I repeat, however, that much of the Book of Acts and several of the writings of Paul are not considered authentic and simply represent spurious works attempting to bring authoritarian literalistic conformity to the established Roman Catholic Church.

In short, Paul's letters written in the later part of his life and ministry influenced Luke's gospel based on Mark and Quella. How can Acts, which was obviously produced at a later time than the Gospel of Luke, report to be an earlier account of Paul's life and ministry? Acts could be written after Paul's letters if it was simply a matter of historical research done by the author of Acts, but not years after Paul's death. About fifty years after Paul's letters were actually written, the writer of Acts claims to have been a traveling companion with Paul during his early ministry.

One of the key questions of the record other than the contradiction about Paul going to Jerusalem, is the matter of recording the activities and nature of the Holy Spirit. (Acts 2) In Acts 19: 1,2 Paul questions the church at Ephesus: "Have you received the Holy Spirit?" They reply to the effect that they had never heard of such a thing. The book of Acts was written circa 100 CE and Paul was writing his letters to the church at Corinth while he was in Ephesus circa 55 CE. The author of Acts claims to have been with Paul when he first met the church at Ephesus circa 50 CE.

This assumed eyewitness story of Paul's question to the church at Ephesus, whom he supposedly just met, was written fifty years after his established relationship with that church. It is untenable that a first hand account would be delayed by fifty years, for Luke would have been almost eighty years old.

One must raise the question of supposed eyewitness accounts with regard to several stories recorded in Acts; the ascension of Jesus, the tongues of fire and speaking in tongues at Pentecost, Paul's presence at the stoning of Stephen and the account of Paul's Damascus road conversion.

In regard to Paul's conversion on the road to Damascus; in Acts 9:7, we are told that when Paul received his vision of light and heard a divine voice, *his companions heard the voice but saw no one*; yet in Acts 22:9, when Paul tells of his same conversion experience, *his companions saw the light but did not hear the voice that was speaking to him*, which is just the opposite.

In considering the question of speaking in tongues, Paul in his letters was not concerned with receiving the Holy Spirit or the gift of tongues. In fact, in I Corinthians 13 he states that tongues will cease and seems to consider those speaking in tongues as more of a liability than an asset. In short, the historical accuracy of the book of Acts is in doubt and the writer, rather than being a companion of Paul, was most likely an editor of stories about Paul as well as other stories about Peter and the early church. Its purpose was likely to defend the positions of the Roman church; especially the idea that apostles were eyewitnesses to both resurrection and ascension, which validated the concept of Apostolic succession.

Paul in I Corinthians 13, speaking of the contrast of outer show with inner reality in regard to glossilalia (speaking in tongues) has given us a profound statement about the nature of Love.

[1] I may speak in all the languages of humankind or even as a divine messenger, but if I do so without Love then I am ordained to sound like noisy brass or a tinkling cymbal.

[2] If I could predict the future, were aware of all secrets, knew science completely and had the absolute conviction to carry away mountains; yet if I am unable to love I have no reality.

[3] If I give away every thing I have to nourish others or sacrifice my flesh to the fire; if I do not act in love they are useless acts.

[4] Love patiently endures and acts benevolently, Love is not jealous; Love does not brag or act arrogantly;

[5] Love has good manners and is not selfish; is not quickly exasperated and does not consider others as worthless;

[6] Love does not bid godspeed to injustice but is glad for the truth,

[7] Love patiently endures any situation, is unfailing in trust, does not give up hope and has no limit to its endurance.

[8] Love never, ever, loses its Way.

Paul argues that special powers and gifts will ultimately fail, for when the perfect manifests, the partial will cease to exist. I think this substantiates my belief that there is no eternal to be found in the temporal. When Love comes as our *daemon* the father within does the work, which is the *being* of love and not the *doing* of the *eidolon*, which is without true value.

Paul continues his statement emphasizing the difference between childish behavior and a mature, spiritual view of the world. Again, this is support for enlightenment as true spiritual rebirth. "I put away childish things."

[12] For now we see through a mirror in a temporal way; but then as presence: now I know a portion; but then I shall be fully acquainted.

[13] And now endure Conviction, Confidence and Benevolence, these three; but greatly better by much is Love.

One of the most intriguing drills I was ever challenged with, was the task of exchanging the word 'love' in this definitive section with the personal pronoun 'I'.

[4] I patiently endure and act benevolently, I am not jealous; I am not a braggart nor do I act arrogantly;

[5] I have good manners and am not selfish; I am not quickly exasperated and do not consider others as worthless;

[6] I do not bid Godspeed to injustice but am glad for the truth;

[7] I patiently endure any situation, am unfailing in trust, do not give up hope and have no limit to my endurance.

[8] I never, ever, lose my Way.

Chapter Six—Spiritual Libraries
Ancient and Modern

The Way in World Religions

The sacred Library of the Hebrew/Christian tradition (the Bible) contains a good deal of material helpful in understanding the spiritual path. In addition, other devout literature of the world has much to offer in understanding the Way.

Many sages have experienced and taught the spiritual path of oneness. Teachers of: Tao, Ch'an Buddhism, Zen, Sufism, Vedanta, Jewish and Christian mysticism, and Gnosticism, represent the ancients. Different designations, such as Krishna consciousness or Christ consciousness, only indicate the culture and language of the visionaries who follow this path. Lesser-known writers of recent days, including a few referred to as New Age, also present a non-dualistic teaching.

The faith of the Buddha, Jesus and other religious sages from around the world was experiential. Christ Mind, Buddha Awareness, and Krishna Consciousness are simply different names for an internal awareness of divine Presence; a reference not only to the experience of the founders but an encounter available to their disciples as well. However, as developed religions, Christianity, Buddhism, Islam, and Vedanta have for the most part become external religious and political institutions.

Aldous Huxley wrote of these common teachings in his book "The Perennial Philosophy". According to Huxley, Liebniz coined the phrase, 'Philisophia Perennis'. Huxley asserts, "Only the transcendent, the completely other, *can be immanent without being modified by the becoming of that in which it dwells.*" "The Perennial Philosophy teaches that it is desirable and indeed necessary to know the spiritual Ground of things, not only within the soul, but also outside in the world and, beyond world and soul, in its transcendent otherness – 'in heaven'."[126]

---

[126] The Perennial Philosophy, Aldous Huxley page 2

The Nature of Ponderable Matter

"Genuine philosophers concur in holding that whatever the real world may be, it is at least modified by the senses so that what man directly experiences is something different. Also, for the twentieth century physicist, ponderable matter, that is, *matter and form as given through the senses, is definitely known not to be the actual physical reality.* The ultimates of matter are apparently wave-systems of essentially the same nature as electromagnetic or light waves; and, further, these systems cannot be correctly imaged in any sensible model. Only mathematical equations are capable of representing the reality, whatever that may be, in a manner that is consonant with observed effects...

"When Shankara speaks of destroying the universe, he does not have in mind a physical cataclysm but a Transition in Consciousness such that the apperceptive Subject realizes Itself as Lord over the universe, instead of being a victim of it. The individual soul that has attained this position may choose continued cognizance of the universe, but the essential power of the latter over the former is destroyed unequivocally."[127]

The Sages of the world, often referred to as Mystics, Masters, Avatars or Enlightened Ones, have given us a profound heritage of spiritual insight. Unfortunately, as is the case with all religious institutions, form and ritual to a large extent have replaced the creative teachings of the founders. Buddhism, Zen, Vedanta, Islam and Christianity are not exceptions.

If these ancient Sages could be brought together in one room, I have no doubt they would have a joyous celebration of oneness. Regrettably, (except for the Buddhists), if a sample of the majority of their traditional or literalistic followers were likewise assembled, historical experience has shown that because of conflicting dogma, form, and ritual, they would undoubtedly, eventually seek to kill one another.

The ultimate expression of the perennial philosophy would be in learning the Buddhist lesson that when our inner reality finds union with the reality of the unmanifest Ground of Being, it is not the case of an ocean consuming the dewdrop but rather the dewdrop incorporating an ocean.

The eternal cannot be objectified in the visible world of space/time, and must remain invisible. Our visible manifest world will never confine the invisible; at best it can only be used to uncover it. Jesus taught that we are in and not of the world; as enlightened dew drops in the world, it is up to us to demonstrate what he taught. By being open to Spirit, we accomplish the awareness that we are not of the world. Spirit leads us to the still point

---

[127] Pathways Through to Space, Franklin Merrell-Wolff: pages 155-157

where space/time dissolves into the timeless; and the dewdrop reveals the ocean it has absorbed. There is no eternal within the temporal.

Spiritual healing is based on letting go of the self-erected blocks that prevent our spiritual vision, so that we can once again see what is real. The task is complicated by our common assumption that we will see this reality in the outer, with our physical eyes, rather than with sagacity of Spirit. There is a Real World of Spirit that we must learn to see with eyes and heart of Spirit. Our problem is that we have blocked our spiritual vision with fear, judgment, and mistaken beliefs, all centered in an unforgiving attitude toward the past. The Buddha taught his disciples this different way of looking at the world and had great influence on the spiritual teachings of the Far East. In addition to the ancient spiritual libraries, there have also been writings incorporating the subject of the Perennial Philosophy in more modern times. Religious and philosophical authors deal with the subject, as do poets and scientists as well. In developing an understanding of the witness of these many teachers, both ancient and modern, I think it best when practical to allow them to speak for themselves:

Hermetica

Hermes, an Egyptian Sage, attributed his work to the god Thoth. To distinguish him from their own Hermes, the Greeks called him Hermes Trismegestus (thrice great). Thoth is dated from early Egyptian times; The Hermetica was translated into Greek circa 200 CE. but the Egyptian version was probably several hundred years old by then. It became a foundation for the Greek mystery religions and may have been known to Pythagoras as early as 500 BCE. Its theme is the perennial philosophy of the invisible reign of god within. Following are selections from "The Hermetica" translated by Timothy Freke and Peter Gandy.

Rebirth...Pg. 140: "This is the only road to reality. It is the way our ancestors trod to discover the Primal Goodness. It is sacred and divine, but a hard highway for the soul to travel in a body. For the soul's first step is to struggle against itself – stirring up a Civil War. It is the feud of Unity against duality, the one seeking to unite and the other seeking to divide.

"He who is reborn communes with the All-Father who is light and life. You will only experience this supreme vision when you stop talking about it, for this knowledge is deep silence and tranquility of the senses. He who knows the beauty of the Primal Goodness perceives nothing else. He doesn't listen to anything. He cannot move his body at all. He forgets all physical sensations and is still, while the beauty of Goodness bathes his mind in Light and draws his soul out of his body – making him One with eternal being. For a man cannot become a god whilst he believes he is a body. To become divine he must be transformed by the beauty of Primal Goodness."

Secret Teachings…Pg. 146: "This is the journey of knowledge. Speed towards this knowledge, for although it is hard to let go of the familiar and return to the old home from which we originated, Atum's grace never fails and there is no end to his bounty. He is by nature a musician who composes the harmony of the cosmos and transmits to each individual the rhythm of their own music. If the music becomes discordant, don't blame the musician, but the lyre-string he plays, that has become loose and sounds flat, marring the perfect beauty of the melody."

Gnosticism

Although Gnosticism is an integral source of the earliest Christian writings, the fact is, we have not had exposure to their understanding of the teachings *of* Jesus until very recent years. The foundation of actual triune thought is that god intends, logos expresses, and the world results. Space/time manifestation is the result of Spirit expression. According to Gnostic teaching, the mind is not within the body; the body is within the mind. Likewise the soul is not within the mind; the mind is within the soul. The soul, individuated in personal expression, is unified and universal within the total Impersonal Self.

In Chapter Five, "The Biblical Library", we have already written a great deal about the Gnostic influence on early Christianity. The gospel of John and the Q document of Luke and Matthew are testimony to this influence.

The gospel according to Thomas is the best known of the Gnostic gospels discovered in the Nag Hammadi library. It is a Coptic text; an Egyptian dialect with borrowings from Greek, and is the language used today in the liturgy of the Coptic Church. The book consists of 113 very short logia or sayings; the following quotations are all logia from the gospel according to Thomas according to several translators.

Logion 3: "Jesus said: If those who lead you say to you: 'See, the kingdom is in heaven, then the birds of the heaven will precede you.' If they say to you: 'It is in the sea,' then the fish will precede you. But the kingdom is within you and it is without you. If you will know yourselves, then you will be known and you will know that you are the sons of the Living Father. But if you do not know yourselves, then you are in poverty and you are that poverty."

This statement attributed to Jesus is a reaffirmation that the kingdom of god is within us and if we don't know this awareness, then we truly are impoverished. It is a mirrored reflection of the logia that speak of recognizing the poverty of the material world. (54 and 69)

Logion 29: "Jesus said: If the flesh has come into existence because of the spirit, it is a marvel; but if the spirit has come into existence because of the body, it is a marvel of marvels. But I marvel at how this great wealth has made its home in this great poverty."

To see the spirit as the source of the body is to recognize a great wonder. But to suggest that the body is the source of the spirit is nothing short of ridiculous. This great wealth or Pearl is concealed within our bodies.

Logion 44: "Jesus said: Whoever blasphemes against the father, it shall be forgiven him, and whoever blasphemes against the son, it shall he forgiven him; but whoever blasphemes against the Holy Spirit will not be forgiven, either on earth or in heaven."[128]

The concept of blasphemy against the Holy Spirit has always been difficult to interpret. In order to understand the nature of this blasphemy, it is important to understand the trinity of creation, according to Gnostic philosophy. As in our previous overview of John's gospel, we are dealing with the creative trinity of Source, Means, and Effect. At the highest level is Source, which through means of energy and intent produces the manifest world. This is to say, that heaven by means of logos produces earth. Thus it can be understood that the Sonship by means of the Holy Spirit is manifested from the Father. Gnostics taught that the *appearance* of sonship was not its reality; the reality of space/time sonship is the Holy Spirit expressing from the Father. One may speak against heaven or against earth from ignorance (i.e. we don't understand either of these if we have not been enlightened), and this ignorance can be forgiven. We can only be aware of the connection between heaven and earth when we are enlightened through the Holy Spirit. If we know this awareness, then we are alive. But if we know the Holy Spirit as the Reality of life, then no one who knows this Life, can curse Life. If we've blasphemed heaven or earth, then we have done so through ignorance. But if we are truly Alive through the knowledge of the Holy Spirit, we cannot possibly curse that Life or blaspheme that Spirit. Thus there is no reason to be forgiven either in heaven or on earth.

Logion 48: Jesus said: "If two make peace with each other in this one house, they shall say to the mountain: 'be moved,' and it will move."

Being able to move a mountain is a symbol or idiom for the possession of great power. From the Gnostic standpoint, if two people are truly able to make peace then they obviously know their oneness. This knowledge of

---

[128] See also Mt 12:31

oneness places them at the center of Reality, where the material world and its mountains are of little consequence.

Logion 53: "His disciples said to him: Is circumcision profitable or not? He said to them: if it were profitable, their father would beget them circumcised from their mother. But the true circumcision in spirit has become profitable in every way."

This logion demonstrates how little concern the Gnostics had for ritual. True circumcision is a change of the heart and mind; it is an inner happening, not an outer convention.

Logion 54: "Jesus said: Blessed are the poor, for yours is the kingdom of heaven."

Logion 69b: "Blessed are the hungry, for the belly of him who desires will be filled."

To say congratulations to the poor suggests a different meaning for the word poor than we commonly give it. If, by entering the inner kingdom, we have discovered the impoverishment of the outer world, then to be poor is to have no investment in materiality, and we thus deserve to be congratulated. These are the mirror image of logion 3.

Logion 56: "Jesus said: Whoever has known the world has found a corpse, and whoever has found a corpse, of him the world is not worthy."

The same concept of corpse is restated in logion 80 as carcass or body. This is the same sentiment as logion 54. The material world is gladly exchanged for knowledge of the inner kingdom. The material world is a carcass and if you discover this fact, then you are to be congratulated. In consciousness, we lose the entire nothing we thought we had, in order to gain the 'Pearl of Great Price' and the 'Hidden Treasure'.

Logion 67: "Jesus said: Whoever knows the All but fails to know himself lacks everything."

Logion 70: "Jesus said: If you bring forth that within your selves, that which you have, will save you. If you do not have that within your selves, that which you do not have within you, will kill you."

We can fill our heads with all the learning of the material world that we possibly can cram in; and if we direct all our energies toward the outer material world and its possessions, it will kill us. The true experience of life is to discover the power within; without that power, life is meaningless.

Logion 90: "Jesus said: Come to me, for easy is my yoke and my lordship is gentle, and you shall find repose for yourselves."

The key word in this logion is repose or rest. In Gnostic philosophy, the word rest is a code word for true rest; repose or peace can only be part of our experience if we know the reality of Spirit. In Gnostic philosophy, god as the source, the ungenerated forefather, is ineffable, invisible, and eternal depth. Depth gave rise to a female counterpart named Silence and together they energized the world by means of extensions called Aeons, one of whom was Wisdom. In some of the Gnostic material, Eve, who was the daughter of Sophia – the goddess of wisdom, was the mother of Adam and thus the mother of all human life. True knowledge is achieved when we merge in consciousness with Depth and Silence, thus finding rest and repose.

Of these selections Logion 29 and Logion 70 are my favorites.

Vedanta

Vedanta is a philosophical system in India based on the Sanskrit word Veda (ancient Hindu scripture [knowledge]). The underlying principle of Vedanta (fulfillment of the Vedas) is *tat tvam asi*, the Sanskrit words for "thou art that". The ultimate reality to be realized is the identity of the Atman or Impersonal Self, with the Brahman, expansive Source and impersonal Absolute as written in the Upanishads circa 400 to 200 BCE.

To Shankara, an eighth century teacher, *tat tvam asi* (thou art that) meant that the Impersonal Self is fundamentally identical with universal being; and that the outer world of personal experience has no independent reality, for reality is a single principle. He taught that we are tied to the familiar world by the bonds of karma (action/reaction), which are the accumulated consequences of actions in many lifetimes.

Shankara describes Enlightenment thus: A man is said to be free even in this life when he is established in illumination. His bliss is unending. He almost forgets this world of appearances. Even though his mind is dissolved in Brahman, he is fully awake, free from the ignorance of waking life. He is fully conscious, but free from any craving. Such a man is said to be free even in this life. For him, the sorrows of this world are over. Though he possesses a finite body, he remains united with the Infinite. His heart knows no anxiety. Such a man is said to be free even in this life.

Shankara founded the branch of Vedanta referred to as non-dual (Advaita) Vedanta; this branch has an essential teaching of knowledge (Veda) not unlike the early Gnostic Christians. Did Jesus, who taught the Kingdom within, have contact with the idea of *tat tvam asi* (thou art that)? This statement agrees with Jesus' argument, "You are gods."[129]

On the surface, Vedanta would seem to have a belief in a multiplicity of gods. It is as if the Hindu followers had a ladder full of deities that would enable them to ascend from the primitive to the most transcendent. Vedanta incorporates the Hindu idea of levels of gods, or rather, *levels of the idea of*

---

[129] John 10:34

god. These are attempts to state levels of the philosophical understanding of god and godhead. In our culture, the Roman Catholic tradition of directing prayer to saints or Mary or the Sacred Heart of Jesus would be analogous.

One of the major books teaching this non-dualistic inner doctrine is the Bhagavad-Gita, which draws heavily on the Upanishads (mystical Vedas). This is the story of a prince, Arjuna, who is led to fight a battle against many friends and relatives and is trying to weigh the ethics, right or wrong, of his situation. He is drawn into a dialogue with the god Krishna.

The following excerpts are from "The Inner Doctrine"; Part II of the Bhagavad-Gita compiled and adapted from numerous translations by the Yogi Publishing Society.

"Know thou, 0 Prince of Pandu, that there never was a time when I, nor thou, nor any of these princes of the earth was not; nor shall there ever come a time, hereafter, when any of us shall cease to be."

"That which is unreal has no shadow of Real Being, notwithstanding the illusion of appearance and false knowledge. And that which has Real Being has never ceased to be – can never cease to be, in spite of all appearances to the contrary. The wise have inquired into these things, O Arjuna, and have discovered the real Essence, and inner Meaning of things."

"Know that The Absolute, which pervades all things, is indestructible. No one can work the destruction of the Imperishable One."

"Of a truth, none can slay – none can be slain."

"Take unto thy inner mind, this truth, 0 Prince! Verily, the Real Man – the Spirit of Man – is neither born, nor does it die. Unborn, undying, ancient, perpetual and eternal, it has endured and will endure forever. The body may die; be slain; be destroyed completely; but He that has occupied it remains unharmed."

"As a man throws away his old garments, replacing them with new and brighter ones, even so the Dweller of the body, having acquitted its old mortal frame, enters into others which are new and freshly prepared for it."

In poetic form "The Song Celestial" by Sir Edwin Arnold puts it:

> "Never the spirit was born; the spirit shall cease to be never;
> Never was time it was not; End and Beginning are dreams!
> Birthless and deathless and changeless remaineth the spirit
> Forever;
> Death hath not touched it at all, dead though the house of it
> Seems!
> Nay, but as when one layeth his worn-out robes away,
> And, taking new ones, sayeth, "These will I wear to-day!""

So putteth by the spirit lightly its garb of flesh,

And passeth to inherit a residence afresh."

"Many are they, who, saturating themselves with the letter of spiritual writings and teachings, and failing to catch the true spirit thereof, take great delight in technical controversies regarding the text. Hair-splitting definitions and abstruse interpretations are the pleasures and amusements of such men. Such are tainted with worldly lusts, and, therefore, incline toward a belief in a heaven filled with objects and employments in accordance with their desires and tastes, instead of the final spiritual goal of all great souls. Flowery words, and imposing ceremonies are invented by these people, and, among them, there is much talk of rewards for this observance, and punishment for lack of it. To these whose minds incline to such teachings, the use of the concentrated, determined reason and the still higher Spiritual Consciousness is unknown."

"Free thyself from the pairs of opposites – the changeful things of finite life; and careless about the same dwell thou in the consciousness of the Real Self. Be free from worldly anxiety, and fierce cravings for material possessions. Be Self centered and uncontrolled by the illusions of the finite world."

"When you shall rise beyond the plane of illusion, then you shall cease to disturb thyself regarding doctrines, theology, disputations concerning rites or ceremonies, and other useless trimmings upon the cloth of spiritual thought. Then you shall be liberated from attachments to sacred books, to writings of learned theologians, or to those who would interpret that which they fail themselves to understand; but instead, you shall fix your mind in earnest contemplation of the Spirit, and thus reach the harmony with the Real Self which underlies all."

"When a man finds satisfaction in the Real Self within himself – such a one has attained Spiritual Consciousness. His mind is disturbed neither by adversity nor by prosperity; accepting both, he is tied to neither. Anger, fear and worry have been cast off by him as discarded garments. He is worthy of the name of Sage."

"When a man has attained true spiritual knowledge, he becomes like unto the tortoise which is able to draw within its shell its limbs, for such a man may withdraw his faculties of sense impression from the objects of sense, and shelter them from the illusions of the sense world, well protected by the armor of the Spirit."

"Wrapped in contemplation of the real, the unreal exists not for him."

"He who has gained freedom from attachment to, or fear of, objects of sense; he who finds his strength and love in the Real Self; he gains Peace.

And in that Peace which passes all understanding, he finds release from all the pains and troubles of life."

"There is no true Knowledge possible for those who have not entered into this Peace."

"That which seems real to the man of the sense-world, is known to be illusion by the Sage. And that which seems unreal and non-existent to the crowd, is known to the Sage as the only Reality. Such is the difference in the powers and vision of men."

"If having attained the blissful state of spiritual consciousness a man dwells therein unto the hour of death, He passes straight to the bosom of the Father."

"The illumined soul thinks always: 'I am doing nothing.' No matter what he sees hears, touches, smells, eats. This he knows always; I am not seeing, I am not hearing. It is the senses that see and hear and touch the things of the senses."

Tat tvam asi (thou art that), is reflected in the Quaker use of the word thou instead of you; using thou because persons are not considered other. There is a case to be made for the use of thou and thee in our language.

> I am That which Thou art,
> Thou art That which I am,
> And That, which I am,
> And That, which Thou art,
> Is One and the Same. [130]

Taoism

Taoism is both a Chinese philosophical system and a religion. Its essential philosophical tenets are from the third century BCE, found in the "Tao Te Ching" attributed to Lao Tzu, and in the works of Chaung Tzu.

The Tao (way) according to Lao Tzu is the unnamed Source of All-That-Is and expresses itself by means of the Te (natural potential spontaneously actualized) or Virtue. We can witness this process in reverse, i.e. from virtue to Tao, as a means; in order to uncover and experience the Tao, which is our center. The life of Virtue or Power is lived by means of effortless effective activity, or *wei wu wei*. Do not do!

Chaung Tzu taught patient observation of the changing flow of life, and advocated non-linear thinking instead of rigid logic and the proscribed

---

[130] From a meditation led by William R. Parker.

views of tradition. The Tao cannot be stated in words or explained by discursive thought. As a philosophy, Taoism asserts that one should seek harmony with the underlying pattern of the universe. There are many moons reflected in a quiet pool of water; as many as there are viewing the reflections. Yet there is but one moon.

Under the influence of Ch'an Buddhism, with its similar philosophy, many adherents readily embraced the teachings of the Buddha. For this reason, relevant philosophical sayings of both movements often can be grouped together. Taoist wisdom has an ancient history as the Chinese concept of the flow of life. It is sometimes called the Watercourse Way. As an analogy, water always finds its own level, flows unceasingly, and over time is an irresistible force.

Taoism historically has been divided into three different movements, Religion, Physiology and Philosophy. Taoism, as a religion, developed many offshoots devoted to various interpretations of the path of virtue. Under the influence of the "I Ching", a book of changes, some groups pushed divination into complex forms of magic. Others pursued physical longevity by means of breathing techniques and exercise.

Originally it seems to have begun as a philosophy based on an understanding of the Tao. The Tao is the unseen, transcendent being-less source of all being. One cannot name or explain the Tao; one simply recognizes and allows the Tao to express itself through life. The spirit of Tao refuses to make judgment on the flow of life. Taoism teaches patience and a sense of expectancy. A classic story illustrates this philosophy.

A certain farmer had a beautiful stallion that one day ran away. His neighbor took a "my ain't it awful" attitude and shared with the farmer that this event was a terrible thing to have happened – that's bad. The farmer's response was to wait and see. In a few days the stallion came back to the farm followed by three mares, the neighbor's observation – that's good. The farmer's – we'll see. A few days later the farmer's son was trying to break one of the mares, was thrown off and broke his leg. The neighbor again cried, "my ain't it awful." The farmer again took the stance, we'll see. The next week the army came by, conscripting soldiers for a war but did not take the farmer's son because of the broken leg. As usual, the neighbor said, "That's good" and the farmer said, "We'll see." He who structures his life will destroy it. He who frees his life will empower it.

In applying the principles of the Tao to the human body and the flow of life, the second aspect of Taoism became an emphasis on energy and healing. The disciplines of this form of Taoism involved practice of exercises such as Tai Chi and martial arts.

Because Taoism placed heavy emphasis on the overall political flow of life, the "I Ching" began to be used more and more as a means of divination. This magical approach to life, along with attempts to find an Elixir of life by means of a spiritual alchemy, resulted in Taoism's third movement, the present day religion of Taoism. Religious Taoism, with all its incantations and magic, seems to be a far cry from original Taoist philosophy.

"The Secret of the Golden Flower" is a Taoist – Buddhist manual of meditation. It is a form of Chinese yoga involving techniques described as a conscious means of opening the resources of the unconscious. The psychologist Carl Jung found it intriguing and wrote a commentary connecting this Chinese yoga technique to his studies of the unconscious.

The major emphasis of "The Secret of the Golden Flower" is to describe the effort of the personal self, needed to create a spiritual entity with identity that will survive beyond bodily death. Buddhist philosophy, for the most part, taught that when the physical material body dissolved in death, the personal ego dissolved as well, and the energy of the personal spirit returned to the flow or Tao from which it came. Because at this point, Buddhism believed that the personal ego did not survive bodily death, there was in this yogic practice an attempt to create a spiritual identity for it in the realm of eternal reality. In a very real sense this yogic practice was the spiritual equivalent of the search for a kingdom of god within. This discipline of spiritual awareness presents us with two differently understood pathways to the experience of enlightenment or new birth.

The first comprises those who believed that the human spirit already has an eternal dimension and the new birth is simply coming into awareness of that which has always been. To be born-again is to realize a potential that is already present as an eternal expression of the source or Tao.

The second suggests that because persons who express into the material realm have no eternal dimension, when the material dissolves, so do their personal expressions. However, if such personal egos seek to center their animal energy within, rather than express it without, they have the potential of actually creating for themselves an eternal spiritual identity. In a way, this is a much more dramatic understanding of being born again. That which is in the present, born of water and flesh, by the germination of the Golden Flower has now the ability to become eternal Spirit.

The creation of the golden flower is dependent upon generative energy. It is referred to as backward flowing energy. The normal use of sexual energy is a flow outward in procreation; the secret proclaimed by the text is the reversal of sexual energy in order to plant the seed of the golden flower. The analogy of the outward flow changed to backward flow seems to be a highly masculine one and the author does not seem to have much encouragement for the enlightenment of women. By conscious intent and action the personal ego or animal nature is able to achieve a breakthrough into the realms of eternal Spirit. I am reminded of the Gnostic statement in logion 29 of the gospel according to Thomas: if flesh has produced spirit, it is a marvel too great to be believed.

Because I am dealing with a philosophy from a different cultural bias, it may be that what appears to me to be a literal concept of creating the spiritual soul, may well be an exercise to uncover an eternal reality (The Golden Flower) already present but unknown as yet to the person.

Buddhism

At the beginning of my ministry, I was reading The Encyclopedia Americana and in the section on Buddhism I discovered a recorded prayer of a Buddhist woman directed to the Buddha. I could not help but be impressed with the fact that the prayer of the Buddhist woman was identical to prayers that I had heard for years in prayer meetings of the mainline Protestant churches I had attended. The only difference was that the prayers were directed to the Lord Buddha instead of the Lord Jesus.

Siddhartha Gautama was born into a ruling family about 563 BCE near the present Indian-Nepal border. His father was a chieftain and the young prince was raised in sheltered luxury. His father attempted to shield him from life's harsh realities. After marriage and the birth of a son, he became reflective on the suffering he had observed in the lives of others. His life was overtaken by a profound need to discover life's meaning.

He first attached himself to two Brahmin hermits and followed a path of deep meditation, but this venture did not achieve the goal he sought. He then joined a band of radical ascetics and for several years lived a life of drastic denial. This path nearly brought about his bodily death.

Tradition has it that he overheard a musician giving instructions about playing a stringed instrument. The phrase that captured his attention was guidance on tuning the strings. If one tightens them too much, the strings will snap; if one leaves them too loose, they will not play. From this precept he became convinced that to produce harmony, life should be lived on a path he called "The Middle Way".

His first sermon contrasted the two extreme paths: indulgence and desire with hardship and self-torture. The middle way leads to enlightenment.

He taught the Four Noble Truths: (1) Life is suffering. (2) All suffering is caused by ignorance of reality and the craving, attachment, and grasping that result. (3) Overcoming ignorance and attachment can end suffering. (4) The path to the suppression of suffering is the Noble Eightfold Path, which consists of right views, right intention, right speech, right action, right livelihood, right effort, right mindedness, and right contemplation.

The experience of the seeker follows the reverse order of the presentation of the Four Noble Truths and the Noble Eightfold Path. The means to the suppression of suffering is a lifestyle of righteous living based on the Noble Eightfold Path. This 'right approach' brings about the overcoming of ignorance and attachment, which in turn eliminates the cause of all suffering and results in enlightenment that opens the way to living in Spirit beyond the limited dimensions of this world of suffering.

There are many variations in the religious expression of Buddhist philosophy. There is the cultural aspect of Buddhist prayer wheels, a practice with which we are unfamiliar. When I lived on the Sioux reservation in South Dakota, I became aware of how many differences there can be between another culture and our own. On Bear Butte, a site sacred to the Sioux, worshipers left prayer cloths and prayer stones lodged in the crotches of growing trees, eventually to be swallowed by growth and permanently in place for the life of the tree. The meaning of prayer is its intent, in spite of cultural differences; wei *wu wei* – flow doesn't force.

Buddhists believe that, although we can leave the circle of lifetimes, we can also choose to return to assist others. This is expressed in the Bodhisattva vow.

"However innumerable beings are, I vow to liberate them;
However incomparable the Truth is, I vow to actualize it."

When Buddhism migrated from India to China, a great many Chinese disciples of the Tao, as well as many meditative practices of Taoism, were assimilated by the Buddhists. This form of Buddhism was referred to as Ch'an Buddhism. Ch'an is the Chinese form of the Sanskrit word for meditation, Tsen. Ch'an was later exported to Japan, and there the word became Zen. The Ch'an teachers of China taught relatively small groups of students. In Japan following the conversion of the Emperor to Zen, thousands of teenage sons of the upper classes were sent by their families to the Zen monasteries to be taught the new religion. This tremendous influx of adolescent boys demanded a much more stringent discipline based primarily on the need for keeping regimented order in the schools as well as spiritual direction. As a result of this and other cultural differences, Ch'an and Zen have major differences in spite of common roots. Ch'an Buddhism today is much closer to its roots in Taoism. In fact, Zen is considered by some to no longer be part of the Buddhist religion.

An insightful author, who has advanced my thinking about non-dualist reality, writes under the pseudonym Wei Wu Wei. He follows the Ch'an tradition of Buddhism and also incorporates teachings from Taoism and

Vedanta. The works of Wei Wu Wei include "The Tenth Man", "Open Secret" and "Posthumous Pieces".

The interesting title "Posthumous Pieces" is written as a kind of literary pun on the idea of coming from the state of non-existence. Nobody existed to write it. The sense of attending one's own funeral is expanded with regard to the unreality of the personal self. We need to learn to attend our own ego's funeral. The book develops a viewpoint that the author does not really exist at this level of the illusion, and for that matter neither does the book. Reality exists only in the spiritual sphere of non-temporality. There is no eternal in the temporal. He says, to call Ch'an 'Chinese Zen' is like calling Judaism 'Jewish Christianity'; and of god, "I am the light that falls on ten thousand specks of dust so that each may shine." "For without me they cannot appear, and without them I cannot be known."

"The Tenth Man" is only one of dozens of stories in the book of that name. It seems that there were ten monks on a journey who fell into a lake. When they crawled out they could each see one monk reflected in the lake; and each could count only nine monks standing on the shore. The conclusion was that one monk had drowned; the moral is that they each lacked self-identity to such a degree that none could tell that it was himself who was missing in the count.

Sufism

Sufism is the mystical branch of Islam; most Sufi mystics follow a path that includes abstinence, renunciation, poverty, patience, and trust in god. Sufis strive to attain the Divine Presence and seek to live in peace with the rest of the Islamic community. The Persian poet, Jalal al-Din Rumi, Maulana (Our Master), instituted devotional dances, particularly those of the whirling dervishes. In addition, many wandering Sufi mendicants appeared over the centuries.

Rumi traveled with his family during his youth and eventually settled in what is now Turkey. Rumi hoped to devote his life to creating poetry expressing his feelings for his spiritual master Shams al-Din, a dervish (devotee of Sufism) from Iran. All translations are by Jonathan Star.

In The Arms of the Beloved
After going to all the shrines of Jesus,
The Buddha, Krishna and Mohammed,
The highest courts, the greatest libraries,
"He was not there."
Then I looked within my own heart

And there I found Him.
He was nowhere else.
He made the door.
He made the lock.
He also made the key.

Black Soot

What a wonder! The beloved is in love with the lover
What a miracle! From black soot grows a paradise.
You have two hands, two legs, and two eyes.
But if your heart and the beloved are also two,
What good is that?
You call out "I am the lover", but these are mere words.
If you see the lover and the beloved as two,
You either have double vision, or you can't count.

Your Triumph Song

On that final day – When my casket moves along
Do not think my soul – will stay in this world.
Do not weep for me, crying Tragedy, Tragedy.
You will only fall into the snares of delusion
Now that's a tragedy!
When you see my lifeless body go by –
Do not cry out, Gone. Gone.
It is my moment of union. –
It is when I come upon –
    The eternal embrace of my beloved.
As I am lowered into the ground – Do not say,
    Farewell, Farewell.
For the grave is but a veil –
    Covering the splendor of Paradise.
Having seen the fall – Consider the rise
What harm ever came to the setting Sun or Moon?
What appears to you as a setting
Is for me a rising.
What appears to you as a prison,
Is for my soul an endless garden.

The love affair with the body is over.
Having tasted the water of life
We've become the immortal Sufi.

When all you had was him

We are scraps of iron. Your love is the magnet
  That draws us near.
Why should I seek? – All I need do is love…
Rest now my soul, Leave behind your religion
And your empty show of faith.
Remember when you had no religion?
Remember when all you had was Him?
Don't talk about night anymore!
In our day there is no night.
In our religion of love there is no religion or love.
Love is the endless ocean of God.
Yet thousands of souls, drowning in that ocean,
Cry out – "There is no God."
0 seeker,
These thoughts have such power over you.
From nothing you become sad.
From nothing you become happy.
You are burning in the flames
But I will not let you out
Until you are fully baked,
Fully wise,
And fully yourself.
Silence already!
He gives us wine to taste, Not to talk about;
He gives to taste, He gives to taste. He gives to taste.

The Sufis are famous for their teaching stories about the nature of god
and the practice of religion. One of the most familiar is the story of the
blind men and the elephant. One blind man felt the elephant's side and
declared it to be like a wall; the next grabbed the tail and affirmed it to be
like a rope. The third thought the trunk was like a snake. Another felt its
leg and identified its similarity to a tree. Then it was claimed to be a spear

by one who felt a tusk and the last holding an ear compared it to a fan. The story was about those of us who claim to fully understand the nature of god; in our blindness we become arrogant in our limited experience of the truth.

Another story tells of two monks traveling together. They came to a stream and a very beautiful woman was seeking a way across. One monk picked her up in his arms and carried her across the stream. After traveling along in silence the one who had not carried the lady accused the other of immoral behavior and of being guilty of endangering his vows of celibacy; to which the other replied, "I sat her down on the opposite bank, but you are still carrying her."

The next story is about a very learned theologian who was rowing over to an island in order to visit two ascetics who lived there in a life of prayer. After arriving at the island, he heard them in prayer and discovered that they were pronouncing the word 'amen' incorrectly. He indignantly corrected them, and after a time began to row back to the mainland. He was not far out on his return trip when the two solitary monks appeared beside the boat, walking on the water. They both apologized profusely because they had already forgotten the correct pronunciation. (Enough said.)

The Metaphysical Movement

An 18th Century forerunner of present day New Thought was Swedish scientist Emanuel Swedenborg, who had mystical visions and wrote profusely about his experiences. Swedenborg was a genius in his own right. His father was a Lutheran Bishop in Sweden. Swedenborg became highly trained in several areas of science, including cosmology, geology, astronomy, engineering, metallurgy and anatomy. He published a paper in 1715 on the subject of determining latitude by using the phases of the moon, before chronographs and Greenwich Mean Time became a solution.

He hoped by his scientific knowledge to prove the reality of god, but in mid-life (1744), at 55 years of age, began to have extensive visions of a spiritual world. He lived in waking, daylight consciousness of the material world and the spiritual world at the same time. He concluded that the material world is a fallacy of the senses and that thought from the eyes closes up the understanding, but thought from the understanding opens up the eyes. He taught that Love and Wisdom, are the real and actual substance and form, which constitutes the subject itself.

In 1759 Emmanuel Kant described Swedenborg's vision, shared with friends while in Germany, of a huge fire in Stockholm some three hundred miles distant.   The conflagration stopped only three houses from Swedenborg's home; confirmed several days later by news from Stockholm.

A major challenge to contemporary theology was his writings questioning the traditional Trinitarian formula of god, which officially separated the godhead when the Son became a sacrifice in order to placate the Father. Swedenborg took the statement of Paul, "In him dwells the fullness of the godhead bodily", and argued that the traditional Trinitarian formula was false because it was obvious that the full trinity resided in Jesus. The Father was within and Jesus expressed the Holy Spirit to his disciples with his breath. To Swedenborg the invisible realities of Trinitarian symbolism *all* resided in the one manifest Son, Jesus.

In Helen Keller's book, My Religion, she describes her six years as an animal, having no words with which to either think or communicate until the breakthrough occurred with her teacher. Miss Keller makes an interesting analogy between her years of sensory deprivation and the early part of Swedenborg's experience before his breakthrough into an expanded awareness of another world.

To a large extent, the discovery of animal magnetism by an Austrian physician, Franz Anton Mesmer, in 1778, and the use of 'mesmerism' (hypnotism) in 1784 by the Marquis de Puysegur, were the root of a developing awareness of the complexity and hidden resources of the human mind. De Puysegur had a subject named Victor, who, when hypnotized, fell into a deep sleep and while unconscious demonstrated a rare ability of clairvoyance. Victor and other somnambulists (from sleepwalk) as they were called, in their trance state could make medical diagnosis for other patients brought to them, as well as occasionally see events at a distance and see future events. The movement was considered a fad by the physicians of the day, and soon fell into disrepute among them. In 1841, James Braid of Manchester, England coined the term hypnotism based on the Greek word for sleep (*hupnos*). Braid discovered that the effect of the sleep state was heightened suggestibility on the part of the subject, and no magnets (as used by Mesmer) or other devices were necessary. The state was not energized by any outside force but was a resident quality of the human mind.

Both Swedenborg and Mesmer influenced a young 19th Century clockmaker in Maine named Phineas Parkhurst Quimby. At the same time Ralph Waldo Emerson left the traditional ministry, and inspired by the works of Swedenborg as well as Hindu Vedanta, developed a kind of Nature Mysticism. The New Thought movement, like the New Age movement, is a 'mixed-bag', but I include it in this discussion because many of its ideas support the Perennial Philosophy.

Quimby used hypnosis in bringing about physical healing. He came to view Mind or Wisdom as *the underlying reality of material form*. Like the Marquis de Puysegur, he also used a young man as a somnambulist to diagnose and suggest treatments for his patients. Another early somnambulist of the time was Andrew Jackson Davis, called the Poughkeepsie Seer. He is often referred to as the Edgar Cayce of his day.

Although Christian Science does not now consider itself part of the New Thought Movement, Mary Baker Eddy's life and times are at the heart of New Thought's development into its present day forms. Mary Baker was born July 16, 1821 (Mary Baker became first Mrs. Glover and then Mrs. Eddy). In 1862 Mary Baker traveled to Portland Maine to receive treatment from Phineas Parkhurst Quimby. Quimby called himself a 'magnetizer'. Quimby had written ten volumes of manuscripts on his theories of hypnosis, calling them "The Science of Health". Quimby was a sincere man but not educated and his writings were unclear. Working with Quimby, she found her neurotic symptoms were allayed, and she became his secretary and assistant.

When Quimby died of an abdominal tumor in January 1866, Mrs. Glover took Quimby's manuscripts and, though unlettered herself, she began copying and editing them. These became the foundations for her book "Science and Health with Key to the Scriptures". Although she later disavowed any form of hypnotism, Quimby's work as well as much of the language of these early metaphysicians became part of her language.

In 1882, Mr. Eddy died of heart disease. The attending physician called by Mrs. Eddy, Dr. Rufus K. Noyes of Boston, performed an autopsy and showed the diseased heart to her. She would not accept this reason for the death, and claimed that her husband had died of arsenic poisoning 'mentally administered'. Mrs. Eddy believed the arsenic had been 'thought' into him by enemies. This was in her mind a case of 'malicious animal magnetism', a concept that Mrs. Eddy could not shake. It is a strange contradiction to me that the person, who based her whole teaching on right thinking, feared the invasion of her mind through the malevolence of others.

Early Christian Science practitioners were allowed to operate independently of Mrs. Eddy; but she abandoned the loose Christian Science Association and formed the Mother Church in 1892, a kind of matriarchal autocracy. In her speeches, she advocated celibacy and would not allow either marriages or funerals to take place in the Christian Science Church. The Church Manual gave her almost dictatorial powers over the 'official' movement from then on.

Many independent Christian Science churches existed alongside the official churches. These independent groups united with others to form New Thought alliances. Some Christian Science teachers were ousted from the Mother Church; notably Emma Curtis Hopkins, and later Joel Goldsmith, founder of the 'Infinite Way' movement.

Emma Curtis Hopkins was involved in the training of Ernest Holmes, author of "Science of Mind", and founder of the Religious Science Church. She also ordained into her earlier Christian Science School, Charles and Myrtle Fillmore, who became the founders of Unity School of Christianity. Unity School of Christianity and The Religious Science Church, along with independent Christian Science groups and others united to form the International New Thought Alliance.

These several groups differ in how closely they align with the Christian tradition, their view of the relation of mind to body, and the role of the subconscious mind in regard to physical healing. On the whole, New Thought groups co-operate with Medical Science; but Christian Scientists term the body mortal error, and except for surgery and broken bones, discourage members from using medical advice or medication. Most of the New Thought groups would affirm some basic teachings of Christian Science while taking exception with many others.

Some quotes from "Science and Health with Key to the Scriptures":

Page 472-3 – "We learn in Christian Science that all inharmony of mortal mind or body is illusion, possessing neither reality nor identity though seeming to be real and identical...God is everywhere, and nothing apart from him is present or has power...Jesus is the name of the man who, more that all other men, has presented Christ. Jesus is the human man, and Christ is the divine idea; hence the duality of Jesus the Christ."

Page 468 – "There is no life, truth, intelligence, nor substance in matter. All is infinite Mind and its infinite manifestation, for god is All in all. Spirit is immortal Truth; *matter is mortal error*. Spirit is the real and eternal; matter is the unreal and temporal. Spirit is god, and man is His image and likeness. Therefore man is not material; he is spiritual."

I would not choose the word error, but recognize the need to state that the illusions of matter or appearance are not real. We need to look beyond the frame and learn to see the picture, while still being aware of the frame.

My favorite phrase in the text is "Emerge gently from matter into spirit. Think not to thwart the spiritual ultimate of all things, but come naturally into spirit through better health and morals and as the result of spiritual growth." (Pg. 485) The word 'gently' speaks of the way in which Spirit leads. It reflects Jesus' statement about his easy yoke.

I also need to affirm that the relationships I have had with individuals in the Christian Science Church have been very cordial and helpful. I have enjoyed the quiet dignity of their worship and find the experience on the whole more uplifting than the traditional Christian Churches that are still hung up on sinfulness and blood atonement.

Modern Metaphysical Works

Another prolific author in the support of non-dualism was Joel Goldsmith. Goldsmith had a background in the metaphysics and healing practices of Christian Science. He emphasized the unity of the Impersonal Self and Impersonal God. His school of thought is called "The Infinite Way". He published many titles and his lecture series continues to be printed posthumously. Just a listing of some titles will give a good sense of the areas he covered. Joel Goldsmith titles include "The Infinite Way", "Conscious Union with God", "Living Between Two Worlds", "Practicing the Presence", "The Mystical I", "A Parenthesis in Eternity", "God, the Substance of All Form", and "Realization of Oneness". The consciousness of Joel Goldsmith was such that he could well have authored "A Course in Miracles". All of his work is well worth the discipline of study. I especially enjoyed "The Infinite Way" and "The Mystical I".

Some quotes from "The Infinite Way": "In cultivating our spiritual sense we become receptive to thoughts which come to us from within…We become so attuned to Spirit that we feel the divine harmony of being; we feel the actual presence of God. Having transcended the five physical senses, our intuitive faculty is alert, receptive and responsive to the things of the Spirit, and we begin our new existence as a result of this spiritual rebirth…Spiritual consciousness is the release from personal effort in the realization that harmony is. This consciousness, with its release from personal effort, is attained as we find the Christ within us a present reality…Wherein then is lack except in the belief that we are humans? We must give up this belief and claim our true identity…The Life which is God is our life. There is but one Life and this is the life of all being, of every individual…Our consciousness of this truth is the healing influence within us…Material consciousness is the false finite sense which beholds the universe and man as being both good and evil. Spiritual Consciousness is the awareness of the individual as God-being, as having only the mind of God and the body of Spirit…We must not live as though we were effect with something operating upon us. Let us remember to live as the Law, as the Principle of our being…Stop trying to apply Truth: Attempting to apply Truth is the action of the human thought. Truth is infinite; therefore there is nothing to which you can apply Truth. It is the reality of being, and there is nothing inside or outside for Truth to act upon: Truth is self-acting and self-operative…Seeking guidance from God at this stage of your unfoldment will set up a sense of separation from God; It gives a sense of God and someone needing help, direction, or wisdom. Actually, *you need to let God be your life* – then It lives, acts, performs, *and IS your very being*."

Channeled material is not just a phenomenon of our time. At the turn of the century, during the heyday of the Spiritualist movement, there were a great many books and novels produced by the unconscious process of automatic writing. There were tomes such as Urantia and Ohaspe (purported histories of human civilization that go back thousands of years), and novels such as those by Patience Worth. Today we have the Seth material by Jane Roberts, and two separate sources for Michael, the archangel. Historically it is supposed, the Koran of Mohammed, and the Book of Mormon by Joseph Smith are to a degree also in this category. To channel information, one must tap the unconscious mind. There is certainly a similarity to the effects of hypnosis, although self induced. If we understood more of the inner dynamics of the process, I am sure we could make a link to prophetic utterance in all religions of every age.

This is a good place to take up the whole question of channeling through the unconscious. In the matter of channeled material the question always arises as to the nature of its source. The psychic Eileen Garrett, founder of The American Parapsychology Society, had much to offer in our understanding of this question. Mrs. Garrett had herself and her two psychic controls psychoanalyzed. In the process she discovered that she had produced these subconscious controls as a device to avoid the responsibility of any message or advice that she might give. The controls were a product of her own mind, and were a self-constructed device to separate her from the information that she produced. It is unfortunate that no one ever raised this question with Helen Schucman, scribe for "A Course In Miracles". I refer again to Phillips Brooks' statement that when conveying truth through personality, the channeler behaves as a stained glass window contributing its own colors. This has been an age of much written material claiming to be channeled. A great deal of it is attributed to some external authority or source, and is presented as if the consciousness of the individual channels were not involved; however, I believe there is no such thing as an ego functioning as a perfectly clear channel.

One problem that needs to be recognized is that, in a sense, all words in whatever context, we have received from somewhere else. It has been said, we furnished only the string to tie up our packages. From exposure to books, conversations, teachers, lectures, news reports etc., all of us have gained what we would call insights. Some internal process gives rise to any new idea or awareness. These unconscious processes are all filtered through our conscious minds, and no one is a perfectly clear channel for any material, no matter what may appear to be the source.

Richard Bach's "Jonathan Livingston Seagull" is a beautiful parable about Christ Consciousness, and it too, according to the author, came from outside his own personal awareness. In this best selling book there is a conversation with a friend and colleague, Sullivan, about his going back to earth. Jonathan speaks. "If our friendship depends on things like space and time, then when we finally overcome space and time, we've destroyed our own brotherhood! But overcome space, and all we have left is here. Overcome time, and all we have left is now. And in the middle of here and now, don't you think that we might see each other once or twice?" (Pg. 63)

Albert Einstein still leaves us dealing with the subject of time and space as illusion. We have not understood the ability of thought to instantly transcend the boundaries of space and time. We are stuck with materialistic concepts of eons of time and light years of space. Jonathan speaks prophetically when he instructs Fletcher to overcome time and overcome space; but his statement is short on the 'how to'. We need to learn how to live with the unsolved mysteries of our lives.

Hear the delightful poetry from Richard Bach's book "Illusions", called: The Messiah's Handbook - Reminders for the Advanced Soul

"Remember where you came from, where you're going, and why you created the mess you got yourself into in the first place.

Learning is finding out what you already know.

Doing is demonstrating that you know it.

"Your only obligation in any lifetime is to be true to yourself. Being true to anyone else or anything else is not only impossible, but the mark of a fake messiah.

"Your friends will know you better in the first minute you meet than your acquaintances will know you in a thousand years.

"You are led through your lifetime by the inner learning creature, the playful spiritual being that is your real self.

"There is no such thing as a problem without a gift for you in its hands. You seek problems because you need their gifts.

"Imagine the universe beautiful and just and perfect, Then be sure of one thing: the Is has imagined it quite a bit better than you have.

"The world is your exercise book, the pages on which you do your sums. It is not reality, although you can express reality there if you wish.

"The original sin is to limit the Is. Don't.

"Every person, all the events of your life are there because you have drawn them there. What you choose to do with them is up to you.

"Here is a test to find whether your mission on earth is finished: If you're alive, it isn't.

"Don't be dismayed at good-byes. A farewell is necessary before you can meet again. And meeting again, after moments or lifetimes, is certain for those who are friends.

"What the caterpillar calls the end of the world, the master calls a butterfly."

David Spangler has written a book for the college of the Findhorn community called "The Laws of Manifestation". The Findhorn group is a community of people who have a unique mindset. By means of openness in their consciousness and attitudes, they seem to communicate successfully with the spirit of plants and animals. The community resides on poor soil, in the cold climate of the northernmost parts of Great Britain on the shores of the North Sea, yet has produced a world famous garden. David offers some cogent views on manifestation and abundance. Some of these views, he supposedly channeled from St. Germain, whom he called, "the Master, the Lord of civilization". This is his view on abundance, which applies to concepts of prosperity as well.

"Viewed by the personality, abundance is a measure of quantity. It means plenty, a multiplicity of things and forms. To the soul, however, abundance is a quality. It means the one essence within all things, from which all things spring. To have a consciousness of abundance, on a soul level, does not mean having a sense of access to many things, seemingly stored in some treasure house, but rather being at one with the essence behind and within all things. True abundance is a consciousness of wholeness, oneness and quality, not of separateness, multiplicity and quantity."[131] Sometimes, metaphysical groups teach a 'prosperity' that is bogged down in materiality.

Edgar Cayce was born in Kentucky in 1876, and became one of the best-known psychics of our age. My first contact with Edgar Cayce's life and teachings was picking up a paperback titled "Edgar Cayce on Dreams", by Harmon Bro. I had no idea who Edgar Cayce was but I once had an interview with Dr. Bro when he headed a department of religion at Syracuse University in N.Y. I was curious to see what he had to say about dreams. His book introduced me to the whole area of psychic phenomena and broader fields such as hypnosis and clairvoyance.

Edgar Cayce had much to say about the unconscious mind as an avenue of enlightenment. Many of Cayce's readings with regard to the unconscious, favor the approach of Carl Jung. The unconscious mind has several different levels of awareness.

---

[131] The Laws of Manifestation, David Spangler: page 20

Cayce suggested that there was a great deal of garbage in the personal unconscious; and if we were to break into this area like a thief who does not come in by the door, we could create all kinds of problems for ourselves. Cayce taught that there were two legitimate or royal roads to the unconscious: dreams and meditation.

In Bro's excellent book on dreams, he recounts Cayce's ability to tune in psychically and recall for individuals dreams they themselves had forgotten. According to Dr. Bro, Cayce taught that dreams have three basic levels of meaning. The first is a physical level. One client came to Cayce recounting a horrendous nightmare, and wanted an interpretation from him. Cayce told him that the only meaning the nightmare had was that the man had been too sedentary and needed exercise. The horror of the nightmare served the purpose of increasing his blood flow and his heart rate, and that's what his body needed. The second level of dreams deals with our personal affairs, and often reconstructs symbolically the situations and complexities of our daily experience. The third level is visionary and comes from a level of the unconscious that might be termed superconscious. The superconscious is a psychological term that is the equivalent of the kingdom of god within.

Thomson Jay Hudson, in his book "The Law of Psychic Phenomena" (recommended by Cayce), taught that the conscious mind is both *in*ductive and *de*ductive, whereas the personal unconscious is entirely *de*ductive. This is why a consciously held belief serves to program the unconscious, which thus effectively outpictures situations for which we see no apparent cause.

We don't understand the root cause of these actions because we have lost awareness of the beliefs that connect them to what we term unconscious action. Edgar Cayce taught that "mind was the builder" of our life experience; he also suggested that after bodily death the personal unconscious becomes the consciousness of the entity.

Roberto Assagioli has written a great deal about the superconscious. He founded a program of Psychosynthesis, and along with Abraham Maslow, was a pioneer in the school of Transpersonal Psychology. Both see humanity as something more than a material function.

The Seth material began with Jane Roberts of Elmira, N.Y., experimenting with an Ouija board.[132] Eventually Jane's messages, identified as coming from a discarnate entity called Seth, began to come through her as a medium without the use of the board. Jane Roberts was a gutsy lady who did her best to tell it like it is, based on her own life experiences. If we consider Edgar Cayce as directed toward the field of

---

[132] The name Ouija is from the French and German words for 'yes', Oui and Ja.

medicine and healing, we would deem that Jane Roberts and 'Seth' pursued a more theoretical and scientific bent.

The religious approach of Jane was directed toward personal growth, in the sense that "in reshaping our gods, we reshape ourselves."[133] "Attend to what is directly before you. You have no responsibility to save the world or find the solutions to all problems – but to attend to your particular corner of the universe. As each person does that, the world saves itself."[134] In her book "The God of Jane", she reflects on the ways in which her experience with 'Seth' helped to reshape her own religious thinking. "Transposed into religious terms, then, we are each continuous with what 'God' is…This isn't to say that we are each 'God' in absolute terms, but that we are expressions of 'God's' essence. We are part of All-That-Is, and All-That-Is is also the medium in which we exist. We are made of 'God stuff.'…

"We might picture All-That-Is in superhuman terms, personifying it as Him or Her – praying to Christ, for example; a Christ quite legitimate as a reflection of our own limited understanding, a Christ quite effective insofar as he would stand symbolically for us in our relationship with All-That-Is as best we could understand it. All-That-Is, however, is no parochial spirit – it is the force behind and within all species and beings and could be projected quite as legitimately as superbeast or superplant, or whatever."

"According to Seth, All-That-Is is the entire creative pattern from which all realities of any kind emerge."[135]

One of the more profound bodies of channeled material is a set of books called "A Course in Miracles". The course consists of a Text, a Workbook for Students (a 365 day study book), and A Manual for Teachers. I have referred to the course a number of times thus far; and in spite of some limitations, I find it a cogent, helpful teaching directed to members of the Christian tradition.

A colleague, William Thetford, assisted the scribe Helen Schucman; both were psychologists. Interestingly, Helen was Jewish in spite of the Christian tenor of the course. One day's dictation to Helen from her unconscious was corrected the next. Sections of the first five chapters of the first volume or Text were apparently corrected several times by her 'source'. It was only after a considerable period that the flow of transmission seemed to get into its stride. One statement in the first section, I find particularly inane, is an interpretation of the story of the creation of Eve from a vital part of Adam. In the Bible, the statement is made that god caused a deep sleep

---

[133] The God of Jane, Jane Roberts: page 63

[134] From Dreams: Evolution, & Value Fulfillment: – Jane Roberts

[135] The God of Jane, Jane Roberts: page 60

to fall upon Adam. The course suggests simplistically that the problem of humanity is that Adam went to sleep, and nowhere does the Bible say he ever woke up.

I believe the course suffers because there are those who attribute its authorship directly to Jesus. At times Helen wrote as if Jesus was speaking, such as follows: "You stand below me and I stand below God. In the process of "rising up", I am higher because without me the distance between God and man would be too great for you to encompass."[136]

This is not the historical Jesus speaking, but is a construct of Helen's cultural beliefs, based on the *religion about Jesus* as a mediator between god and humankind. This statement flies in the face of the ministry of Jesus. Did his teachings of the kingdom within accomplish nothing? Has no one since, learned anything? The kingdom is within us all! Jesus deified, as mediator, is what the church has taught *about Jesus,* not what Jesus taught!

To forestall the idea of a special relationship, the Buddhists teach "If you see the Buddha on the road, kill him"; which, translated to this situation, means if you see Jesus as author of the course, expunge him. If less emphasis on Jesus as author had been pressured upon Helen, she perhaps would have understood that her vision of Priestess was her source. "God has no secret communications to anyone for everything of god is perfectly open and freely accessible to all, being for all."[137]

Some of the metaphysical principles presented in the course:

"A universal theology is impossible, but a universal experience of god and love is not only possible but necessary."[138] We may not journey any distance to find the consciousness or awareness of love – but we must be willing to remove our blocks to the awareness of its presence.

"The one wholly true thought that one can hold about the past is that it is not here."[139] for only an experience of 'Now' can be tied to reality. "Nothing has meaning except the meaning we give it."[140] therefore all our perceptions are the result of judgments; and events we experience are understood as the meanings we give to these situations. These meanings become our memories, which in turn are perceived as past events; the past then finds its source in the meaning of memories. When the meanings given to memory are meaningless, the meaning of such memories are but fearful fantasies, and the past, thus understood, is only a negative 'fact' of

---

[136] A Course in Miracles, Text – page 8
[137] A Course in Miracles: Text page 274 (295.11)
[138] A Course in Miracles: Terms page 77
[139] A Course in Miracles: Lesson 8.2
[140] A Course in Miracles: Lesson 51.1&2

awareness – when in reality this 'fact' doesn't exist. Forgiveness consists of the experience of letting go of perceptions of the non-existent, or letting go of the unreal. A basic principle of the course is that what is the same is the same, and what is different is different. All manifest appearance is the same and is not reality. All reality is the same for its source is the one invisible Spirit. All Reality is always different from all appearance and all appearance is always different from Reality.

The following excerpts from the "Workbook for Students" include some of the most beautiful poetry in the work.

"Lesson 189.7. Simply do this: Be still, and lay aside all thoughts of what you are and what God is; all concepts you have learned about the world; all images you hold about yourself. Empty your mind of everything it thinks is either true or false, or good or bad, of every thought it judges worthy, and all the ideas of which it is ashamed. Hold onto nothing. Do not bring with you one thought the past has taught, nor one belief you ever learned before from anything. Forget this world, forget this course, and come with wholly empty hands unto your God.

8. Is it not He Who knows the way to you? You need not know the way to Him. Your part is simply to allow all obstacles that you have interposed between the Son and God the Father to be quietly removed forever. God will do His part in joyful and immediate response. Ask and receive. But do not make demands, nor point the road to God by which He should appear to you. The way to reach Him is merely to let Him be. For in that way is your reality proclaimed as well.

9. And so today we do not choose the way in which we go to Him. But we do choose to let Him come. And with this choice we rest. And in our quiet hearts and open minds, His Love will blaze its pathway of itself. What has not been denied is surely there, if it be true and can be surely reached. God knows His Son, and knows the way to him. He does not need His Son to show Him how to find His way. Through every opened door His Love shines outward from its home within, and lightens up the world in innocence.

10. *Father, we do not know the way to You. But we have called, and You have answered us. We will not interfere. Salvation's ways are not our own, for they belong to You. And it is unto You we look for them. Our hands are open to receive Your gifts. We have no thoughts we think apart from You, and cherish no beliefs of what we are, or Who created us. Yours is the way that we would find and follow. And we ask but that Your Will, which is our own as well, be done in us and in the world, that it become a part of heaven now. Amen*

Lesson 46.1 God does not forgive because He has never condemned. And there must be condemnation before forgiveness is necessary.

Lesson 49.4 Listen in deep silence. Be very still and open your mind. Go past all the raucous shrieks and sick imaginings that cover your real thoughts and obscure your eternal link with God. Sink deep into the peace that waits for you beyond the frantic, riotous thoughts and sights and sounds of this insane world. You do not live here. We are trying to reach your real home. We are trying to reach the place where you are truly welcome. We are trying to reach God.

Lesson 157.9 Into Christ's Presence will we enter now, serenely unaware of everything except His shining face and perfect Love. The vision of His face will stay with you, but there will be an instant which transcends all vision, even this, the holiest. This you will never teach, for you attained it not through learning. Yet the vision speaks of your remembrance of what you knew that instant, and will surely know again.

Lesson 164.4 There is a silence into which the world can not intrude. There is an ancient peace you carry in your heart and have not lost. There is a sense of holiness in you the thought of sin has never touched. All this today you will remember.

Lesson 182.8 When you are still an instant, when the world recedes from you, when valueless ideas cease to have value in your restless mind, then will you hear His Voice.

Lesson 184.8 Think not you made the world. Illusions, yes! But what is true in earth and heaven is beyond your naming. When you call upon a brother, it is to his body that you make appeal. His true Identity is hidden from you by what you believe he really is. His body makes response to what you call him, for his mind consents to take the name you give him as his own. And thus his unity is twice denied, for you perceive him separate from you, and he accepts his separate name as his.

Lesson 188.6 Sit quietly and close your eyes. The light within you is sufficient. It alone has power to give the gift of sight to you. Exclude the outer world, and let your thoughts fly to the peace within. They know the way. For honest thoughts, untainted by the dream of worldly things outside your self, become the holy messengers of God himself.

Lesson 189.5 What would you see? The choice is given you. But learn and do not let your mind forget this law of seeing: You will look upon that which you feel within. If hatred finds a place within your heart, you will perceive a fearful world, held cruelly in death's sharp-pointed, bony fingers. If you feel the Love of God within you, you will look out on a world of mercy and of love.

Lesson 205.1 I want the peace of God. *The peace of God is everything I want. The peace of God is my one goal; the aim of all my living here, the end I seek, my purpose and my function and my life, while I abide where I am not at home.*

Lesson 248.2 Father, *my ancient love for You returns, and lets me love Your Son again as well. Father, I am as You created me. Now is Your Love remembered, and my own. Now do I understand that they are one."*

There are some parts of the course that I do not agree with and some statements are confused, ambiguous and contradictory. But in other places the poetry is majestic and sublime and speaks to the condition of my heart, such as above, "Is it not He who knows the way to you? You need not know the way to Him." We do not know the way to god, but god has not forgotten the way to us.

I am reminded of one of my teachers at Evangelical Theological Seminary, Professor Radamacher, who emphasized the principle of coherence. In the principle of coherence, when a new truth challenges an old one, we are faced with a choice; for truth is one and only one truth can be held at any one time. Anything we believe to be true must be in agreement with all other things we believe to be true.

In his books Neal Donald Walsch addresses questions to god that trouble him and god obliges with answers. The answers are courageous, cogent and often witty and humorous.

"As I have already explained you cannot demonstrate love until you can demonstrate not loving. A thing cannot exist without its opposite, except in the world of the Absolute. Yet the realm of the Absolute was not sufficient for either you or me. I existed there, in the always, and it is from where you, too, have come.

"In the Absolute there is no experience, only knowing. Knowing is a divine state, yet the grandest joy is being. Being is achieved only after experience. The evolution is this: knowing, experiencing, being. This is the Holy trinity – the triune that is god."[141]

Walsch even has god question channeled authority.

"How do I know that what you were saying is true? How do I know that this is even God speaking, and not my overactive imagination?

"You have asked that before. My answer is the same. What difference does it make? Even if everything I've said is wrong can you think of a better way to live?"[142]

---

[141] Conversations with God, Neal Donald Walsch – Book 1: page 30
[142] Conversations with God, Neal Donald Walsch – Book 1: page 108

As if to illustrate my point that all channeled material is altered by the channeler, god tells Walsch that Walsch is a filter for the material and not all that gets through him is as god intended it. To add insult to injury, god even makes a mistake when he talks about speaking through the scribe for "A Course in Miracles". "I'm saying what I said through Judith Schucman in "A Course in Miracles": You teach what you have to learn."[143]

C'mon god! Helen Schucman was the person who recorded the material and Judith Skutch was the one most responsible for its publication. God seems to have transposed their names.

In a letter regarding this 'mistake' Neal Donald Walsh states, "The error simply points out, glaringly, what I have been saying all along in these books: Do not make this your 'Bible'. I am not infallible, and this material has been brought through an imperfect filter." "Your God and your Wisdom Source will be found within. Do not give your power to any source outside yourself. Not to a book, not to a religion, not to anyone or anything that does not originate within you – for that is where the Holy Spirit dwells, that is where God will be found, and is where God's Son is, once again, made flesh, in, as and through you."[144] I couldn't agree more, but I would caution that it is also possible to have a concept of god separated from ourselves, to whom we give our power.

Again, god offers Walsch a rationale for our experience of the illusion.

"You've entered the relative world – what I call the Realm of the Relative – in order to experience what you cannot experience in the Realm of the Absolute. What you seek to experience is Who You Really Are. In the Realm of the Absolute, you can know this, but you cannot experience it. The desire of your soul is to know itself *experientially*. The reason that you cannot experience any aspect of Who You Are in the Realm of the Absolute is that in this realm, there is no aspect you are not.

"The only way for you to experience the magnificence of being One with everything is for there to be some state or condition in which *not* being One with everything is possible. Yet since everything is One in the Realm of the Absolute – which is the ultimate reality – something not being One with everything is impossible.

"What is not impossible, however, is the *illusion* of not being One with everything. It was for the purpose of creating this illusion, then, that the Realm of the Relative was created. It is like an Alice-in-Wonderland world, in which things are not what they seem to be, and in which things seem to be what they are not."

---

[143] Conversations with God, Neal Donald Walsch – Book III: page 185
[144] Letter response, Neal Donald Walsch – NL #35

"...what you are trying to do is use the illusion of separateness to better comprehend and appreciate the experience of oneness, which is Who You Really Are.

"If you are using the ego as a tool with which to ultimately experience the only reality, it is good. If the ego is using *you* to *stop* you from experiencing that reality, that it is *not* good.

"Only when you had enough of the separateness, enough of the illusion, enough of the loneliness and the painfulness will you seek to find your way home, and then you will find that I will be there – that I am *always* there."[145]

Elia Wise has produced a fantastic book, in more ways than one. Her book, "Letter to Earth" is not channeled material, which gives it a decided advantage in logic and consistency; she accepts personal responsibility for her testimony. However there is another dimension to her work; she had an exceptional teacher who worked with her for a number of years. The teacher demonstrated awareness in other areas of time and space and was able to allow Elia to expand into the universal dimension of her soul's reality to experience many dimensions of consciousness. The mentor was able to give Elia direct experience rather than a spoken message; Elia was told that explaining the experience was her job. She came to believe that the whole cosmos is a vibrational expression of the energies of god or All-That-Is. It is a powerful book but perhaps not designed for everyone.

Elia speaks with firsthand knowledge of other sentient beings beyond earth in the universe. I have no personal experience to substantiate these claims, but I emphatically state that I also have no rational basis to dispute them. They may be a symbolism needed for our time or they may well be a literal reality of the space/time dimension. I can only witness that her work is inspiring, cogent and helpful. It is one of the most coherent statements of the many facets of our life's purpose I have ever read. The scope of the work is too encompassing to summarize, so I will only lift some statements from Chapter Nine, which have direct bearing on the new gestalt of our world since September 11, 2001.

It is helpful to understand 'increased amplitude' as meaning a stronger vibration (more volume); 'decreased magnetism' as decreasing inertia to change; and 'auto-immune system' as reluctance to change. Vibration is not only an indicator in the electromagnetic spectrum, but the area of psychic awareness as well.

From Pg. 86 ff. Excerpts, "Why do people get sick, have diseases and experience pain?"

---

[145] Friendship with God, Neal Donald Walsch—pages 78-80

"There are two profound changes in progress in the nature of your planet that temporarily heighten your physical vulnerability, while producing the alchemical conditions for planetary transmutation into a more enlightened state of being: a change in Earth's frequency amplitudes and a change in Earth's magnetism. Both are well underway...Because of this planetary increase in frequency amplitude, you are likely to feel that there is not enough time to maintain the reality you constructed at a lesser amplitude, perhaps just a year ago...

"This adds new dimensions, dynamics and complexity to your existing awareness – without increasing your time for integrating or exploring them...Having no additional time to process and integrate your increasing awareness causes you to feel a relative lessening of time. Unless you have already simplified your life in order to stay attuned to rhythms of universal integrity, your restful showers have gone the way of homemade bread...

"Until you break pace with escalating complexity of the outer-directed world and reconceive yourself and your life in response to the emerging rhythms of planetary integrity, you are likely to feel overwhelmed, rushed, and out of sync...Your individual and collective consciousness is being entrained by the planetary phenomenon of increasing frequency amplitudes and decreasing magnetism...

"Those who are intimate with the rhythms of integrity, harmony, gracefulness and beauty will be among the first to recognize this change in frequency amplitudes and to align with it. Simplicity is the key to this adjustment...

"Earth's magnetism is breaking down. It is becoming more penetrable in order to enable new coordinates of magnetism and new amplitudes of frequency to instate...

"Simply put, it will get harder to successfully consume hope and other natural resources or to garner support for greed, competition, control, separatism and other inverted values.

"As individuals integrate the increasing amplitude of their own axial values, and all frequencies that constitute their reality, their insight and behavior will further align with Universal values. Such a population will change the social environment and, eventually, what is called reality.

"This process has been happening for more than half a century and it will progress over the coming years at an accelerated rate...

"Imaginal cells are those that amass until they finally take over and transmute caterpillar to butterfly. Those of you who embody the axial values of increased frequency amplitudes critical to each process of human transformation are humanities imaginal cells...When you who embody and express the values of the future come together to effect a common purpose, you will be irresistible...

"When new models emerge, people will feel safe acknowledging that what we have always called reality is just one set of choices from the menu of possibilities. With this acknowledgment the externalization of values and the externalization of authority will diminish. The reclaiming of authority from dysfunctional systems will enable new societal systems to emerge, consistent with Universal values and facilitated by those who embody those values with integrity...

"The window is opening. There is no need to push it. The resistance of old and unenlightened ways is not an obstacle; it provides critical control to the rhythms of transformation. Humanity must be able to survive this process without the breakdown of all physical bodies and without dissolution into personal and social chaos. Those who write you off as powerless, immature, or idealistic, are not your adversaries. They are your collective immune system...You cannot afford to have the new invading culture – no matter how elevated or universal – consume your old body politic, your old body of thought or your old three-dimensional bodies...not quite yet...The future is still developing, using the resources of the current, unenlightened collective body...

"You have not yet recognized the vastness of your number and collectivized to satisfy your basic needs...Get practical...

"Transmutational energy manifests in your system as both a strength and a weakness...An immune system functions on the premise that all is not one, that forces of change are invaders rather than transformers of life, and that the reigning system is superior to any other...

"People are interpreting their power as creators to include responsibility for illnesses that have been genetically programmed through countless generations. Fueled by the human inclination toward guilt, this misconception is difficult to unravel. As an individual you are no more responsible for such illnesses than you are for the fact that you eat candy and get cavities and someone else eats candy and does not. Your responsibility begins when it becomes clear that you are cavity prone. Then do you stop eating candy?...

"The strength of the bridge you have built between your Being and your behavior is a measure of your immediate ability to self heal..."

From Pg. 110 ff. Excerpts, "Is there validity to predictions of catastrophic changes to the earth?

"Collectively you have come to the end of your capacity for denial and avoidance of your internal disruption. You can no longer maintain the schism between your Being and your behavior...

"Rather than die, the old can transform into the new. Transformation would be better for everyone, but transforming is much harder than dying...It takes far greater courage, trust, love and intelligence to reincarnate without a death. You are being asked to do this. Your cities and nations, whose disruptions of integrity and of community are reflected in the Earth's breaks and upheavals, are being called upon to do this. Your economic systems and the values they derive from are being called upon to do this. Their challenge is to regenerate without death. The opportunity at hand is more than a call for transformation. It is the universe-empowered opportunity for transmutation, a phenomenon of grace that will swell from the transformational movement.

"Who will be the first to break the momentum of the old ways? Those coveting power and manipulating the economy to their ends? Those professing to hold spiritual or intellectual domain, implicitly limiting direct knowledge and exploration? Those counseling others in the many therapies that teach people to negotiate, compromise, and adapted for success, rather than to seek and follow their own inner direction?...

"Only you can free yourself from the vested interests and learned positions, to live as you feel. Only you can invent your future integrity...Those who succeeded in aligning their heartfelt values with their actions are way-makers, bridge builders to an integral way of life. Everyone who crosses the bridge adds to the magnetism of love, hope and courage that draws the next sojourner across...

"You're not only a person. You are also a frequency and a value that permeates the universe. When the choices you make in your daily life and quality of love you demonstrate in your daily life are consistent with your essential nature, your actions impact more than you knowingly touch. They impact the movement of All-That-Is. Most people do not believe they are this important because they do not perceive themselves as essential participants in the greater universe.

"If you think of yourself as part of the universe, your experience will embrace the universal...

"If you cannot see what you can do to contribute, rest assured that your way of being in the world has equal impact...Your tasks will become clear to you when their moments arise...

"Each time you express your highest truth and support others in expressing theirs, you are moving the world. Each time you allow inner direction to make your path, you build the infrastructure of peace...This job belongs to each and serves all. It is a job of claiming personal integrity. Live as if the world were already as you wish it would be and it will be so."

I was especially impressed by the comment that, "People are interpreting their power as creators to include responsibility for illnesses that have been genetically programmed through countless generations." (Pg. 98) For my part, I know some very good people who suffer from over-extended expectations for healing. One of the difficulties of healing is to suggest that if we trust god we will be healed; and then if we are unsuccessful we blame our 'lack of faith' and become dejected by guilt. Elia Wise suggests that some of the apparently negative experiences have been programmed into our experience as lessons we need to learn. I personally have run the gamut from Shingles to Kidney Stones to Prostate Cancer to Bell's Palsy and am learning to accept the powerful lessons that these illnesses have taught me.

Many other sources reflect the perennial philosophy as well. Current authors from the medical and educational fields abound. They have published numerous books, which detail aspects of healing, meditation and mysticism. They include Deepak Chopra, Bernie Siegel, Larry Dossey, Wayne Dyer, Joseph Campbell, Ken Wilber and many others. Fortunately, many of these have given lectures on Public Television (PBS) that has helped raise the consciousness of our generation.

Scientific researchers support many aspects of the mystical view. In the field of Physics, Shrodinger expressed his belief that the quantity of minds in the universe is just one. Werner Heisenberg taught that the force that connects particles separated by vast distances in the universe is in instant communication; in effect a journey of thought or mind greatly exceeding the speed of light.

In the field of Biology, field theories have been suggested with regard to intelligence surrounding all living things; a kind of biological aura. Because every cell in a body has the same genetic code or DNA science has developed the art of cloning. This has been demonstrated by substituting the nucleus of an intestinal cell of a frog in place of the nucleus of a fertilized ovum. The parent of the donor cell was replicated. This process has now gone on to higher farm animals.

The genetic code in all cells being identical, how does an individual cell discriminate in the role it will play in the function of the body? In other words if a cell of blood, a cell of bone, a cell of muscle and a cell from the cornea of the eye have the same information, which information do they decide to use? The suggestion of field theory is, that there is a field of intelligence surrounding the body with energy patterns of design, which instruct individual cells as to which developmental path to follow. There are some that suggest the possibility that when cells run amuck as in cancer, something has gone amiss in the field.

This field of intelligence is the metaphysical field of the Tao. The entire material world is based on the power of Te. Te is the intelligence and mind supporting all of creation. On Palm Sunday when Jesus said, "Even the very stones would cry out",[146] was he referring to 'Field Theory'?

The field of legend and Fairy Tales is replete with teaching with regard to the inner sources and is a source for the Perennial Philosophy.

The legend of the Holy Grail is filled with meaning, not the least of which is the awareness that the grail itself is the *sacred container within each of us* that is the residence of the Christ. The wine of spirit is the heart of Christ within us. The quest is what it takes to learn that the goal is not outside ourselves, and all the external seeking is fruitless until we discover that we already posses that for which we seek.

We can include "Snow White and the Seven Dwarfs" as well as "The Wizard of Oz". Snow White as mentioned before as a symbol of purity is assisted by the seven Chakras of Eastern meditation, interpreted in modern thought as the seven ductless glands of the endocrine system.

Consider the story of Snow White in reference to our discussions on the conflict between the outer world of appearance and the inner world of spirit. The story opens with the wicked stepmother obsessed with the magic mirror to which she unrelentingly addresses the question, "Who is the fairest in the land?" As a stepmother representing the outer ego, she is not the real parent of the child, who represents the inner spirit. Eventually, the ego begins to recognize that outer appearance (the image in the mirror) is illusion and there is a reality that may be known. At this point the mirror answers that the fairest is not the wicked queen but the child Snow White. A huntsman is directed to kill the child but allows her to escape into the forest. The inner spirit is indestructible and is often hidden from view. At this point the seven Chakras of meditation appear. The dwarves were working deep in the earth in order to mine the gold, a discipline that enables an outworking of the inner process. Then again, the ego seeks to kill the inner child, but the attempt is thwarted and the child stays alive even though she is in a deep sleep. What's next! Prince Charming, who as love, provides the way. He symbolizes the power of the inner Christ who inevitably brings about resurrection, with the result that the inner spirit united with the spirit of god lives happily 'ever-aftering.'

The Wizard of Oz is also full of guidance and symbology. One begins by battling with the 'wicked witch'. Along the path of the yellow brick road, we meet a cowardly Lion who must find his courage; a tin man without a heart, needing to find love and feeling; a scarecrow or straw man,

---

[146] Luke 19:40

very vulnerable, needing to find a brain along with intelligence and wisdom. And Dorothy, with her magic red shoes (perhaps a symbol of understanding), is looking for home, a place of purpose. All are seeking outside of themselves, looking to Oz, trying to find what they believe they lack. The outer source, the Wizard of Oz, is a fraud and a joke. He is in no way able to meet their need. After the sham is uncovered, assisted by the 'good witch', they discover that the true source of salvation lies within.

When any of us move from the polarity of the ego to the polarity of the One, separation ceases to exist, and we then experience the state that Jesus taught, "That they may be one even as we are one." The statement "Thou in me and I in them", does not mean god in Jesus and Jesus in us, as the language could imply. There is no us, and there is no I, there is only, as the poet Ella Wheeler Wilcox said, "Nothing at all but Me."

Illusion

God and I in space alone and nobody else in view.
"And where are the people, O Lord,' I said,
"The earth below, and the sky o'erhead,
And the dead whom once I knew?
That was a dream; God smiled and said,
"A dream that seemed to be true.
There were no people, living or dead,
There was no earth, and no sky o'erhead,
There was only Myself – in you."
Why do I feel no fear,' I asked,
"Meeting you here this way,
For I have sinned I know full well,
And is there heaven, and is there hell,
And is this the judgment day?"
"Nay, those were but dreams,' the Great God said,
"Dreams that have ceased to be,
There are no such things as fear or sin,
There is no you – you have never been -
There is nothing at all but ME."

Ella Wheeler Wilcox

Chapter Seven—The Power of Silence
The Unity of Spirit

"If the Son has set you free, you shall be free indeed."[147] When considering what it means to be set free, I think of the song "Tradition" from the musical "Fiddler on the Roof", a song celebrating the myriad attitudes and behaviors demanded of us, because we have always done it that way.

In the New Testament, one of the best illustrations of distortion of the record by tradition is the Christmas story of the three wise men. The actual record simply states that magi from the east came to search for the king of the Jews and were led to the house where the child was. The magi are referred to in no specific number or sex; they could have been a mixed group of men and women of indefinite number. The reaction of the Jewish king Herod to the questions of the Magi suggests that this contact occurred within the first two years after Jesus' birth. In fact, King Herod died in 4 BCE and may have been deceased before Jesus was born. Over the years this story has been closely associated with the story of the shepherds at the manger. The three gifts that were brought have become three men in the role of kings. Later stories supplied the men with names familiar to most people as Melchior, Balthasar and Gaspar. Their claimed relics or bones are interred at the Cologne Cathedral in Germany. These traditions are relatively harmless to the story, but it does suggest that whatever the original event, it became heavily embellished beyond the original record in Matthew.

Consider the story of a woman taken in adultery and brought before Jesus for judgment and condemnation by the Jewish law. This story is not present in many ancient manuscripts and when it is present is most often found in manuscripts of the gospel according to John.[148] No one who has seen Cecil B. DeMille's early Hollywood rendition of this story in the movie, "King of Kings" (1927), can help but realize that the legalistic prejudice of this case was extremely negative and those who brought the

---

[147] John 8:36
[148] John 8:1-11

woman forward for judgment were terribly hypocritical. The men probably carried stones with them as they came to test whether or not Jesus would follow the letter of the law. When Jesus was faced with the accused woman, he wrote, on the ground. In the midst of his writing Jesus said, "He that is without sin among you, let him first cast a stone." No one knows what Jesus wrote, but DeMille had no compunction about adding to tradition when he conveyed the idea that Jesus' writing was linked to the sins of those who carried the stones. As the sin of each was revealed they dropped their stones and slinked away. The story ends with Jesus asking the woman, "Where are your accusers?" When the woman answered that there were none he replied to her, "Neither do I accuse you". There are very few gospel stories that carry the spirit of Jesus as well as this one does, but scholarship is clear that this story is a very late addition and does not lend much support to the event as having any historical connection to the life of Jesus. The event may have occurred, but if so, it was a rather obscure oral tradition that kept it alive; for it was incorporated quite late into the compilation of the gospel stories.

In exception to the western empire-based church interpretation of salvation by Jesus, the Sages of the world taught that transformation was a change needing to be accomplished within the mind and outlook of the individual. The Gnostic concept of Jesus supports other sages holding the Perennial Philosophy. It was the western Jesus movement which claimed he did a work that could be substituted vicariously for others. It was a work that supposedly effected external salvation rather than internal transformation. A rather cheap salvation, some would say.

In effect, salvation from this standpoint has nothing to do with transformation in our lives. It is strictly a result of vicarious merit being transferred from someone else's account to our own. One negative side effect of this concept is the teaching that we are totally unworthy of entering into god's presence on our own. In fact, without Jesus' shed blood, if we were left to our own devices god would send us to an eternal punishment of hellfire and brimstone. Shouldn't we wonder when teachers who claim that the true nature of god is perfect Love teach this tragic doctrine to us?

This construct suggests that god has either created beings totally unworthy of god's presence, or we as finite beings have successfully destroyed what god has created. How different, to accept the realization of the grace and love which god extends as the essence of our true being! It is the extension of Love that transforms awareness as the life of god within us.

Later Buddhists were like the Roman Jesus movement, in that as they became more religious they did the same thing to their understanding of Gautama. This man, who taught the four noble truths and the noble eightfold path as means to enlightenment, became a mediator. Buddha could now be invoked to bring vicarious salvation and act as a passport to heaven.

The legalistic position of the traditional church is that the blood of Jesus was shed to cover our sins so that god would overlook them. All that was required to be saved was to accept the gift of god's grace granted by Jesus' sacrifice. The problem with this system was that it gave the hierarchy of the church vast power; it also began to teach that the Roman church was the only vehicle of salvation and could by its power of excommunication send to hell any opposition within the ranks. Religion may have some strength in common insights, but in its lust for power it is subject to uncommon corruption. In the Perennial Philosophy spiritual insights are shared. In the corruption of power politics materialistic form separates the followers, and faith is no longer held in common. Our different religious forms create barriers of prejudice and animosity.

The Roman church was held in the grip of the power it assumed. This power was the authority of the priests over the laity and of the bishop over the priests. As the Roman emperor had been considered divine, so now the bishop of Rome ruled over the church with the same imputed divinity. For this system to work, vows of absolute obedience were required. As a result, the Church of the Empire wiped out Gnostic influence and all other opposition in the early Jesus Movement. The present day institutional church as a whole still suffers from the same authority complex. The institutional church today is a very powerful force and has many functions and vested interests. It serves: as a vehicle for personal renovation, for behavior modification, for social reform, as a poor man's country club, as an extended family, as a social stepping stone and as support in matters of like-minded belief and prejudice.

In social reform, the institutional church seems to act in judgment and attack based on complete belief that this approach is the way to change the material world. Some years ago it was popular to argue the waste and supposed inefficiency of feeding grain to beef cattle in order to fatten them for human consumption, rather than using the grain for human food. "My mind is made up, don't confuse me with the facts." In a United Church of Christ Conference meeting I attended, a Missouri farmer, ironically from the 'show me state', listened to this argument, then challenged the remarks being made. He stated his land was too poor to raise wheat for human consumption but could raise Milo that beef cattle ate and humans couldn't.

Can we always be sure we are fixing something, even if it's not broken? We are prone to make judgments on the world and believe we know what is best for others. Robert Ornstein, in his book "The Roots of the Self" tells the story of several children who were born blind because of opaque ocular lenses, which only allowed diffused light to reach their retinas. Because the retinas, and optic nerves were still functioning, the children were given inter-ocular implants such as adults who develop cataracts receive. The children had all been blind for a period of at least ten years. Everyone involved believed that when the lens implants allowed images to focus on their retinas, the children would miraculously receive their sight. After the operation, none of the children were able *to learn* to see. The new images on their retinas were painful and dazzling. Instead of the operation bringing them sight, it almost killed them. All became depressed and some even committed suicide.[149] "The road to hell is paved with good intentions."

Institutional religion will be around for a long time. Its overwhelming inventory of buildings, property, pension investment and building funds in addition to ever-present demands for continued institutional existence are too great to be set aside. An individual may understand Jesus' words about losing one's life to save it, but I think these words are far too harsh for a religious institution to hear. While the establishment can bend to change, to what degree it can bend remains to be seen. Even the ultra liberal Unitarian-Universalist Association has established a kind of humanistic orthodoxy consisting of a pattern of intellectual skepticism and social activism.

For the present, hope seems to lie in the manifold assortment of small study groups. At least they have little financial investment; and if a small group fails to fulfill its purpose people are able to walk away. All kinds of resources are available, from personal growth groups based on psychology and encounter, to groups based on spiritual healing and those based on the works of specific authors or systems of learning. They include Joel Goldsmith's – Infinite Way, Jane Robert's – Seth Material, Edgar Cayce's – Search for God, and "A Course in Miracles" to name but a few. Some are more avowedly into the Perennial Philosophy than others. A few churches even allow groups such as these to use their facilities without demanding that they conform to preformed orthodoxy.

The metaphysical system presented by most institutional Christianity is a house of cards. It is not god's purpose to send anyone to a hell created for the eternal punishment of sinners, from which none escape. Hell is a construct of our own making. God's creative plan for restoration is universal and certain. The knowledge that we are already god's beloved children is all that is needed for our own healing, and it is this ultimate realization that sets us free to understand god. Inevitably, people will come to understand that god is not our judge but our advocate.

---

[149] The Roots of the Self, Robert Ornstein: pages 10,11

Above all, it is absolutely necessary to focus on the positive values of Spirit and not on the negativity of religion. God is the only power that is, and thus is reflected in the power of the inner kingdom. It is the power within you. It goes without saying; if god has not lost anyone then there is absolutely no need for any external legalistic salvation. We need to learn to see as god sees. God is too pure to behold evil, which means god looks beyond the judgment of appearances. Blessed are the pure in heart for they shall see god, for they see as god sees. Judge not and you shall not be judged, suggests that it is not god's worldview that judges, it is ours. A clearer understanding is discovered when we affirm, "I want to see differently"[150] and "Above all else I want to see."[151] External salvation is based on the idea of meeting god's needs and changing god's attitude; but it is not god that needs to be changed! Inner healing occurs when we see differently by learning to see as god sees.

It is misleading to say that everything has a history; this is not true of the Timeless, where everything is now. God has no history, and god has no future, god is now. The clarity of the Timeless, allowed to unfold in perfect expression, will meet all real needs of our space/time experience. God is no respecter of persons, is not without witness and works within all our lives. We need not seek to plan or control but only to allow the Spirit to manifest itself freely with great expectancy and no pre-set expectation on our part.

The church, as an institution of judgment and as a vehicle of limited legalistic salvation, will one day cease to exist. For its own survival, humankind must and will come to understand that humanity exists within god's expression of Love and Spirit; and that there are no outsiders and no exceptions to the rule. Salvation will come to be understood by all society as the need for individuals and groups to appropriate the Grace of god, which is the ground of their own existence.

Each person will understand the freedom of grace, as the illusion of separation falls away and they come to know in themselves the unity of All-That-Is as god's expression of Itself. The power of inner silence will become the authority of concord as each one experiences the guidance of inner Unity. Prayer will be reaching out to others, especially if they have temporarily forgotten their connection to Spirit. Prayer will not be a plea to use god, but will be rather an exercise in touching our own spiritual reserve (which is inner awareness of god), and extending energy from that source to those who have temporarily lost their own sense of universal spirit.

---

[150] A Course in Miracles, Workbook: Lesson 21
[151] A Course in Miracles, Workbook: Lesson 28

It may seem a contradiction to speak of the power of silence in conjunction with prayer because we often consider prayer as speaking, rather than an attitude of awareness or simple silence. We have a need to transform our understanding of prayer.

In my experience, in our religious culture we center on god as the external mechanism of prayer. By means of our prayers we focus upon an external object god who needs to be informed, persuaded and in some sense directed in order that our perceived needs and desires may be accomplished. One could diagnose the logic of this traditional kind of prayer as a triangle. God is at the top and we, with our desires, are the two ends of the base. When we find ourselves unable to go directly to our goal we initiate prayer toward god whom, in turn, we believe is energized to effect the desire of our prayer by achieving the answer we seek. By this means, when we pray for someone or something, we understand the mechanism as praying to god that god may bring about our intent. Prayer based on our will is woefully inept.

I believe that this externalized view of god and prayer is inadequate, ineffective and erroneous. Instead of our using god to accomplish our perceived needs, we would gain a much better understanding of effective prayer if we were to change the direction of energy *from us through god* to a flow that is *from god as us*. Thus, effective prayer for someone is not to pray to god for him or her, for as Jesus said, "I beseech not the father for you, for god himself loves you."[152]

Effective prayer for a person is not a prayer to god for that person; it is rather god extending as us, bringing healing to the need. In union with god we are also one with those we hold in prayer. Our unity of faith enables the Father to work within us. Jesus prayed for his disciples on many occasions, and his source of spiritual union became a source to lead them into truth, spirit and unity. His prayer did not try to change reality for some supposed distorted benefit. We can help others remove the barriers they have constructed that keep the Principle of love from their awareness. When we know god's love for us our friends are helped to know that love as well.

Effective prayer is not getting god involved; it is getting us involved. In true prayer, the triangle effectively becomes a single unitive point. In traditional ineffective prayer, we seem to believe that it is our responsibility to inform, request and persuade god to accomplish what we believe should occur. This is the all too common fallacy of believing we know what the will of god is, and that now *we* must seek to have god accomplish it. A potent adage says, "A lot of people want to serve god, but only in an advisory capacity." This is a popular modality in our culture for

---

[152] John 16:26,27

accomplishing our plans. To strive to do, rather than be, is carried over into our religious practice of wanting first to know and then to do. Religion is first motivated – then activated.

By this view, we become in our egocentric perception the energy that accomplishes god's ends. The subtlety is that these words could be an accurate description of prayer if we could only understand that the energy of god's accomplishments is not our own, but god's. A sense of separation has entered into the equation when we presume to accomplish god's will for god. We need to understand the application of the Taoist principle of *wei wu wei*, which means doing through not doing; for it is the Father that does the work. We only allow god's means, using god's energy.

The difference in the two kinds of prayer is whether we perceive ourselves as using god, or god as using us. Is the intention god's or ours? Do we become an instrument god designates, so that the personal self by its energy and will accomplishes what in its judgment it now believes to be the will of god? Harmony results when we allow god to be in charge. We can offer only what god has given us.

Consider this scenario. God has no needs, and only knows the perfection of All-That-Is. In prayer, when we ask for something to be given to us there is a separation implied because we believe we have a lack. We need not ask for a special something. If we negatively affirm what we believe we do not have, we have created an awareness of separation. Even asking god for help, as an external, drives deeper the wedge of apparent separation. We need to know that we are one with All-That-Is, and All of Spirit is ours to give.

We need do nothing, except not to interfere. Not interfering is undoing. We need not do, we need to undo! We need undo the illusion of separation. Divine Principle is not aware of our perceptions or judgments and their resulting illusions. God knows who and what we are as extensions of its own Being. God cannot lose that which is part of its own whole.

To pray for someone is not in any sense valid if we perceive prayer as trying to make divine Principle aware of need. First, god has absolute awareness of all that is real, and second, god has no knowledge of the illusion of need. For god cannot have an awareness of need. Because god knows no need, we practice futility when we try to inform god of our need. Harmony is our co-operative affirmation of what god knows to be true.

To pray for someone is to support them in opening to hear the voice, or feel the love of god through our knowledge of divine Principle. Because of judgments and resulting illusion, persons feeling lack or need have temporarily lost sight of their connection with wholeness (Holiness). Thus through our knowing god's resource in prayer, the person in need can be helped to become aware of the total supply available.

Divine Principle is always available to anyone, but there are times when we may lose awareness of its presence. By our awareness of the presence in others, we enable them to remove their blocks to the awareness of Love's presence. We do not pray to motivate god – we pray to build an awareness of the resource which is available to the one who may be temporarily experiencing the illusion of separation and need. We cannot pray to motivate god, for god as Principle is already as involved as it possibly can be. God Principle is love, truth, ground of being, and All-That-Is.

If a person believes two plus two equals five, they will suffer the results of that error. To pray to god to change something for a person in error is like asking Principle to make two plus two equal five in order to bring harmony to them. We do and can pray for others who are in the pain of error, but it is not to change god but rather, to enable change in them and us. We do not ask Principle to make two plus two equal five. We affirm in our own minds for others that true awareness is two plus two equals four. Because all minds are joined, to affirm for another the Principle of love is to make healing available to them. In this case, we are not using god Principle in a distorted way, rather we are allowing god Principle to use us. God Principle using us to help others is the proper way to extend healing to others. Many pray to god as if they were asking Principle to accommodate error. One does not pray in order to change god. We pray in order to change ourselves, that in so doing we may be truly more helpful to others.

While it may be true that the Holy Spirit takes ineffectively stated prayers and uses those to change us in the best way we will allow, those prayers are still burdened by the inappropriate images we carry about the nature of god. When we understand the dynamics of god Principle, our energies are far more coherent and more effectively directed. If sin (*harmatia*) is missing the mark, then ineffective prayer is part of the problem, not part of the answer. Effective prayer does not debilitate us in our concern for others; rather, it empowers and revitalizes us by its energy as well as opening avenues of trust to those for whom we pray.

This Principle applies to healing. Healing must be of the mind, for mind focused on problems simply reinforces the error of two plus two equals five.

On the other hand, the evasive action that is assumed by some trying to bury their problems under a pile of positive thought is tantamount to whistling in the dark. It cannot hide the fact that the reason we are whistling is because we are afraid of the dark. In a similar fashion, affirmations or facades of 'truth' do not hide the fact that we are expressing these affirmations because of roots in fear. We need not, indeed cannot, cover

over our fears no matter how valiant our efforts. We can, however, replace them with the experience of love.

It is often said, "As you think, so you become." While it is true that our beliefs do 'press out' to form our perceived worlds, we are often not clear as to the actual beliefs that underlie our statements. We may be thinking, "I want to be rich" when in fact our actual heartfelt position declares "I am fearful of being poor." In this case, it will be the latter fear as our true thoughts that will actualize. We may assume an affirmation that appears positive when in fact we have chosen it because of our fears. In this case, which consideration are we actually manifesting? Our assumed affirmations may appear to be that which we want, when in fact they represent what we fear. We may actually affirm fear through expectations, when we really need to discover how to affirm trust in expectancy. This does not mean that we can not use an affirmation effectively by consciously making an effort to change our thinking and beliefs.

When we start with an affirmation, it would be helpful if it were that which we can not help but believe. If we get to the root of our true beliefs and affirm them, our faith will grow in the direction of more powerful beliefs that we cannot help but affirm.

To experience love we must remove the walls we have erected which hide its presence. Our anger, judgment, and unforgiveness can lock us into general negativity and trap us by our own attitudes. It may be that *our general theory of negativity* carries as much or more significance in our lives than does Albert Einstein's general theory of relativity!

Forgiveness basically needs to be practiced for us, not others. We can recognize when we are ill or suffer. We accomplish little or nothing by denying the experience, except perhaps to muddy the waters of our spiritual awareness. It is a fallacy to maintain that people of faith do not get ill. Illness is often, or perhaps always, a teaching device for those of us who have need to learn. If we were in the world to teach as perfect souls with nothing to learn, perhaps one could argue for a faith that would deny the possibility of illness.

Rachel Remen, in her book, "My Grandfather's Blessings" suggests that there is a difference between healing and curing; curing applies to symptoms whereas healing goes to the root of the problem. She also criticizes the church for not learning to ask the right questions and giving answers to questions it has not yet learned to ask. It has become a business with a product and its product is its simplistic answers. In her view, from the edge of life, we have the capacity to bless the lives around us. Our focus must not be on the problem but the Resource.

I am reminded of Michael J. Fox's testimony regarding his experience with Parkinson's disease. He stated that he had been healed with regard to that affliction, but had not been cured.

Not long ago while sharpening a butcher knife I sliced open the back of my hand. After a trip to the doctor's office and about seven stitches, I came home to await the healing process. It was then I asked myself the question, "What if we were responsible for all our own bodily healing?" Today I can hardly find the scar and I know that I had no conscious part in the bodily healing process, except not to interfere. Of course I could have hindered healing by damaging the stitches, or caused infection by not keeping the wound clean; but why would I have acted so stupidly? I simply trusted a process that I do not fully understand.

Fear that the body wouldn't heal would have produced a debilitating sense of separation. There is a lesson here for the spiritual life. A house divided by interference with the flow of life is fractured. When we separate self from Impersonal Self by ignoring the natural healing resident in the universe, we destroy the natural flow and our house divided will not stand.

Again, we need do nothing, except not to interfere. The Principle of the Universe is friendly, and when we let go of enough personal garbage we will begin to grasp that fact. Healing comes about by trusting the Universe, not hiding from it or attacking it. The Universe is the energy of god-principle that expands and expresses itself through us.

As Jesus taught us to pray – we must allow god's Universe to express itself in Majesty through our lives – "Let thy kingdom come" – and not thwart its unfolding, because of our isolation or fear. To paraphrase John 1:1 again, There is an ancient communion. That communion is in the presence of the divine and has the intent and character of the divine. That ancient communion still energizes the world of our experience.

The valid question now becomes: how does the purpose or will of god effect Itself through us? The answer is that we allow it (*wei wu wei*) as effortless fulfillment. We must remove the blocks to the awareness of love's presence, which are our blocks of fear, anger, judgment and lack. When our awareness knows the Love, Peace, and Grace of god, then because all minds are joined, our minds become a channel through which the purposes of god can flow as true prayer. We do not need to know the will of god in order for it to be accomplished. We need only be willing and open channels through which the energy of god can flow in order to accomplish its purpose. We need not know or even suspect what is accomplished when our minds and love become unified with the One that always Is. The real question remains, "Who is doing the work, the separated ego or the Father within?" Is it the self-righteousness of religion and sacrificial religious devotion, or the Spirit within? In the self-righteousness of religious ritual we believe we can use god. In opening our hearts to love, spirit and healing, god energy will flow as us. In self-righteousness there is separation; in love there is unity. It is god as One-ness established in true being that is at the heart of all effective prayer. The miracle of love is not under ego control.

In order to understand our need for silence, it will help if we look at the busyness involved in our lives. We are like a hen trying to lay an egg on an escalator; much scurrying around, but not much getting down to business.

One of the problems in religious discipline is our anxiety, which lacks the patience to allow god to move in the fullness of time. We are often advised to make an effort for god instead of the more sage advice to wait upon the Lord. One such expression is the challenge "Fake it till you make it." Faking it can only be an act of doing, never of being. All reality, however, is Love. We are love and we must learn to act as love, doing so from within our own being. There is no way to fake an 'as if' of being. We must learn to do as an unconscious expression of that which we are. We can't fake who we are, for that would just add another layer of unreality to the barriers already overlying our true being! To act as if you love, as an ego discipline, may be attempted; but Love is not an act. The fact remains we can choose to love! Choosing to love may be a new learning experience for us, but it will not be a fake one. We are love; and an act of will can demonstrate that fact. We can let go of judgment! It is impossible to fake letting go of judgment, just as it is impossible to fake forgiveness. Real forgiveness is a choice based on the knowledge that we are one with those who only appear as *other*. Affirm that which you can not help but believe!

He who sees the face of god will surely die. In the face of the Impersonal Self the personal self cannot continue. There is no personal god because there is no personal self; the release from the personal self is a release from personal effort. The father within does the work. As Jesus said, "My yoke is easy and my burden is light." The easy yoke is the father's Love expressed within and through us. Failure comes from the belief that in our ego self we can express god. This is never true, in the personal self we do not express *for* god; it is only in the Impersonal Self that we can express *as* god. God as Mind is forever expressing Itself.

What god did not extend creatively does not exist and everything that exists, exists as god expressed it. The outer world we see is, at best, a reflection of reality. Perception is of our own making and in itself is not real. No object or experience has any meaning for us except the meaning we bring to it. Our past beliefs are projected outward to define the world we believe is out there. The metaphysical question remains, "What is it that really appears out there?" We need to learn that even in the most apparent 'tragedies' nothing real has been threatened. Every outer event or appearance has only the meaning we give it.

We are the energy of light, yet we perceive in the separated outer only darkness. In perception the darkness and the light seem to have become one. We need to look past the unreal darkness to the reality of light. Light does not exist to the blind man. The vibrations are present but there is no eye to experience sight. In like manner, Spiritual reality does not appear to the spiritually blind. We need to look past the unreal appearances.

Light is a fascinating subject; the speed of light according to Einstein is the one constant of the universe. Yet it is obvious that light passing through glass can be absorbed, leaving only one color to pass. A prism of glass affects light according to the amount of material it passes through, creating a spectrum of color. Spectrums of wave or speed of particle; it depends on the role of the observer to bring awareness into being.

I have asked questions about the nature of light. If objects approaching the speed of light lose dimension in space and shorten interval in time – would not a photon obviously traveling at the speed of light cease to occupy space and no longer have duration in time? If so, how can one speak of light years of distance – when the photon has no space/time dimension? Perhaps it is in this area that understanding of the space/time illusion exists.

We are the observers of the outer world, and what we see depends upon our expectation. Choose to see a world of material reality and that is precisely what we will see. Choose a world of Spirit and we will see the reality of Spirit. Which world does god see? God does not see as an observer but knows as Participant. Pure being, Spirit, Is-ness, is unfiltered presence. To think of Pure being in normal terms, i.e. space/time, duration and form, is to be unaware that Spirit has no duration, is-ness has no duration; it is timeless. Our space/time consciousness is one of the blocks or filters preventing our experience of Pure Being.

Edgar Cayce stated that thoughts are things and mind is the builder. In teaching about our world awareness he also made the unique statement that the world is not only composed of time and space but patience as well; a world of time, space and patience. Judgment and prejudice are things in space/time, form and duration; perhaps it is in the exercise of patience that we allow learning to unfold.

To attempt to be in charge of the outer world is not being, it is doing; and a doing that is separated from All-That-Is. We are not capable of taking charge. Perhaps we need to discipline our inner lives praying, "Be Thou in charge at my request."[153] All doing is in form and duration. Space/time 'reality' is doing – manifestation and form. The unmanifest, the formless, the timeless – is the reality of pure and total being. God is Alpha and Omega, Timeless Spirit, and so are we. Perfect Love casts out fear, so "Teach only Love for that is what you are."[154]

True correction is not accomplished in time and duration. It is accomplished in Spirit. We change or correct our world when we change our belief systems about it. We experience the universe as a holographic projection of our beliefs, pre-judgments and expectations. Spirit, pure Being, has intent but no form. It has no boundaries; it is clean, timeless and formless. Insight is the flow from pure being to interior thought made manifest in our awareness. Christhood is not something we must strive to attain; to be in Christ means simply that the fullness of our Being is recognized and realized. The Yoke is easy...Never sacrifice anything you value until you find a better value to replace it. The world is crushed with the false values of religion that demand sacrifice. Sacrifice is not the Way.

The fundamentalists are still wrestling with the concept of Evolution vs. Creation. The real problem is that the church has not yet come to grips with the physicists' concept of time and space as illusion. If space/time is an illusion, then so also are all phenomena dependent on time and space including the myriad actions of all humankind. Thou art that, *tat tvam asi.*

Once I visited a charismatic group and although I was not impressed with all the anxiety demonstrated in the desire to speak in tongues, a young lady with a beautiful voice sang a song that she said Spirit had given her. It was based on the statement made by the apostle Peter when he observed Jesus miraculously walking on the surface of the Sea of Galilee. The words sung to a beautiful melody were, "Lord, if it be Thou, Bid me come to Thee on the water." The sense of the song was simply to know the Source and seek that its will be expressed. When we are in a state of child-like grace we are able to trust the good intent of the Father; for it is always god's good purpose to give us the kingdom. To paraphrase a common affirmation,

> The light of god shines through us,
> The Love of god flows from us,
> The Presence of god is in us,
> The Power of god expresses as us,
> Wherever we are, god is.
> When we drink from the fountain of Life,
> We have drunk from the fountain of eternal life.

---

[153] A Course in Miracles: Workbook—Final Lessons 361 – 365
[154] A Course in Miracles: Text 6, III, 2:4

Two extraordinary stories became a very real part of my understanding of prayer; the first came from Ambrose Worrall and is told in the book, "The Gift of Healing", which was written with his wife Olga. The second comes from a study of the nature of prayer and its effectiveness at Redlands University. It is detailed in the book; "Prayer Can Change Your Life" by William Parker and Elaine St. Johns.

The first story that caught my eye was about an individual Ambrose Worrall knew, who was an executive in a Baltimore manufacturing company. He had a six-year-old daughter, Kay, who was very ill. In his need, he came to Ambrose and told of the intensity of his daughter's illness. She had contracted measles, which had progressed into encephalitis (sleeping sickness), and resulted in her being in a catatonic state or coma for sixteen days. She was paralyzed, rigid from head to foot with little hope of recovery, as patients seldom survived many days in that kind of coma.

The man asked Ambrose if he could help his daughter. She was in quarantine, so the father gave Ambrose a picture to focus upon. It was a custom for Ambrose and his wife Olga to have a time at nine o'clock in the evening to focus on healing requests that they had received. That evening, when 'tuning in' to become one with the little girl, Ambrose began to feel a healing force flow to the man's daughter from his solar plexus and then felt it blocked by a barrier surrounding the child.

As a psychic, he relaxed and saw in his mind's eye a picture of the father sitting beside his daughter's hospital bed; the father was concentrating intensely on something. Ambrose was certain the father's concentration had something to do with the blockage of the healing energy.

The next morning Ambrose asked the father what he had been doing at nine o'clock the previous evening. The father explained that his daughter had a feeding tube through her nostril, and her throat was so tight it could not be removed. As a result he was praying for her in her discomfort, concentrating that at least the throat muscles would relax. Ambrose's response to the father was "Don't do that". He instructed the father to visualize some happy occurrence for her that evening, such as her attendance at a birthday party or out playing with her friends; some way to picture her in perfect health. When Ambrose meditated that evening, he felt energy flow through him and it was not blocked as it previously had been.

The next morning, the girl's father told Ambrose that she had awakened and opened her eyes for the first time in eighteen days. Her fever had subsided and the paralysis was cured as far down as her waist, and she had about ten percent of her vision restored. The physicians told her parents that there was little hope the condition would improve, but after a few days allowed her to go home as she was no longer contagious.

Kay's condition did not show any sign of change in the next several weeks, and the father asked Ambrose to visit her at home. When Ambrose came into the room, she was trying to read a child's book with very large print, held very close to her face. Ambrose picked her up and very gently tried to stand her up, but her legs sagged like those of a rag doll. He held her in his arms, talked with her and rubbed her back.

The next morning when her father came in to carry her to the bathroom, she waved him away and told him, "Daddy, I don't need you to carry me." She got out of bed by herself and walked to the bathroom.[155]

Sometime later I was able to attend a seminar with Ambrose and Olga Worrall, and in personal conversation with him I asked questions about the story just related. I told him that my understanding was that the prayers of the father had actually served to block the healing process. I asked him if I was correct in that perception. He replied that I was absolutely correct; that the *anxious* prayers of the father had effectively blocked Kay's healing.

He went on to say that much of that which passes for prayer in the traditional church is simply nothing more than pious worry. We energize the negative we are concerned about. After filling me in on the story, Ambrose reached into his pocket, and showed me a picture of a young mother with two small children. The mother pictured was Kay!

The Redlands University study in regard to prayer involved participants selected from faculty, student body, and townspeople. These were divided into three separate study groups. The first group worked with the practice of prayer only. The second group worked with principles of psychotherapy only. The third group was comprised of those who took the principles of psychotherapy and combined them with the practice of prayer. All three groups were given psychological profiles before and after the study. The purpose of the profiles was to determine what, if any, change might have occurred after a disciplined period of application.

After the study concluded, the psychotherapy group had some degree of improvement following the period of involvement. The combined group evidenced the most improvement in their psychological profiles. The amazing thing to me was that the group working only with prayer showed a worse profile at the end of the study than they did before it began!

William R. Parker, who co-authored the book and headed the study group, suggests that the evidence seems to say that people who involve themselves only with traditional prayer appear to spiral in negativity. They seem unable to break free from the vicious circle of their own negative

---

[155] The Gift of Healing, Ambrose and Olga Worrall: pages 17-21

concerns. Worrall's observation about traditional prayer and pious worry seemed to hold true in the Redlands' study.

One can use all the traditional forms and say all the correct words, but if there is not a positive attitude of trust and intention, results are diminished or the situation exacerbated. It is possible for religion to have all the right words, but for all the wrong reasons. Someone has said that great ideas are not just to be used as bumper stickers; they must be effectively integrated. It makes a difference whether we are trying to *address* a god that is outside ourselves, or whether we have learned to *express* god from inside.

Psalm 91 states, "A thousand shall fall at your side, ten thousand at your right hand, but it will not come near you." If we consider this statement in light of levels of awareness, we may understand that the thousand represents conflicts at the material level and that the ten thousand represents conflicts at a mental level; however, at the absolute level of Spirit there is nothing that challenges one's own Spiritual Self. Appearances in the space/time world will change and at times appear to threaten, but one's spiritual reality will not be harmed. Spirit is invulnerable.

If we are Followers of the Way and healed by the transformation of Spiritual birth, we understand that god is no respecter of persons. In the Law of One, separation dissolves and we are all One and the Same.

Separating cause from effect is a form of dualism, for invisible cause and visible effect are one. The illusion reverses reality when we think that the external visible is cause and the internal invisible is effect. To see them separately and apart is not to see the Real world. We can feel the love of god expressing in us, and we can know the love of god expressing as us. We are the Light of the world only in the proportion that we realize that there is no darkness in us or in the world!

Rene Descartes, a 17th Century French philosopher, is famous for the words, "Cogito, ergo sum." ("I think, therefore I Am."). In his philosophy, he held nothing true until he had grounds for believing it true. He used his statement of thinking and being, to argue the existence of god. I believe there has been much energy wasted in examining the question of the existence of god. The existence of Source is not the question. Source exists if we do. We should focus on the question, "What kind of Source exists?"

If we start with the obvious, "Does a world, or do we, exist?", then we must recognize that being exists. We can question the nature of that being but not its very existence, even if that being is seen only as a dream state. We must ultimately explore the nature of being, and the first question becomes, "Given a state of being, what is the source of that being?" There must be of course a ground of being, and if we choose we can label this ground of being god. Being exists; ground of being exists. Up to this point we have only stated the obvious. Being exists and so does its source; but not one aspect about its nature or description of source has been stated except its existence. We again raise the question of dualism; is being other than ground of being, or are being and ground of being the same?

The most avowed atheist would have to accept the concept of a starting place even if the source is without cause itself. There are many concepts held about god that I do not believe; therefore, I would be a non-believer in those particular gods. Atheism needs to define the god it doesn't believe in. A-theism depends upon the kind of theism one is a or negative about. The question of the existence of Source remains. What is the nature of Source? Call it by any name, but don't deny its existence. The real problems arise when we begin to grapple with the relationship existing between the ground of being and the manifest world. Can ground of being be considered a thing or object and still include the nature of Spirit? Source is Spirit and Spirit is "The Living God of *No*-Thing, and *No*-Where". (a book by Nels Ferre)

I remember Nels Ferre playing word games, saying that the wasness of the is (past) exists, but that the isness of the was (future) does not exist. These are simply temporal expressions, whereas the reality of god is transtemporal. I think that the spirit in its now, encompasses all that was and is, in an eternal now. Like many aspects of the real, there is no adequate language that can contain or label what is essentially ineffable.

If one acknowledges the reality of the timeless and the spaceless, as Einstein avowed the unreality of time and space, then our sense of the present, moving along a timeline from past toward future, is the foundation of the space/time illusion and the foundation of bodily experience. The time line of past and future does not encompass Spirit, which is the Reality of god and all reality. Past and future do not exist as Realities. The now is not coming into being and then passing out of being, as a time line would demand. The now of Spirit Is. Einstein commented that "people like us, who believe in Physics, know that the distinction between past, present and future is only a stubbornly persistent illusion."

The Sages of the world speak of god as Spirit: no space, no time, no thing; invisible, empty and timeless. God is not an invisible object or thing, not even a non-thing (a kind of non-object). God is, but is *non*-existent as an object in space/time; Spirit is, but is also *non*-existent as an object. Things exist as objects but god is unmanifest. There is no god as object. The *no*-god that is, is unmanifest and not a manifest thing. God is spirit, unmanifest, empty, and non-existent in time and space. If you fully comprehend this paragraph, quit reading; you must have graduated.

Jesus said, "Worship in spirit and in truth." and Buddha taught, "God is, but there is no god (as object)." God cannot be worshipped objectively or even non-objectively, for non-object is a classification derived from objectivity. God can be worshipped only in spirit and in truth. To worship god in spirit is not to worship any form, visible or invisible. There is no existent god to worship. Spirit cannot be worshipped objectively. Spirit can only be known. When god is worshiped in Spirit and Truth god is not worshiped as other. True worship is union with god!

This is why we are enjoined not to worship god in objective form but to experience god subjectively. The goal we are to seek is not worship of god as an outside object but union with god as inner Source of our own being. It is not the 'worship of god' that is possible in truth; it is union with god and union with the experience of Spirit. There is no god demanding worship.

True worship is not related to an object, but is the knowing of Subject. True worship is the experience of Subject as our Spirit and our Truth, for the kingdom of god *is* within us and is experienced as non-object I AM, the Impersonal Self. We can feel the presence of no boundaries.

The seeker is that which is sought; but the seeker cannot be sought as object, for the seeker is spirit in nature, i.e. non-objective. The 'I am' awareness cannot be objectified; it is empty of all form. In the outer we experience form, but we cannot call Spirit *it* or object. Spirit is Source and Reality of manifest appearance, and is the unmanifest subject but not the separated object of appearance. The kingdom is within. The Kingdom Is.

God is – but there is no god! This is the sound of one hand clapping. Subject without object! Unity is the Whole in spite of apparent diversity. The *other*, with its myriad appearances of diverse form, is manifested from One Spirit. But even an objective sense of oneness is not the source, for Spirit is emptiness and formlessness. The Sages have referred to this as, "The fullness of the void and the voidness of the full." The only god we ever know is the god within the Impersonal Self.

Larry Dossey in a recent PBS broadcast remarked that the Void is the plenum of fullness and that the mind is loose in time and space. He spoke of a Princeton University experiment with telepathy at a range of up to six thousand miles. Computers selected pictures that were sent by human transmitter to human receiver. Remarkably, in some instances the image was received three days before it was sent! His other comment would aptly concur with my understanding of being meditated instead of meditating. Dr. Dossey commented that the ability to be effective in biofeedback is not accomplished by doing, for we cannot be successful by trying. *We have to give up trying in order to attain the goal and allow it to arrive.* (*wei wu wei*)

Form gives many appearances of other. Form is what appears different but is not divorced from the Source; its source is the One. Hence there is no judgment on the different by what is the Source. The One by means of Love expresses the many.

The Source is at peace and the Same sees the different, from Peace and without judgment or condemnation. The Real World is the awareness of the Same bound with appearance of what is different. The Spirit is on earth as in heaven. Heaven is experienced as within-ness, and heaven is both the Seeker and the Sought. The Sought is the Seeker and the Seeker is non-known until the reality of the One is realized. It is the Same – The Seeker which is the Same now experiences the different not as an illusion of – out there – but as a reality within. The different is still different, but it is experienced from the perspective of the Same. The world of outer illusion is now seen as a fact from the Self within. We now experience the unified dualism of flesh and spirit.

When one discovers that, that which is sought after is the seeker, then the seeking no longer objectifies whatever is sought after. The sought is not found, it is realized! But as an adolescent is a part time adult, so the seeker becomes a part time Sage – no longer hooked permanently by the illusion of a separated other or the different. Now with a center core of realization, illumination, and enlightenment, the apparent personal self, or ego, subsides. It does not disappear while we live in apparently separated bodies, but it can experience the healing of knowing the Sameness, and thereby blesses the apparent world of difference.

We learn to live in the world of the inner/outer split, and at the same time, to live with a spirit of inner/outer integration. Walter Starcke, a student of Joel Goldsmith, wrote a book called "This Double Thread", in which his basic thesis was that we walk as if we had one foot in each world. We have one foot in the world of appearance and one foot in the world of Spirit. We are in the world even though we are not of the world.

The question, or Experience, of One and other is perhaps understood best in our own personal sense of body/mind duality. We must learn to reference the two as one and relate to the unity of both. Pain in the body is experienced by the mind as separation, and unless we learn to dissociate from that kind of separation, we will not see body/mind oneness or bring healing to the conflict. This is a reflection in the microcosm of the problem of dualism in the macrocosm.

God potentiality as subject is pervasive, and potentiality as object is non-existent. Spirit cannot exist as form, and once we perceive an expressed form, potentiality in the form no longer exists. In our desire to heal outer situations, we often think that we can effectively send healing thoughts from the wholeness of our Impersonal Self, to that in the outer where we perceive the need. By buying into the illusion of dualism, we

217

unfortunately create level confusion. We cannot use Real Mind to heal a separated body, for Real Mind does not know separation. Such attempts are always from the ego level. We can, however, heal a mind of error by choosing to know the truth. It is in knowing the truth that minds are free; and when we are free indeed our world will reflect that freedom. The son shall make you free. Only mind is healed by Spirit, and then only mind willing to be healed.

In the silence, meditation opens our awareness to the Unmanifest Source. A flow of energy comes in the awareness that we are truly known; and from that inner voice springs an intimation of knowing. Paul understood that one day we shall know as we are known, but the time does not yet seem to be. Insights always come from the inner source. The Impersonal Self functions in spirit – not the personal ego. It is not I, but the Christ within. The father within does the work.

The unmanifest is Spirit; the manifest is matter. It is illusion to perceive manifest matter as reality; for it is the reality of the underlying Spirit and our externalized perception, upon which matter is totally dependent. How do you say god is, but does not exist? It is appropriate to say that the object form of god does not exist. But the mystery of god can not be described either as existence or non-existence. It is best to say simply, *god is*.

The Silence of meditation is learning to be The Still Point. The purpose of meditation is not only to let go of the outer world of phenomena, but to learn to avoid the inner world of thoughts as phenomena as well. However, we can gain insight through the contemplation of our inner worlds.

The primary question we ask ourselves is, "What do we have to do in order to be?" The answer is nothing; we already are pure being, pure in the sense that being is an effortless given. We are – we have always been – we will always be. Confusion comes from such questions as, "What do you want to become?" In this, we are dealing with roles and perceptions. When we believe we must strive to achieve in order to become, we are seeking for a means to the goal – a way to effect place – we think the proper use of time is doing, in order to be. We need do nothing, except not to interfere by blocking the flow of love. In our doing, we lose sight of the pure being that god is expressing, and forget who and what we are. We say we want to experience god. The problem is that we speak as if god is some outer or some other that we want to come into our awareness. Spirit is not about other; it is about the true inner Self.

Spirit is not an outer, it is our essential inner. Whatever we are now experiencing, in its origin, is god or Source. The problem is that we experience god through the filters of our own imposed judgment, comment, beliefs, and control. We must remove these filters or blocks before we can realize with clarity, the extension of god that is being expressed as our Impersonal Self. God is spirit. Those that worship in spirit and truth are not worshipping in a traditional sense. They are experiencing union.

"When the student is ready the teacher appears" does not mean that when the student isn't ready, a prosecutor appears. The spirit leads; it does not argue. The prosecutor is the pain, confusion, and fear produced by the personal universe our separation has generated.

One conundrum that exists in regard to meditation is the question, "Can we spend so much time in striving for silent reality that we neglect the lessons that we have come into the illusion to learn?" It is in context of life that we learn. Awareness is reciprocal; we cannot truly believe that Christ is in us, until we truly believe the same Christ is in all others. Meditation is not striving; it is not something we do; it is something we are.

The question of striving raises the problem of shoulds and oughts. Are we free or are we constrained legalistically to meditate? We can't legislate Joy or Peace but we can forbear acts that block our joy and peace. If meditation is approached as a legalistic chore, we start with a wrong setting. A chore of meditation is an oxymoron. We must find within ourselves a sense of positive affirmation. The chore is in removing our blocks to joy. It helps to be aware that god has not lost the way to us. When our blocks are silenced our way is opened.

One helpful technique to let go of a racing mind is to focus on breathing. Breathing is automatic, and focusing on it gives the mind something to do without creating a disruptive challenge. When sitting in silence, do not attach to thoughts and do not detach from thoughts, for to focus on avoidance is doing. In practicing non-attachment to thought, be an observer of the process without being snared into doing anything. The one thing silence teaches is that loudness is not reality. Loudness is always external to the silence, deafening by definition.

Meditation comes in as many forms or shapes, as there are meditators. I remember Herb Puryear of the Association for Research and Enlightenment, in a workshop on meditation, telling the story about a girl who had been meditating for five years. She said that, in that time, nothing had ever happened, *except her whole life had been changed*. Akin to that illustration is the young woman who told Ambrose Worrall that she had been meditating for five hours each day but her life did not seem balanced. Ambrose told her to cut her meditation time down to five minutes per day. The implication of his instruction seemed to be that although Silence was required in our lives, we still need the balance that life desires to teach us. I believe we are dealing with our daily bread.

When a newborn opens its eyes it may take awhile to focus and see clearly. An adult with eyes closed need only open them in order to be able to see. Meditation is like learning to open one's eyes to an expanded sense of seeing. Once you have seen the stillness, brief periods of opening one's eyes to it may suffice. It is as if we were walking with our eyes closed and must learn to take time to open them and see reality before we move on.

The ability to focus our eyes must be learned. A baby takes a long time to learn to focus and follow objects – to connect. When we begin to explore the inner awareness of Spirit, we need to take some time and discipline in order to open to the Silence. I think it was Rumi who said "Brush the sleep from my eyes master."

There are as many ways to god as there are people to experience them. Perhaps it is, that spirit manifests to us in as many ways as is necessary. We give voice to as many paths as are recommended by our understanding of the experience of the unmanifest.

These all may be of particular help, but there is a giant presumption inherent in the thinking of most of us. We seem naturally to generalize from the particular, i.e. we believe that a particular path we have walked is the same light in which everyone ought to be able to walk. Reasoning from particular to general is the biased idea that if this is the way for me, it must therefore be the way it is and the way it must be. In that frame of mind, we presume it is obviously the way for others as well. Each tub must set on its own bottom. We must paddle our own canoe![156]

Studies with regard to shamanism make many references to experiences of an underworld. Those capable of such experiences testify to the great diversity of both guides and obstacles encountered. Those teaching shamanistic approaches demonstrate many pathways: drumming, chants, and drugs like Peyote and LSD. These are all, in a sense, guided tours of the underworld of the unconscious; yet sometimes teachers suggest that the way they have learned is the only correct way. The Spirit is a very gifted teacher and is always able to take us from wherever we are to wherever we need to be.

I have heard spiritual searchers speak about experiencing the 'White Light', especially in their practice of meditation. They assume that in order for meditation to be valid, because they have had this kind of phenomenal experience, everyone should have the same experience. It is like the presumption that only those who speak in tongues receive the Holy Spirit.

It is evident that in this testimony of my journey I may well be guilty of this exact fault. I do continue to experience growth in my awareness; and

---

[156] *"Pas de Lieu Rhone que Nous."*

am not trying to argue that I have arrived. But I must witness that when I test my beliefs against the teachings of the Sages of the world, I find support for my journey. There is a Way and it can be found, or perhaps more correctly, if we are willing it will find us.

Jesus said, "My teaching is not mine but of the one who sent me. If anyone wills to do the will of god, that one shall know if it is of god or if I am speaking on my own. Do I speak for my own glory or the glory of the one who sent me?"[157]

Many commercial groups offer to teach about the experience of enlightenment. Their graduates are given the right to assume titles such as Master and Adept. I'm sure that there are valid learning experiences involved, but at times the advertisements suggest enlightenment for a price. Interestingly, many of these movements are directed toward the 'well-to-do'. People are attracted to workshops and they do cost money to conduct.

Altered states of consciousness have many causes: hallucinogens, low frequency rhythmic sounds such as drumming, and out of phase sounds produced by hemisync earphones, in addition to light forms such as strobes and mandalas. The circle is a very common symbol in mythology.

Many of the adherents of these particular disciplines mistakenly believe them to be the universal means and not just limited to themselves, or a particular psychological type. Too many searchers on the path are impressed with the belief that this is so. Because one person can dissociate by looking in a crystal ball does not mean that all persons can.

I well remember sitting in with charismatic groups who appeared to believe that the only true manifestation of the Holy Spirit was the ability to speak in tongues (glossilalia). In that context: I have never had, wanted, or seemed to need that particular experience. I have been saddened by the sense of failure of those in such groups who wanted the experience so badly they could 'taste it'. They were unwilling to give in to fakery, or a cheap substitute for the real thing; so rather than being honored for their personal integrity, the judgment of the group was that they were in some way defective. I can not believe love would draw such boundaries of separation.

We must be aware of the anomaly that there are those in traditional frameworks who have allowed love to express itself, and there are those that have not yet learned to live in love. Others who seem much closer to the Perennial Philosophy than to orthodox tradition, for some reason, in spite of more integrated thinking, have not made the commitment or the decision to make their beliefs operative. They have changed their surface thinking but

---

[157] John 7: 16-18

there has as yet been no real transformation of the mind or life in their belief system. Fear and judgment still prevail.

Those with a mistaken theology believe they are still dependent upon it for their own salvation and cannot alter it because of their own fear. Only when their salvation becomes based on non-threatening beliefs can they afford to alter their outlook about god. When one's salvation is based upon a god who has not lost anyone, holds no anger or judgment, and elicits no fear, then it is safe for one to change theological beliefs. Faith as an inner resource is motive enough to tolerate a paradigm shift in our beliefs about the outer. Faith based only upon outer orthodoxy does not feel safe to change. This is the problem of new wine in old wineskins.

Jesus said, "Thou art gods."[158] We can venerate and deify Jesus and in doing so miss the whole point of what he was trying to teach. We are one with the Father! The Father within does the work. The Father and we are one. The Christ is the Universal Self of all. The Logos is expressing us; and we are one with the Living Word.

The silence within is the silencing of discursive thought. So, silence projected without brings a Real world to vision. This new world is not judged by past memory; it is seen as god's manifestation. The body and all things are neutral; waiting to be seen in the manner dependent on whether or not we apply our memories and judgments from a personal past or the vision of the Tao, which is god's Logos or Word.

To experience Tao in relation to the manifest world is to bring to it the miracle of true awareness. Situations, persons and things are seen differently, and because a new awareness is brought to them, the possibility of a new response from us opens before them.

Deepak Chopra has said, "It is not the loneliness of the Ego, but the solitude of the Seeker, that will dominate our awareness." Life is all interconnected; it is not a jungle out there. According to Chopra, the life force is irresistible – effortless ease. According to Jesus, the yoke is easy and the burden is light.[159]

As we begin to think about the nature of god, we become aware that inherent in the use of language is the division between subject and object. It is impossible to use language without expressing a context of separation. This is also a characteristic of our thinking for, whether we realize it or not, it is apparent that all of our thoughts are in language. Perhaps this is why the experience of knowing at a deep level of awareness is more an 'aha!' of feeling, rather than some contrivance of intellect.

---

[158] John 10:34
[159] Matthew 11:30

Intellectual concepts about god, by their nature inevitably must express god as an object; and in this very expression any perception of union with god is denied. A conventional relationship with an objectified 'other' is the best that the tradition of language can invent. The witness of Jesus, "I am one with the father", cannot be defined in discursive subject/object terms. If we, with Jesus' expression as a pattern, are to experience the same union as he, it will not, indeed cannot, be experienced at the level of words. One of the major problems in understanding the scriptural traditions of the world is that they are by very definition stated in words subject to limitation. The experience of words is something very different from the 'Living Word'.

I believe that the Universe responds to our awareness and attitudes. The word Universe is for me an acceptable symbol for an awareness of god. I am not embarrassed to talk to the Universe, and I am convinced of its ability to respond cogently. I do so in the awareness that the reality of the Universe and I are One and the Same. True communion is immersion in the reality of All-That-Is, and All-That-Is must be understood as the ground of Energy and Intelligence and not the appearance of space/time.

Indeed, the Spirit who is our Spirit communicates in a reality beyond words that can be uttered. This is the Thunder of the Silence and the Fullness of the Void. Externals in the form of words may symbolize the clarity of prayer or intent for us, even when in truth it is the power of the internal silence that actually follows through.

The Universe in its Wholeness and oneness is aware of us as its expression; the very hairs of our head are numbered and its eye is on the sparrow. The Universe in its Being is the energy of Love – Unconditional Love. There is no fear and no judgment in its relationship to us. In Love and lack of judgment Forgiveness is expressed – Unconditional forgiveness.

We Abide in God's Heart
Early on I determined
To walk as near to god
As I was presently able.
My determination remained solid
But I discovered the nature of god
Changed the Presence that I sought.
It dawned I need not be concerned
With any of my attachments to god
For god was absolutely attached to me.
Bonding; my love toward god
And god's love toward me
Became one and the same.
These are not two
Appended as one.
For god is always the same.
We may *believe*
That god's love
Abides in our hearts.
But we can *know*
We truly abide in the Love
That is the heart of god.

George E. Fandt

Chapter Eight—The Future of Faith
Being Right or Well

Healing Judgement

We are now at a point where we need to understand our role in the Illusion. We have faced the principle that we need do nothing, except not to interfere. At the same time, we need to learn how to achieve by not doing.

At the level of the real, it is clear that there is nothing to be done, for All-That-Is is complete. At the level of the absolute there is no journey, but if this is true, then why are we here? The answer of course is that in our space/time dimension there is much that can be accomplished. It needs, however, to be an effortless accomplishment, if we are to honor the principle of doing by not doing, or to accomplish from our being.

We are told not to judge the world in the form of condemnation and separation. However, there is much useless pain and suffering in the space/time world and it can be healed by the miracle of Love. Again I am reminded of Walter Starcke's 'double thread' i.e., one foot in each world. The secret is learning to be *in* the world without being *of* the world.

We can be at peace, knowing that nothing real can be threatened, and still be aware that there are those who are still temporarily of the world who are experiencing much needless pain and suffering.

This is where the miracle comes in; it is not under conscious control and we have no need to be told what to do, because doing is not the answer; however, the state of our real being is. Again, how to *be in* the world of illusion and not *be of* it. There is a reference in "A Course in Miracles" to what is called healing judgement. This is not in any sense a form of condemnation. For Spirit to use us in this approach to healing we must be fully aware that those temporarily in need are part of same Sonship as us.

Healing judgement is being truly helpful. It is like telling someone, "If you step off this cliff your body will suffer excruciating pain and may likely be killed." This is not a judgement of the worth or value of a person temporarily in the belief that they *are of* this world.

We are not asked to be clever and fix things as if we knew the right or wrong of it. We are simply directed to choose to be helpful in healing with understanding that is not up to us to know how to do. It is after all *not doing* that is required, rather, a deep Silence of knowing who we are. Silent because this is not a role of the personal self that is committed to doing, but rather, the function of the Impersonal Self that is silent in its being.

This is a lesson in how to fix it, *"Don't fix it,* it ain't really broke."

Some years ago I heard a story about a motto hung on a wall in a halfway house established for the benefit of those recently discharged from a mental institution. The words of the motto were these, "Would you rather be right or well?" These words, addressed to recovering patients with psychological needs, essentially address the question, "Are your belief systems going to make your conditions better or worse?" The need of our egos to be right can destroy our wellness; do we want to pay that price? I am reminded of the 'prayer only' group in the Redlands University study.

Mental health is based on a principle of proportionality. Do we overreact, or maintain a sense of balance? When we view our outer world, most of us still have a need to categorize and make value judgments. It is understandable that reasonable persons will likely come to differing conclusions. When we enter into spiritual silence, we give up words, and concepts, categories, and judgments and are on equal and identical footing with others. Our ability to live with others in co-operation depends to a great extent on the sense of worth we offer to one another. This sense of worth is often expressed as one meaning of love. We *can* see our world without judgement! Our judgements may not change the world, but they will change us and destroy our sense of Peace.

If we choose to love one another, we will thereby be enabled to live together in harmony and wholeness. This is the setting in which we come to understand the meaning of being right or well. If we are so convinced that we are right that we choose to act without respect for other persons, whose sense of right may be different from ours, then we will lose the wellness that could exist in our relationship. Unfortunately, we have structured an adversarial society and have been conditioned to believe that 'winner takes all'. If our sense of personal worth is limited, we may believe that we must win at all costs. If we are in harmony with the Universe, we don't have to win; we will have discovered that it is impossible to lose.

William Folts, a close friend of mine for many years, was not much interested in sports, and being a 'Scientific American' type, once offered me his opinion that sports were basically an exercise in 'synthetic crisis'. As I reflect on his insight, I cannot help but agree that all things in the outer world to which we give anxious attention fall into his designated category.

They are all synthetic crises of our own projected invention. Soap opera consciousness, so-called professional wrestling and most, if not all, of that which we call entertainment indicate our devotion to synthetic crises. Even our news broadcasts are shifting from reporting the news to making the news; a choice for greater effect. How many 'synthetic' laws and rules have we enacted to create a security blanket by defining our rights and wrongs?

In our own nation, the impeachment trial of President Clinton taught us many of the same lessons. In the presentation before the Senate, some of the House managers were so absolute in their rightness they could not see the harm they were doing to their own political party. Being right is the need to win at any cost. Being well demands accommodation and recognition of the worth of those with whom we disagree.

Some years ago I watched a British television program broadcast on PBS concerning the partition of Palestine and the establishment of the State of Israel. The commentator highlighted the idea that this was a story about 'right against right'. Both sides in this crisis believed irrevocably that Palestine was their land. Both Jews and Arabs were convinced that their god had given them the land. It was theirs by divine right.

In a more recent PBS program on the same issue, called "The 50 Year War", it was stressed that one major problem in the negotiation of any peace settlement was that the Arabs refused to recognize a Jewish state. Because of the need to be right, several wars were fought and thousands of lives were lost. Several decades after Israel was established, and under the grace of Anwar Sadat, President of Egypt, motivated by what he called the power of love, the Arab sense of right began to crack. Anwar Sadat came to believe in the 'rights' of Israel. He later paid for this belief with his life. One might hope that Israel may one day see their wellness beyond their 'rights' to Palestine.

The Crisis in the Middle East

This past number of years, the conflict between Israel and the Palestinian people seems to be at its greatest. The United Nations and many of the world leaders have been doing their level best to mediate some kind of communication between the Palestinians and Israelis in order to put an end to the conflict and bring peace to the region.

We are in effect looking at the results of a blood feud between Semitic tribes that has lasted for thousands of years. The means to the end of the violence, terror and fighting is fully found in the teachings of Jesus of Nazareth, who most would agree is the greatest prophet that Israel has ever produced. The reason his words cannot be heard is that both groups perceive god in the nature of a divine personality, an objective being, and the absolute authority in this world of time and space.

Jewish fundamentalism has its roots in the story of the god of Abraham, Isaac and Jacob, but even earlier than this, is the story of the disparate tribes brought from Egypt through the wilderness and formed into the sons of Jacob. These tribes had several primitive concepts of god based primarily on the geographical region from which they came. Principal of these, for our chronicle, is the war god Yahweh, who was perceived as the military power behind the armies of Israel. One must understand that initially the god Yahweh was not considered as a universal deity but much more simply as a tribal deity, who had a distinct relationship and covenant with the Jewish people. In the early history of the Jewish religion, Yahweh was conceived as a god stronger and more powerful than any of the other gods of the nations that surrounded Israel. In the so-called conquest of Canaan, the watchword of the people was "Choose you this day who you shall serve, as for me and my house we will serve Yahweh". Israel made their choice for a nationalistic, militaristic god, and this god chose them as his people.

From the beginning, this god is judgmental and capricious. According to the acceptability of their offerings, Yahweh judged harshly the first children of Adam and Eve, Cain and Abel. Abel's offering of flesh as a hunter or herdsman honored the tradition of nomadic people, but Cain was a farmer and gatherer and his vegetables were not perceived as a suitable offering. Sacrifice demands a life and vegetables were not perceived as being alive. This plain distinction is the source of the concept of blood sacrifice and the statement that without the shedding of blood there is no remission of sin. At the time the story was written, it may be that the priests of the day were much happier to eat the meat from offerings rather than bake bread from offered grains. The priests did not long favor burnt offerings.

By the time of Jesus of Nazareth, Jewish religion had settled into the practice in Jerusalem of blood offerings brought before god by the established priesthood of the temple. One must remember the words of Jesus, "My father's house is a house of prayer, but you have made it a den of thieves." Many of the Jews of Jesus' time in Palestine perceived themselves to be 'god's chosen people' and sought for a political/military messiah, though a greater number of Jews lived in Alexandria, Egypt, than in Palestine.

In order to understand the wedge driven between the people of Israel and their greatest prophet, it is necessary to understand the roots of the early Jesus Movement. Because Yahweh was a military leader for the Jews and because they were under the yoke of Roman occupation, the Jews looked for a military savior to appear and overthrow the yoke of Rome. Jesus did not perform this role; he taught the necessity of discovering an inner spiritual kingdom, open and available to all without external priests and ritual. The Gnostics, who seemed to understand the teachings of Jesus, did not survive the upheaval between themselves and those in the early Jesus movement who perceived the death of Jesus as fulfilling the Jewish concept of sacrifice. This also resulted in a belated wish for the return of Jesus as a political Messiah. These perceptions were totally unacceptable to Jewish theology. In the midst of these perplexities, there was also a need for early western church leaders to align in political conformity with the Roman Empire.

Many Jews who were Roman citizens and within the western Jesus Movement enraged the Palestinian Jews by refusing to become part of any revolt against the Roman occupation.

To Jesus, god was no longer a personality or objective being; god was the principle of love without judgment and condemnation. The best way that this god could be experienced was in learning to let go of the past, its judgments and grievances. There were no chosen people, there was no objective personality god, the energizing reality of the universe was intelligence, purpose and love available to all beings equally.

What we now know of the Gnostic teachers of the first century is that they at least had a beginning grasp of what Jesus was trying to say. Women were equal, the nations were equal and god was no respecter of persons. Unfortunately, the political ravages of the church's identification with the Roman Empire all but destroyed this witness to the teachings of Jesus in its emphasis on substitutionary atonement and church hierarchy based on the model of the Roman Empire.

In the current Palestinian situation, one can understand that Jewish Fundamentalists, responsible for the assassination of the peace seeking Prime Minister Yitzhak Rabin, now back a most suppressive mind-set toward the Palestinians. There seems presently to be no forgiveness for the past and no accommodation for a Palestinian homeland in the territory of the chosen people. Jewish fundamentalism seems to have no place in its theology for forgiveness of ancient wrongs. Rather, the grievances of the Holocaust are kept alive, with no attempt to let go of the past in forgiveness.

From a psychological perspective, the fundamentalist's fear of the annihilation of Israel by the Muslim world appears to be a projection, based upon the mirror of their own desires for the annihilation of Palestinians from the West Bank of the Promised Land, which they call Samarian Judea.

The Israelis have occupied Palestine for over fifty years. Except for the witness of Anwar Sadat, little has been accomplished in healing this ancient enmity. The United States, in its military support of Israel, has a minimal awareness of the anger we have provoked among Arab countries. Instead of seeking to understand the rationale for the terrorism of September 11, 2001, we have heightened the conflict by our need to seek an eye for an eye.

Did tribal gods give Palestine to the Jews or to the Arabs? Both sides believe that their actions are based on a righteous conviction that they are in the right. Wars are still fought on the basis of such beliefs.

Healing judgement at this point is the recognition that both sides of this issue are filled with the fear of annihilation by the other. There is very little trust and a great deal of anger. Psychologically and karmatically they have created for themselves a kill or be killed situation. Recently I was asked, "Whose side are you on?" I was flabbergasted by the question, and after seeking my center, replied, "The side of humanity." The world is full of such conflicts and we can help most by realizing the worth of the persons on both sides of the conflict. There is a better way than war!

Another illustration of the need to be right, thereby destroying wellness, is in regard to our abortion clinic disasters. The most difficult issues to deal with, social or otherwise, are those in which *right* is opposed to *right*. Concepts and belief systems are the criteria we use in making judgments and taking action. The present conservative traditional theological systems of American Christians, both Roman Catholic and Protestant Fundamentalist, are based on the belief that a human soul or entity is either created or joined to the body by God at the moment of conception. Some Roman Catholic thinkers believe that the entity is from a treasury of souls created at the time of Adam who fell from divine grace along with him.

Having accepted the belief that God has somehow entered into the act of conception in the creation or attachment of a new soul, it follows logically, that to abort a fetus after this divine act has taken place, is to frustrate the purpose of God. The basic question of when a fetus becomes human in these systems is already settled quite simply and completely. In this view, the destruction of this life becomes the moral equivalent of murder. Some of these thinkers seem to have less difficulty in authorizing society to take the lives of adult souls in the form of war or capital punishment. Some do allow abortion to save the life of the mother.

The humanist non-theological group represents another belief system not quite so coherent in structure. From this standpoint one attempts to derive logic from the medical field with arguments about when a fetus becomes viable. In this system of ethics, the fetus is a living organism, but then so are the ovum and sperm. If one is concerned about the potential of the creation of a human entity, then one must consider the issue of the innumerable sperm and egg cells, living organisms that are frustrated in their purpose and die never joining in the act of conception.

Conception in this view is not necessarily the beginning of a human life, but rather the continuing of the potential for human life. It is at this point where the conservative theologians and the humanists take issue on such questions as fertilization outside the womb with the inherent possibilities of the risk of destruction to the fetus.

Another theological position quite common in Eastern religion and with growing acceptance in the west, is the belief that persons are not created at the time of birth but pre-exist that experience, and indeed are spiritual beings with a life from God that is not only eternal on the time line of the future but on that of the past as well. This theological position allows one to believe that the soul does not derive from the act of human conception, and its being is not dependent upon a material body. From this belief system, it is possible to derive a moral imperative to certify that the circumstances of the body are conducive to the well being of the entity that will enter.

The questions asked from this theological belief, have not to do with the possible frustration of the will of God in the aborting of a fetus but rather, as to whether or not the circumstances of the birth of the infant will provide the best means for the soul to enter and accomplish its goals.

With these contrasting religious attitudes toward the morality of conception and birth, it should be clear that although we may be conditioned to favor one or other alternate, no one is capable of producing hard, clear cut evidence as to which position is true. In a society which affirms the freedom of the individual conscience, and affirms the separation of religion from state, such a decision, as to which belief system if any, one should hold, ought best be left to each person.

'Right to Life' would hardly tolerate a decision of the state based upon a theology that accepts the moral responsibility to provide the best circumstances of birth for a pre-existent entity to enter. In such a state, abortion could become mandatory for any circumstance deemed by law to be inappropriate for an optimum life. Yet this would clearly be the moral outcome if the state were to insist that this particular view was the 'truth', and that every citizen should be bound by it.

In a pluralistic democracy, such decisions are best left to individuals, less clearly to religious institutions or movements, and never to government. One person's testimony of belief should not by law or regulation become the test of another person's morality.

Prior to Roe vs. Wade the common Protestant perception of the beginning of human life was the belief that human life began with birth.

In 1923, my mother Fannie Fandt gave birth to a son, Warren John. According to her, the baby lived only three or four hours. When she sought to find a minister to conduct a Protestant funeral service, several refused. Their refusals were based on a belief that the baby had not actually breathed and therefore in their judgment had never been alive. Because these clergy did not believe my mother, they considered the infant stillborn and refused a Christian funeral. My mother was finally able to find a woman minister who conducted a burial service.

This popular theological premise of the day was based on the story in Genesis (2:7) that god formed Adam from the dust of the earth, and Adam became a living soul only when god breathed Life into Adam's nostrils. Further support for this earlier theological stance is that while Roman Catholic nurses were instructed to baptize any fetus in a spontaneous abortion, to my knowledge, the protestant church has never had a funeral ritual for a miscarriage.

I recall that in the mid 90's a 'right to life' funeral director unsuccessfully took the State of Florida to court, when his wife had a spontaneous abortion, trying to get a death certificate for the fetus. I assume that in general, states do not offer a death certificate when no birth certificate has been awarded. It would appear that legal tradition also follows the rule, "No breath – No life".

In human reproductive cell division, it is a biological fact that human ovum and sperm have been continuously alive through parental succession for thousands upon thousands of years. Even before union in conception these cells are alive, although I know of no one who argues that they are "human life". The Roman Catholic tradition that human life begins with conception has a certain logic, which also helps explain their position on birth control. The position of Protestants earlier in the last century that life begins with breath is still held, though perhaps unconsciously, by mainline Protestant churches today and is also logical. Some medical people support the idea that life begins in the second trimester of gestation, a process referred to as quickening.

The psychic Edgar Cayce, who accepting a concept of reincarnation, believed that in some cases the soul of the "entity" hovered near newborn infants, sometimes for days, deciding whether or not to make a connection, puts another less common position forth. Add to these considerations, the almost humorous controversies of divorced couples, over ownership of frozen embryos, held in deep freeze for future uterine implantation; with the implied question of "murder" if the embryos are abandoned.

In the matter of religious freedom, "The testimony of one person's faith should never be made a test of another person's faith." It is my position, that because none of these points of view can be proved to be true, it is not the prerogative of the state to legislate the correctness of any of them.

Although each of these positions holds certain logic in reference to its particular framework, I believe that with one exception, none of these positions are supported by hard evidence. There is no way to know when human 'life' begins. It is simply a matter of which of these religious systems, or others, one supports.

The possible exception occurs when one combines the logical concerns of the discussion of human cloning with concepts regarding abortion. Cloning is the duplication of substitute cellular material when introduced into a same species fertilized ovum. Removing nuclear material from an intestinal cell of an adult frog and then substituting it for the nucleus of an ovum in a different adult frog was carried out in early experiments. The result was a perfect replication of the donor frog. Such experiments have been duplicated in higher primates such as "Dolly", a female sheep.

A great deal of controversy has arisen in regard to the possibilities of human cloning. I am reminded of the movie, "The Boys from Brazil", which was based on the idea of clones from cells of Adolph Hitler. There was also a comedy by Woody Allen based on efforts to replicate an assassinated leader from cells in his nose, the only surviving body part.

The Right-to-Life movement seems to have convinced many politicians that not only physical life but personhood as well, begins at conception.

The issue seems to revolve around confusion in regard to stem cell research and the need for therapeutic cloning in order to provide a new therapy for cell systems that have broken down. Stem cells have not yet been programmed to become part of a unique cellular structure and are free to follow any branch of their genetic code (DNA).

The human embryo at the stem cell stage is not yet a person according to the biological evidence of human cloning as practiced by Mother Nature. The indisputable, simple fact is that nature has been cloning humans for countless millennia. We call these clones, identical twins. Even though twins come from the same fertilized ovum, with identical human bodies, twins do not have identical personalities or psychological characteristics. I suppose it would not create a religious controversy to suggest that they also have separate souls.

In fact, I am a grandfather of identical twin boys, and their parents would make no argument that regarding personality they have as many differences as night and day. I suggest that this puts a considerable crimp in the argument that human life begins at conception. The life of a physical body; Yes, but the personhood of an individual; No! It is evident that there is much more to the formation of a human being, extending far beyond the union of sperm and egg.

Perhaps there is yet more to be argued for the Protestant theology of a century ago, when Protestant theologians believed that god breathed into a newborn baby the "Breath of Life".

The healing judgement understands the sincerity of those who may hold radically different ideas. Most 'Right to Life' people I have been in touch with seem to have a paradigm of a god who can't recover a soul from a physical abortion. I can't explain why, but it seems to be where they are coming from. Nothing real can be threatened; their god is too small.

When thinking about god, we need to understand some of the difficulties inherent in the concept of a personal god. In doing this, we are faced with ideas both about the immanence and transcendence of god. In the awareness of god's immanence we are known in complete personal awareness of our being, whereas perceiving god as an object or as a personality belittles the transcendence of god.

A personal god who functions rather like a personal secretary is a useful concept only when god is needed for status or called on in desperation; but the function of Spirit can be best understood in the sense of god as Impersonal Principle. Perhaps it is helpful when we say that god is not a personality; to remember that Principle goes far beyond personality and has profound personal effect upon our lives. With our human limitations, talking to god as one who hears and responds may have some childish aberrations, but it can also reflect a childlike quality.

Is prayer our being able to control god to accomplish our desires and plans? Or is prayer rather, our willingness to allow spirit to work its plan through us? When we talk to the Universe our prayer is not conforming to an external; it is co-operating with an internal. As the inner, so is the outer; Inner the cause – Outer the effect. The nature of prayer is not making requests to an objectified, manifested god, but rather, attuning to the Unmanifest Spiritual Force of the Real. Attuning is a matter of attitude and feeling. In effective prayer, there is no god withholding grace, no god to persuade or to inform. Yet even without an objective and external god, our words and attitudes do act as a declaration of intent, which is recognized by the inner Spirit. Better that the effective Prayer of the heart also is a meaningful Prayer of the mind. A less meaningful Prayer may still be an effective Prayer, for the intent of the heart is the source of its effectiveness.

Terrorists such as Osama Bin Laden justify the murder of thousands of innocents in their need to be right. The 'rightness' of terrorists is a malignant form of madness, one day to be swallowed up in wellness.

I expect that it is in the nature of our adversarial propensity that we are led to fight wars of 'right against right'. I have come to believe that almost all conflict is 'right against right'. War is uncivilized behavior. That is why the Sages of the world have always said that the solution must be in loving one another. It is the inherent nature of the space/time continuum to categorize all material objects. The need to catalog ideas and concepts follows automatically for the space/time mind. Our adversarial approach conditions us to many pairs of opposites, including: Right – Wrong, Good – Bad, Well – Sick, Pure – Adulterated, Whole – Divided, Healthy – Diseased, Saved – Lost, Holy – Evil, One – Many, Union – Separation, Justified – Condemned, Self – Other. The list could go on indefinitely.

Our belief in the material god Mammon, allows us to go to war: nation against nation, clan against clan and even brother against brother. To let go of the world is not giving something up as loss, nor is it an act leading to poverty. It is letting go of attachment and insecurity. In non-attachment we are free, for we need not deal in possession or loss.

I am saddened when our government attempts to justify pre-emptive attack upon other nations, for whatever reason. A pre-emptive strike is not self-defense, it is analogous to premeditated murder.

We argue that others may develop an atomic bomb, in total disregard of the fact that for more than fifty years no nation has dared to use one in war because it would be total destruction for the land of the aggressor.

Perhaps there is still an opportunity to hear the words of the Prince of Peace in regard to the futility of following the law of an eye for an eye. One day the nations of the world may beat their swords into plowshares. One day as a nation we may come to understand that it is better to be whole and well, rather than to be right and sick to death. Perhaps we are not yet ready to love our enemies, but just maybe, we may become willing to make an effort to understand them.

Unfortunately, Jesus' words about war are still relevant. "You have heard of wars and rumors of war, but the end is not yet". The global village has not yet found its way to peace.

Our judgments against those we consider wrong are always our justification for doing harm. As a nation we attempt to justify our motives. Obviously motivated by projected fear, we proclaimed loudly in Vietnam that we were fighting International Communism. In the Gulf war we protested just as loudly that the war had nothing to do with oil. As Shakespeare wrote, "methinks you protest too much". What consequence, when we believe that being right gives us permission to do wrong?

The judgements behind war rest upon a conditional forgiveness: a forgiveness that comes into being only after the requirements of repentance are met. Repentance as a change of the human will coupled with letting go of judgment, enables one to become aware of forgiveness, but it is not the cause of that forgiveness. Forgiveness is a given in the Reality of Spirit – the simple fact is that the reality which god expresses has not been destroyed by the madness of those who believe that they have lost god or that god has lost them. In our essence we are innocent and very holy (whole) as well.

When one realizes that the Universe holds no judgment upon us, then one understands that god has no need to forgive us. When we understand that there is no divine judgment, we realize the awareness of innocence in the experience of forgiveness. Forgiveness knows that there is no condemnation. It is true that forgiveness cannot be recognized until we give it away. To know forgiveness we must extend it unconditionally without judgment and without condemnation. Like love, from which it proceeds, it must be given before one is aware that it is possessed. Like salvation and integrated with salvation and healing, forgiveness is a given, not to be attained but to be realized.

Love is real and eternal; all forgiveness is temporal and learned through application. The quality of forgiveness does not make innocence – or loveliness – but it does recognize the reality underneath the mad perceptions formed by judgment and separation. "Forgiveness shines on everything as one – and thus is oneness recognized at last." [160] The Tao as unmanifest cannot be intellectually known or defined, but it can be experienced. If we allow, we will know the energy, intelligence, and indeed love, inherent in the unmanifest Potentiality – in its knowing of us.

Love is the ability to see the worth of others even when our belief systems are not in agreement, for perfect love casts out fear. The freedom of the Spiritual journey always is in contrast to the demands of a materialistic society.

We still our minds and our lives. We look out on the world around us with a sense of peace. In quietness and in confidence is our strength. We come from a stillness within that recognizes and realizes the oneness of the world in which we live.

---

[160] A Course in Miracles: Workbook: page 449, 2:4

Chapter Nine—The Nature of Healing
The Energy of Life

In a discussion about healing there is the presumption of a condition needing to be healed. A problem exists to be dealt with, and there is need for change. In our culture it almost goes without saying that the words 'healed' and 'healing' are used with a primary focus on bodily ills and treatment.

We seek to move from discontent and <u>dis</u>ease to a level of contentment and ease. In the practice of medicine, therapy falls into two distinct categories, the treatment of symptoms and the healing of root problems. Physicians also separate the practice of crisis medicine from the treatment of chronic conditions. We can be rescued from chronic symptoms without being healed of the problem. Treatments may even become masks that hide the cause of the problem. In a religious connotation this would be similar to the traditional sense of being saved, as contrasted with being healed.

I recall the first time a medical doctor told me that my blood pressure was elevated. He suggested that I was suffering from essential hypertension. Hypertension, I understood as referring to high blood pressure, but I had to ask what the word 'essential' meant in that context. He told me that medicine used the word 'essential' to indicate that they had no idea of the cause; the point being that there could be multiple reasons for elevated pressure, not the least of which was 'white coat hypertension' or simply being made anxious by the act of having one's blood pressure taken.

The subject of healing raises the question of levels of healing and levels of awareness. I can think of at least three levels to consider. It is convenient to use the categories of spirit, mind, and body. The basic level of understanding is that, at the level of Spirit nothing needs to be healed. At the physical and mental levels is where we feel the afflictions of the body.

We live in a material world, and part of that milieu is our physical body. At the most basic level, physical healing is using means to alleviate pain, injury or disease. We can massage a sore muscle, set a broken bone, suggest a better diet, or prescribe medication. If we feel pain as the result of a sliver in our finger, very few would raise metaphysical questions about the illusory nature of matter. No long debate is needed in regard to an obvious answer. The proper solution is simply pulling it out. Few would consider meditating to cause the sliver to levitate out of one's finger. Some might argue the possibility, but no one would consider it an appropriate course. We may understand that matter and time are illusions of mind; but material action at this level would not be questioned as an appropriate choice. I believe that the evidence for existence of viruses and bacteria is overwhelming. The deadly harm of certain poisons on the body cannot be denied. Yet the efficacy of the immune system and the development of bodily immunity is an area where we still have much to learn.

If we have a rash and it itches, we soon learn that scratching is not a cure. Our culture knows of unguents, salves, creams, ointments, lotions, or other balms that we may apply to the rash for relief. We might even get a shot of cortisone, especially if the rash is the result of contact with Poison Ivy.

When we are dealing with some treatments the question becomes, with regard to possible 'placebo effect', did the treatment work because of inherent chemical effectiveness, or did it work because we believed it would? We are now dealing with the relationship of mind and body. The mind has a strong effect on the functions of our bodies. It is well to remember that the term 'placebo effect' is not an explanation; it is a label. Merely to label an effect does not mean that we understand its cause.

One fascinating aspect of the mind/body relationship is the evidence that many individuals with multiple personality disorder exhibit different allergies and medical symptoms depending upon the personality manifesting in the body at the time. There is also the intriguing religious question: in the case of multiple personalities, which person does religion need to 'save'?

This leads us to healing's function at the level of mind and emotion. Some may regard mental and attitudinal levels as distinct but I see them as the same, for the role of belief and feeling is closely linked. Mind involves both conscious mind and levels of unconscious mind. When there is a lack of harmony (a dichotomy or split), between these two aspects of mind, bodily illnesses often result. The conscious mind incorporates the level of will and choice. When the unintegrated conscious mind is at war with the unconscious, a grievous situation exists for both physical and mental health.

Glenn Clarke used the affirmation, "He will make my feet like hinds' feet, and lets me tread securely on high places"[161] to make the point of our

---

[161] II Sam. 22:34, Psalm 18:33 and Habakkuk 3:19

need to integrate the total mind. His story involves a dude ranch in the mountains where the guide was picking out mounts for the guests to ride on a saddle trip into the wilderness. One of the guests was attracted to an older, gentle and rather slow animal. The trail boss pointed out that this old plodding horse was not suitable for a trip into the hills because the horse's feet no longer tracked. The older English word hind refers to a small red deer, and the hinds' feet track. In correct tracking, the position found by the front hooves is followed exactly by the rear hooves. While the rear feet support the animal the front feet seek out a safe grip and then the hind moves its rear feet to the exact safe position determined by the front feet. Mountain sheep or goats without this ability would not survive for long. Clarke felt that the harmony between the front and rear hooves of the deer is illustrative of the need for harmony between our conscious and unconscious minds. At this mental and emotional level we can speak meaningfully of harmony and order. The biblical affirmation includes the additional meaning that hinds' feet open the dimensions of spiritual heights.

Hypnosis also demonstrates that the conscious mind has the ability to effect, and the unconscious mind, through conscious suggestion, is thereby affected. The conscious mind can take all kinds of varied input and with inductive reasoning construct a scenario. The unconscious mind will accept the scenario and with deductive reasoning, fill out all the details. The unconscious has total recall of events, feelings, and judgments introduced into its experience. A skillful guide can use the power of hypnotic suggestion to uncover conflicts not ordinarily allowed into conscious awareness. The conscious mind may suppress and forget; but the unconscious mind has absolute recall.

A classic story of mind/body relationship told by Sigmund Freud illustrates the results of inner unconscious conflict. The case was about a paralyzed woman who was confined to a wheelchair. By using hypnosis, Freud was able to connect her paralysis to the death of her sister. This woman's legs were paralyzed and she could not walk; but under the hypnotic state she could accept the suggestion to walk. There seemed to be no physical reason for her condition. Her conscious awareness offered no clue to a solution. But; the patient had been secretly in love with her brother-in-law. When her sister died, possibilities opened for the patient to fulfill her secret desires. However, there was a significant conflict between her grief at the loss of her sister and the secret desire that allowed her, in some sense, to be glad her sister had died. She could not integrate the resultant grief, gladness, and guilt, and so, as a solution to her guilt and anxiety her body translated the unconscious conflict into paralysis. Because she was now confined to her wheelchair, she no longer believed that marriage to her brother-in-law was a possibility. As long as she was paralyzed, this put her irresolvable conflict on hold. Emotionally, she could not afford to walk, so as not to act on her desires toward her brother-in-law. This was a tragic way to handle the conflict of guilt and desire. Fortunately, if I remember correctly, Freud was able to bring this conflict to her conscious mind and help her to resolve it. When it comes to conflicts in the human psyche, sex is one area where they abound. Freud seemed to think it was the major area of conflict with his patients. The attitudes and judgments of his city and generation played a large role in the mental problems of his patients.

Marlo Morgan, in her walkabout experience, tells the story of how the 'real people', her aboriginal tribe, demonstrated to her their approach to physical healing.[162] A member of the tribe, while walking on the edge of an embankment, fell about twenty feet onto some rocks and suffered a severe compound fracture of his leg. The bone between his ankle and knee was sticking out about two inches. A tourniquet was immediately applied to his upper leg. A healer made passes with his hands alongside the leg near the break. Another healer explained that the passes were made as a means of reconnecting the former pattern of the healthy leg. They were jogging the memory of the bone into acknowledging the true nature of its healthy state. They talked to the bone to remove the shock of its injury. The healers gathered around the injured person and began to sing a chant for healing. At the height of their song, they gave a shout and the broken bone slipped back into the hole of the leg from whence it came; the leg was set. When I had an opportunity to question her about the story, Dr. Morgan was clear that she could not tell if they sang the leg bone into place or physically pulled it into alignment. The song had to do with focus on the opportunity for the bone to demonstrate its ability to fuse in renewed strength. Dr. Morgan did say that they applied sticky tar made of congealed menstrual blood to the wound. After gluing the jagged edges of the wound together, they covered the whole area of the trauma with the same tar. The result of the incident is that the next day the man was up and walking as if nothing had ever happened to his leg. Within five days, the tar compound fell off, leaving only thin scar lines.

It was not long after first reading this story in her book that I noticed an article in a magazine, telling about recent research having developed glue made as a byproduct of blood. This glue was designed to fasten together the edges of flesh wounds. Modern 'materia medica' was only a few thousand years behind this aboriginal tribe.

---

[162] Mutant Message, Marlo Morgan: Chapter 13 – Healing

This 'Walkabout' story is a good transitional account, for it contains aspects of spirit, mind and body. The tribe demonstrated a cooperative relationship between physical, attitudinal and spiritual healing. One does not get much more 'physical' than a compound fracture of a leg and the use of a compound of 'blood-glue' to fasten the edges of the wound back together. The healers chanted and sang in a positive manner to the bone in order to instruct it as to the opportunity it had to demonstrate healing and effectively become stronger than it was before the break. The story also establishes the value of community support for the patient and the need to express their collective trust in the Universe of Goodness.

The level of spirit is oneness, where there is no polarity, no division, and no separation. There is nothing at this level to be healed; yet this level is a profound source for healing, and one might even say the only source for real healing. Healing at this level consists of pure potentiality and perfect intent, or love. Spirit experienced as Peace and Trust can enable a trust focused upon attitudes and emotions. Spirit is the Intent and Love that can energize a level of perfect order and harmony within our mind and establish a balance between the conscious and unconscious mind.

Treatment at the physical level may have no effect on other levels, but it was by a combined mental and physical technique of hypnotic suggestion that Freud was introduced to his patient's conflict at the mental level. From the other direction, it can be argued that it was the crippling philosophy of a repressive culture and its expectations that created the guilt at the heart of his patient's problem. There is no question that conflict at the unconscious level can cause problems at the physical level.

The attitude we project on our social environment has profound effect on the harmony existing between our unconscious and conscious minds. The mixed messages we receive and accept from authority create these conflicts. Parents tell us to do one thing on a particular occasion, and then at a different time give us contradictory instructions.

When we train a pet we know better than to give contradictory commands. When we train a dog, if one day we scream at it for getting on the living room sofa, and the next day invite it to lie beside us sitting on the very same couch, conflict will result. If one day we feed scraps from the table, and the next day order it from the dining area and command it to stay out while the family is eating; after a lifetime of such mixed messages the dog will end up being neurotic.

How many children with neurotic or alcoholic parents end up with similar conflicts? Old Testament wisdom states that the sins of the fathers are visited upon the children, to the third and fourth generation. What do we present to our children? Are they exposed to a god of Love and Beauty that we are jealous to pursue, or are they exposed to a god of retribution that we anxiously strive to escape? When fear predominates, where is our bliss?

Is god a plus or minus in the celebration of life? In god's presence, do we feel warmth and security, or are we cold and frightened by the harsh reality of our shortcomings? Will god help us overcome adversity, or place it in our path? When sadness occurs, is god a sense of comfort or is god perceived as giving us a test? Our religious outlook and spiritual dimension have a profound effect on our health.

If we can integrate Jesus' message of discovering the realm of god within us, it will become evident that the liberty and cohesiveness of this inner awareness will have profound effect on our mental attitudes. Our attitudes and beliefs will influence not only our physical bodies but our social circumstances as well. This premise is after all the basic thesis of this book.

My experience with an aging body is that after a time, the 'get up and go' doesn't get up to go as quickly as it once did. The transmission has begun to fail, the gears don't always mesh well, and sometimes they just grind and growl. Ed Nelson, father of my wife Lillian, a wonderful old gentleman in his nineties, used to say, "The parts are wearing out."

When I was younger my experience with Shingles (a virus related to childhood Chicken Pox) had always been mild and short-lived. As is common among older people, I have had a long time bout with the neuralgia of Shingles. The blisters have long gone, but the pain along the nerve path has lingered for several years. But as experience shows, wrinkles are also a common sign of age, and should we make an effort to erase them, as well?

In regard to the continuing pain, some concepts of karma suggest that there is a causal connection between the pain I feel, and my beliefs and or mental attitude. The argument is that if I would just change my thinking, the pain would be healed.

There is no question that there are lessons we learn from all our experiences. But, to make the accusation, that we are individually responsible for all our pain and suffering, is not very helpful. This belief can produce a morbid sense of undeserved guilt. All things are lessons to be learned, but not all things are a result of spiritual karma. To reiterate the comment of Elia Wise, "People are interpreting their power as creators to include responsibility for illnesses that have been genetically programmed through countless generations. Fueled by the human inclination toward guilt, this misconception is difficult to unravel."

Some like to quote the phrase, "There are no accidents." Of course, every effect has a cause; but, to insist that there is a spiritual connection, every time we stub a toe or hammer a finger, is somewhat tedious.

What did Jesus mean, when he spoke of those eighteen persons on whom the Tower of Siloam fell? "Do you think that they were worse offenders than all others living in Jerusalem?" Rain falls equally on the just and the unjust. At times, rain falls beneficially and at times in uncontrolled torrents; is god meting out justice? I believe there are material laws existing in the space/time world that operate apart from the spiritual law of karma.

When we catch a cold; is this necessarily a reflection of spiritual imperfection? I think not! The whole tenor of the book of Job is that the trials of this just man were not a reflection on his relationship to god. Disasters need not be understood as acts of god.

Were all who died in the terrorist attack of 09/11/01, suffering some type of spiritual, karmic retribution? Would anyone argue that those killed at Hiroshima and Nagasaki died justly as a result of karmic debt? I hope not! The so-called collateral damage of saturation bombing is not accidental; it is a direct result of war and military aggression.

It may be that there is a level of national or cultural karma that individuals get caught up by. When we come into this life experience of space/time there are certain limitations and risks involved. Synchronicity, as Karl Jung understood it, often occurs in our relationships, after all, at the level of reality our minds are joined, and there is only one son of god. Certainly, we could agree that our degree of mental alertness, and a developed spiritual awareness, would give us an advantage in coping with life. But inevitably, we will leave this life by means of bodily death. Death is never an accident; it is always a result of cause.

I believe that as a direct consequence of bodily experience, we will experience unavoidable pain. This does not suggest that we do not bring upon ourselves, a great deal of needless suffering. Pain and suffering are not the same. Physical pain is an unpleasant physical stimulus. The question of the nature of suffering (unsatisfactoriness) is a keystone to the Buddhist understanding of life. From the Four Noble Truths: "All suffering is caused by ignorance of reality, and the craving, attachment, and grasping that result. Overcoming ignorance and attachment can end suffering."

Karma is not a physical space/time law; it deals with our relationships at the level of Spirit; it can be negative or positive in its effect. Atonement is the undoing of the unreal. Pain is a space/time occurrence in the unreal, we meet with an ability to cope. We meet suffering with healing; a change of attitude and spirit.

Physical problems may or may not be cured, but spiritual suffering must be healed. A major problem results, when negative karma is directed toward outer appearance and 'doing', instead of inner reality and 'being'. Thus, we feel responsible to change behavior, rather than belief. Too often, we pray, "Help me to change the things I cannot accept."

When it comes to the question of pain and suffering, we need to be able to tell one from the other. I am reminded of the prayer of Reinhold Niebuhr often-used in 'Twelve Step' programs:

"God grant me
Serenity to accept the things I cannot change,
Courage to change the things I can,
And wisdom to know the difference."

When we label physical events 'karmic consequence' we see effect but are often unable to understand the cause. In short, we sometimes try to correct an unknown karmic cause when in fact no karma is involved. We need to undo the space/time illusion. Rather than function in the unreal, we need to choose the real and allow undoing with effortless accomplishment, allowing the 'Father within' to correct the unreal.

For me, the hardest thing about self-healing is understanding that the Self is already whole. When we ask for outside help we inadvertently split our minds from the Whole. We need to affirm the wholeness of our lives, and stop trying to fix them with conscious control.

In a strict sense god does not heal us. As long as we construct an *us* apart from the Whole, we have a problem. The separated us we want to heal has become an illusion. At an absolute level god does not heal us; god is the wholeness that we are. As long as we construct an us, apart from the Whole, we have preordained a problem. Total healing is inherent in the wholeness of realizing, or making real, the fact that there is no separated us. Because our physical bodies have root in god's Spirit, when we trust that Spirit, we can have confidence that bodily needs will be taken care of. Seek first the kingdom and these things will be added.[163] The whole Self is our enlightenment. The very act of asking god for help implies that god is other, and that we are not in touch in the absolute supply of All-That-Is.

The self may try to be enlightened, but the personal self cannot be enlightened. In this sense the process of enlightenment is identical with the rationale for spiritual healing. The separated self cannot be enlightened or healed, whereas the true Self already is. When the separation is dissolved, the whole Self replaces it. When the conscious mind is integrated with the absolute mind of the superconscious, the resulting harmony cannot help but be reflected in the physical body.

Long ago and yet to be, in space/time illusion, are the same. Perceived potential does not really exist in the future, but in the now of the real. Alpha and Omega are Real Only in the Now! We may perceive Source as past or future, but reality is now. Returning to love is not a result of having

---

[163] Matthew 6:33

wandered away; it is experiencing what now Is; beyond the space/time of what will be. Affirmations for health and healing must seek to return to the potential of what will be. Return to the future. Return to love, health and wholeness. Realize the reign of Perfect Being within you.

At present we are to a large degree identified with our physical bodies. We have a need to eat, sleep, and take care of physical need. We need to deal with the physical level, and although we can teach and believe that all temporal things are illusions in their form, we must be able to recognize that the god/mind or Logos energizes those temporal forms. We have mentioned before the sliding scale of focus between the transcendental Self and the temporal self. A large part of our spiritual growth involves coming to terms with the fact that we must experience two levels of awareness: the absolute level of the reality of god and the temporal level of space/time existence. We need to integrate this apparent functional dualism of spirit and flesh.

The metaphysical community has struggled to relate these two levels. We have the ability or freedom to misuse that part of the One Mind that is the center of our being. I believe that divine mind underlies the whole physical space/time universe. This is the level of the world's reality; not its form, as we have mentioned before.

God has given humankind a mind so powerful that we can use it either to extend reality or to make illusions. God does not intervene in our use of that mind because to do so would deny the power god has given it. The concept of the non-intervention of god applies to healing as well. If we have made blocks to the awareness of god's presence, god's purpose does not allow god to remove them. Edgar Cayce once made the comment that even god can not heal a man who does not want to be healed.

I am reminded of the excellent film "Resurrection", with Ellen Burstyn, who plays the role of a healer. She comments on one occasion about the complexities involved when a healing does not occur. The scene is a tent where people have gathered to experience her healing touch. She speaks to the family of a lady she could not heal and says, "I'm sorry, best you take her home now." When they leave, her grandmother asks, "Couldn't you help her?" She replies, "Well, Grandma Pearl, some people need their sickness to get love and attention; some people need it to get those things. It's not up to me to judge the right or wrong of it."

For some people there is a payoff in illness and disease. It may have been a device used early on to get attention, and then habit took over. One aspect about illness that seems to resist healing is the simple recognition that in the learning needs of our soul, we may have accepted limitations that are profitable for us. I have already mentioned Helen Keller, and am also reminded of the statement by Elia Wise that there is a futility in attempting to change what has been genetically programmed into our physical experience. In our entry into physical life we may well choose conditions that optimize the journey. Michael J. Fox, who suffers from Parkinson's disease, stated, "My disease is not personal". Michael demonstrates that although he is not cured, he has been profoundly healed.

The Pima Indians of the Southwest suffer from genetic obesity and Type II diabetes. In their original history they survived on cactus buttons, roots and very small fish from the Pima River. The Pima River was dammed and the tribe moved to a reservation. Their diet changed to that of the average American, fast foods etc. As a result of their genetic programming they still store food in their bodies, having come from a background of near starvation in their diet. Their obesity is a result of genetic proclivities faced with the provisions of the modern American culture.

The interplay of divine mind and our minds involves the relation of the various levels of mind. There are several theories or models dealing with descriptions of conscious, subconscious, unconscious, and superconscious. The psychologist Carl Jung constructed a model like a pyramid. Conscious mind was the capstone at the top. The unconscious mind in his approach is divided into several different levels below the conscious. Its upper level could be described as personal unconscious that can be taped for memories and normal patterns of behavior. Below that lies a deeper level of personal unconscious, consisting of forgotten memories from our total experience. At the base, Jung theorized a Collective Unconscious that contains racial memories and archetypes; this level is held in common by all persons. This same model could be transferred to a picture of a sphere with a surface dotted all over with individual conscious locales. Each individual consciousness would descend into the sphere like an inverted cone to deeper and deeper levels, until it finally arrived at a common nucleus. Both models agree with the metaphysical proposition that all minds are joined as one.

Roberto Assagioli, in his concept of Psychosynthesis, added to the dimension of the collective unconscious a cosmic level he called superconscious. This opened the door to the study of the field of Transpersonal Psychology. Edgar Cayce inverted these models. He visualized a spiral that began at the level of the individual's conscious mind and traveled upward in larger and larger circles until it reached the common area of god mind. The one unique facet of this model was that the ascending spiral as it completed each circle contacted the same areas of development, but at an increasing level of awareness.

Stuart Grayson, a Religious Science minister, in his book "Spiritual Healing", pictures the whole mind as a circle divided by three horizontal lines. The base he calls unconscious or Absolute, and equates it as god-mind; the middle he calls subconscious, and the top conscious awareness. Along with Thomson Jay Hudson, he sees the conscious mind as inductive and instructing the unconscious to work out its assignments deductively. His model doesn't touch all the bases of the former illustrations. He makes the point in very strong fashion that the unconscious takes instruction from our attitudes and beliefs, as well as from the archetypes of the universal unconscious, and out-pictures them into our world of experience; i.e. the inner is the cause of the outer. He also makes an excellent observation of the differences between normal impulsive and abnormal compulsive behavior, based on our integration of conscious and unconscious.

I think I would picture mind as a piece of paper divided by three vertical lines. Consciousness is on one side and Superconscious, or the Absolute on the other. The middle would be filled with vertical strata ranging from personal unconscious, to soul memories and collective racial archetypes.

What seems to be our outer experience is actually a construct of our inner attitudes and beliefs. This theory attempts to establish and explain the matrix in which disease is caused and healing takes place. If we consider personal self as the area of conscious mind and Impersonal Self as the Absolute Mind; then, we can begin to understand how our sliding scale of consciousness effects the out-picturing of our life experience.

In its simplest form the Law is, "What we sow, we reap". By exercise of the will, we determine the beliefs and attitudes we will adopt in our conscious experience. The attitudes of our conscious mind circumscribe the world around us according to the prejudice and judgments that we project upon it. But this projection is not truly an effect upon the outer world at the conscious level. The effect of our conscious attitude is instead, a projection into our own unconscious. These are the belief statements, which serve to program the deductive ability of the unconscious mind. Our *word* overwrites the *Word* of the Superconscious, and the resulting conflict is extended outward to construct our experience of the outer world. What we see is what we get; only the energy flow is from inner seeing to outer getting. Seeing what we believe and expect is the cause and the world is the effect. Believing in the inner, results in seeing in the outer.

To change the world, we must choose to change our minds and thus change our seeing. We can choose to love, we can choose to forgive, we can choose to let go of past memories; in short, we can trust the Universe and let god be god. When we do so, the inner mind that builds our world will be healed and the out picturing produced will be love, joy, and bliss; established in the quality of abundance. Our world will be healed because we have owned healing by our own holiness.

The sliding scale of conscious intent and attitude, from fear to love, moves the deductive principle of the unconscious in a range from fear to love. When the Logos or Absolute Mind is free to function as the Ideal of the subconscious, because it has received the permission and instruction of the conscious mind, the Mind out-pictures the Will of god through our will. The kingdom comes forth to our world, as it has always existed within us.

Problems with this out-picturing come about as a result of all the garbage we have constructed in our personal and racial unconsciousness; the blocks to the awareness of Love's presence. God's will is perfect at the absolute level, but we may not be wholly ready for bodily perfection. The condition we wish removed is perceived as an outer or externalized situation. We desire circumstances to be better. We feel victimized by the external situation and believe if only it could be changed, we would be better for it.

Our grievance has already shifted from what we saw as the outer source of the problem, to an inner feeling of being victimized. We have already conceived a cause and effect relationship between what we believe is victimizing cause and victimized effect. The one solid conclusion we mistakenly draw from this scenario is simply that we are not the cause and, therefore, not responsible. The cause is externalized; the effect is internalized. Whatever we perceive as the problem can in no way be pictured as our responsibility, for it now has an obvious outside cause.

I am reminded of Paul's prayer that a thorn in his flesh be removed.[164] He prayed three times that god would deliver him from what he called a messenger of the satanic, but the answer he received was, "My grace is sufficient for you, for my strength is made perfect in weakness." Scholars believe that the thorn in the flesh was poor eyesight as stated in Galatians, "See with what large letters I am writing to you with my own hand."[165]

Life experience is a lesson to be learned. Our ability to learn determines the way in which the lesson is taught. Spirit, as the Perfect Teacher, is able to use imperfect situations as perfect means. One can say that at the absolute level only the Impersonal Self is real and that the personal self is only an illusion. This is a true statement of spiritual reality, but it is not very helpful to leave it at that when dealing with an external world of space/time. The ego or personal self represents where we are when we deal with the temporal. Time provides the context of unfolding or growth. The question is not, "When are we going to die?" The real question is, "When are we

---

[164] II Corinthians 12:7-10
[165] Galatians 6:11

going to live?" In the context of discussion about near death experiences, Bernie Siegel suggested, we need rather to have a near life experience.

"Yet there is a kind of seeming death that has a different source. It does not come because of hurtful thoughts and raging anger at the universe. It merely signifies the end has come for usefulness of body functioning. And so it is discarded as a choice, as one lays by a garment now outworn. We call it death, but it is liberty. It does not come in forms that seem to be thrust down in pain upon unwilling flesh, but as a gentle welcome to release. If there has been true healing, this can be the form in which death comes when it is time to rest a while from labor gladly done and gladly ended. False healing merely makes a poor exchange of one illusion for a "nicer" one; a dream of sickness for a dream of health."[166]

Houston Smith observed a three-week Zen retreat; during the last seven days he experienced a twenty-four-hour intensive with the other monks. Without sleep, he became very upset with his experience, and when he went to speak to the Zen Master he was loaded for bear. Before he could speak, the Zen master interrupted and confronted him with a statement that neither health nor sickness are real. It is fairly easy to think of sickness as part of the illusion, and seek to overcome it with health. But, if health is illusory, then the true healing of illness is not health, but resides in the realm of the Real! Thus we understand that bodily death may become our friend.

Because what is out-pictured from the sub-conscious comes from an area where minds are joined, what is expressed into the experience of the world is a kind of consensual awareness. If our conscious expression comes from our center, from our sense of eternal being, we will move from our power and not from our fear. We can live with a positive trust of the universe.

Social behavior in the outer is a reflection of whatever social attitudes are reflected from the inner. We do not have to follow the way of madness. We can choose the attitude and way in which we view the world. If we let go of judgment and condemnation we will not reap its terrors. The instructions given to us are simple. To know love, teach love; for what we sow, we reap. It is not an external law of retribution; it is the internal Law of One. The fruit of the tree reflects its roots. It is at the root level that the energies of either war or peace are put into motion.

One hard saying of scripture makes sense at this point. "Vengeance is mine; I will repay."[167] The fact is, that the law of retribution is not an act or choice made by an external, angry god. It is simply the principle of the Law

---

[166] The Song of Prayer, Foundation For Inner Peace: page 16
[167] Romans 12:19

of One at work. What we plant into our unconscious will flower into our world of external experience. The law of god is not mocked; sow to the Spirit and reap life; sow to anger and judgment and reap destruction. The law of god takes no pleasure or pain in our foolish attitudes and acts. There is no condemnation by the principle of law but the law will work nonetheless, for we do it to ourselves.

We can take a kind of perverse pleasure in our anger and unforgiveness, feeling victimized by the situation; but the true fruit of forgiveness does not primarily benefit the forgiven; it is rather the absolute source of life to the one who forgives. We find it hard to accept the fact that what we choose to do or be, we do to ourselves.

It is true that beyond space/time we have only the Real and that the Real is based on the Unity of Spirit and Love. But space/time is a platform on which, and in which, we learn and are taught by Spirit. It is as if god/mind knows both reality and illusion and chooses to work where we are; teaching us to allow the unreal of fear and separation to be undone.

The forces of Spirit are operative in the circumstances of our lives. Spiritual reality is totally correct when it teaches us to say, "I am not a body, I am free, I am still as god created me."[168] The Holy Spirit as teacher of the Law of One arranges, through the out-picturing of our consciousness, the space/time physical circumstances in which we can best learn.

At this point in our lives, we are all in a place of out-picturing our mind structure. When we are able to choose and learn, we need but focus on the lesson that is before us to experience needed growth. As the prophet Isaiah taught, our growth is structured: for it is precept upon precept, precept upon precept, line upon line, line upon line, here a little, there a little.[169]

In truth, there are no boundaries and no levels, but by virtue of our prior choices, in practice we have established parameters that we must deal with, and within them we will learn what we must. I think we can become too focused on trying to attain the absolute level while in the body, and confuse the purpose of this particular physical experience.

Although in Spirit I am absolutely free, if I have chosen to learn the experiences that only a male body can teach; I have established space/time parameters that Spirit does not violate. I do not believe that having made these choices, I still have the option of pregnancy and childbirth available to me. Another time, another place, perhaps. I also believe that having entered into physical life, if I stay to complete the full cycle, I have bought into the

---

[168] A Course in Miracles, Workbook: Lessons 201-220
[169] Isaiah 28:10

progressive experiences of infancy, childhood, puberty, adolescence, maturity, old age, and final bodily death.

There are many that may have chosen what some might call a very restrictive bodily experience. Helen Keller, I believe, was surely such a person. Deprived of both sight and hearing, she made a remarkable use of both her mental and spiritual faculties.

We are eternal Spirit with temporary human experience; we are not human beings with temporary spiritual experience. Many questions might be raised with regard to the mentally restricted. Might not the autistic child have a greater feel for reality than the rest of us? Is the person whose intellect cannot categorize and memorize, inferior to those with greater intellect? Or, are those listed by society as the intelligentsia, the ones more to be pitied? Is it possible that persons categorized as low IQ may at the same time have a very strong intuitive identity and awareness of the whole?

We are heavenly treasures in earthen vessels.[170] Does the clay say to the potter, "Why have you made me thus?"[171] One form of prayer I remember well from Unity, "This or something better, Lord." It is understood that Spirit knows our needs better than we do. "From ancient time the living wisdom has existed, wherever god was, the living wisdom was present; the living wisdom witnesses to the reality of god." (John 1:1)

To those motivated by fear and unable to hear the words, "Love your enemy". Hear the words of this poet.

> I have felt the sway of elephant's shoulders,
> and you expect me to mount this jackass!
> Try to be serious.
>
> Mirabi[172]

---

[170] II Corinthians 4:7
[171] Romans 9:20

[172] Robert Bly – Mirabi Versions, The Enlightened Heart—Stephen Mitchell, p. 77

Letting Be!

Doing by not doing and knowing by not striving to know,
We come to understand all the things we know god is not.
We have gained by letting go.
We attain, by the recognition that there is no thing to attain.
The heart of stillness sits perfectly balanced in midst of chaos.
The prodigal son demonstrates the little willingness needed.
When we take a step towards god, god runs toward us.
We discover that god does not love; god is Love.
It is not the matter of a choice that god could make,
As if the two were separable, For god is Love.
Doing effects material change, revolution and armies.
Being effects spiritual change, enlightenment and peace.
The fallacy of doing precipitates need to understand our being.
Thus we discover that there must be a better way.
Thus we discover that there is a better way.
Finding spiritual values in the maze of materialism,
Is a difficult process,
But being born again is a process and not an end.
It is a path and will be eternal.
In our culture it is moving beyond Christianity as a religion,
To the Christ that is our Source;
It is in moving beyond religion to dynamic power,
We lose our 'God' in order to find god.
As a space/time object god has only the meaning we give it.
Such a god is an illusion of appearance;
We must look beyond to see the Reality hidden beneath.
What we believe, or think we believe,
Determines our dimension of human experience.
But we will know as we are known and we shall be like gods
For we shall see god as god is.
We are of One/Source and One expression.
When we see god face to face

George E. Fandt

Chapter Ten—Heirs of God
Epilogue

What a marvel! That a Being Colorless
Displays a hundred thousand hues, shades!
What a wonder! That a Being Void of Form
Enrobes in forms beyond all numbering!
May we behold That Being in all the hues
And in all the forms.
Thus, in the name of That Which has no name,
Yet lifts to every name an answering head,
The name of That Which is the changeless One
Amidst the changing Many,
And within Whose Oneness all this Many is confined,
May we begin our work of Peace.

Sufi Writings[173]

Recapitulation

In the past, my discipline in sermon preparation meant at the very least, the habit of allowing one seed thought each week into my consciousness. The process of listening for such insights still functions though I seldom have opportunity to preach. Perhaps that is as good a reason as any, for the desire I now feel to write.

Is this book a patchwork quilt or a seamless robe? It makes little difference, the choice is yours, and both answers are acceptable. I believe it will be helpful after so much detail to create a synopsis of the viewpoint that has been presented. If we can take the nitty-gritty of what has been said and condense it with clarity, the import of this book will be enhanced. I would

---

[173] Integral Yoga Publications, LOTUS Prayer Book

like to attempt a succinct statement of the basic and germane concepts that clearly demonstrate the issues that are at stake on the spiritual journey.

Neither society nor the church has yet accepted the message of Albert Einstein with regard to time and space. According to physicists, space/time is not real but illusory, and is therefore, interpreted from our own particular mindset and understanding of appearance.

If we accept this space/time world as reality we accept a dualistic reality; i.e. another reality beyond Spirit. When Jesus said, "You cannot serve god and Mammon", he was speaking precisely to this point. Mammon was a pagan deity representing the material world (appearance deified). I accept only the reality of Spirit, and not the dualism of two real but basically incompatible worlds. Spirit is the only reality and is in fact the energy and design that underlies this world of appearance. Because spirit energizes this world, it is paramount that we accomplish a functional but temporal dualism of matter and spirit; then walk as it were, in both worlds simultaneously.

Our Impersonal Self has identity with the reality of Spirit. Our personal self is part of the illusion of space/time, and through the power of mind, projects outward the conditions of the world in which we live. When Jesus said, "We must worship in spirit and truth" and "My kingdom is not of this world," he did not say, "My kingdom is not in this world". I believe he was trying to indicate that his reign was spiritual and that we are not to identify with what Paul called the god of this world. Our Impersonal Self in the world has the ability to see the Real World beyond illusion.

I believe those efforts to change the world of illusion from its outside are mostly acts of futility. When we attack the outer world caused by our own perceptions of judgment and condemnation, we make the dreams appear real. We are trying to change what is unreal in the first place. There is little merit in trying to change the dream. We will only wake up from the dream when we undo the unreal. By giving permission for the inner Father to do the work, we align with the dimension of Spirit, and change that occurs in the outer will be accomplished not by our personal energy but by the Father within. The Real World we thus realize, is a better place to live.

Futility in trying to change the dream also speaks to our approach to prayer. Traditional prayers addressed to grievances and concerns can be labeled 'pious worry'. Directed toward problems, they energize the problems rather than the solution, and make the unreal more real to us.

Modern-day physicists are the prophets for our society, and we must first begin with the relationship between energy and matter. To be converted from a materialist viewpoint to a spiritual one, we must first look at basic laws of matter. This presupposes some understanding of modern physics.

Since Einstein, we have come to understand that matter and energy are not separate entities. The quantum level of energy is at the root of all things. When I was in high school, the understanding we received from the teachers was simply that matter and energy were separate and immutable in their own sphere. By habit we still look at material form as the reality of the world. There is no eternal in the temporal. The apparent world is not real.

The field of science confronts us with overwhelming evidence that the energy beneath the molecular level is the underlying reality; and that outer form is simply an appearance resulting from that energy. The form that appears to our sensory awareness is an illusion. With instrumentation, science can direct us to an awareness of the existence of many kinds of energy of which our senses are unaware. The real paradigm shift that is needed is to become aware that the energy of the universe is intelligent. This primary intelligence is the basis of all forms of energy, and ultimately of all matter and form. The omnipotence, omniscience and omnipresence of traditional theology now faces understanding the concept that the source of all things, All-That-Is, is the energy and intelligence of the universe.

Albert Einstein believed and demonstrated that space/time is illusion. Modern theory holds that matter and energy have a common unnamed, unknown source allowing them to be interchangeable. The demonstrations of the atomic age leave little doubt concerning the reality of this relationship. The sages of science accept matter unequivocally as being composed of energy and space/time. The electromagnetic field, which demonstrates the materiality of both molecule and atom, consists almost entirely of space. The attempts of science to explain electrons and quarks become not only esoteric but poetic as well. The mystical quality of this research has not been lost on the participants. Along with the poets, the physicists are now attempting to express some sense of the relationship between energy and mind. Albert Einstein is exemplary among those physicists with mystical awareness. Philipp Frank quotes Einstein as follows: "The most beautiful emotion we can experience is the mystical. It is the power of all true art and science. He to whom this emotion is a stranger, who can no longer wonder and stand rapt in awe, is as good as dead. To know that what is impenetrable to us really exists, manifesting itself as the highest wisdom and the most radiant beauty, which our dull faculties can comprehend only in their most primitive forms – this knowledge, this feeling, is at the center of true religiousness. In this sense, and in this sense only, I belong to the rank of devoutly religious men."[174]

Metaphysicians and philosophers have tried to explain to us that the world we perceive is an interpretation based upon the meaning or meanings

---

[174] Einstein: His Life and Times, Philipp Frank

we project upon it. The exterior world that we perceive is not the objective material reality that we believe it to be. Our perceptions are not caused by what is out there, but are rather a result of our own beliefs. At the heart of the space/time illusion is the lack of awareness that exterior perception is not cause, but effect.

When we come to understand that our apparent objective material world consists mostly of space, and that its reality, in essence, is energy, we can begin to see more clearly the relationship of that energy and Mind. The physicist Sir James Jeans suggested that at this level the universe might best be understood as a thought.

The sages of the world have taught that this knowledge of all things can be experienced only in a spiritual dimension. Mind and spirit are the source and source is not material appearance.

Spiritual reality cannot be objectified: it is invisible, timeless, and spaceless. The nonobjective source of All-That-Is can be referenced as the Spirit of the universe, the Silence of the beyond, Infinite Mind, or if one would prefer, simply as god. The god of reality is not an object, or thing, but the invisible energy and intelligence of All-That-Is. As Source, god is the only Power, Mind, or Presence in the Universe.

To understand this reality of spirit, we must let go of our death grip on outer material reality. We must experience a transformation of our minds and our beliefs so that we may let go of our conviction that the space/time world is real. The world the body sees is not real.

Jesus emphasized that we cannot serve two masters. The principle of coherence demands that we make a choice. In short, Jesus tried to teach us that we must choose between the perception of the outer material world as our god, or an awareness or knowledge of the inner Spirit that energizes both the world and ourselves. We cannot commit to space/time as reality, and at the same time experience Spirit. If we are willing to commit to Spirit, then we will understand that time and space hold only the meaning we choose to give them; and we will be aware that what we see 'out there', is our own meaning projected 'out there'. If we accept the inner reign of god, what is 'out there' will take care of itself. "Seek first the kingdom and these things will be added." To put it simply, there is no eternal to be found within the temporal. The temporal world is not real.

It is the Spirit that contains the truth of who we are; yet, it is not as if the ocean of spirit absorbs and destroys the dewdrop, it is the dewdrop that absorbs the ocean and finds its true reality therein. The dewdrop represents the Impersonal Self.

The means by which we align with the spiritual *inner,* and let go of our allegiance to the material *outer,* is simply the recognition that the material outer is an illusion. Undoing material primacy dissolves the hold that the outer has over us. The sense of domination and fear that we allow the outer world to have, is constructed by the judgments that we pronounce upon it. Our judgments make a temporal world seem to be real for us. They are *our* judgments, and we must dissolve them with *our* forgiveness. In judging the world, we miss our spiritual path.

God as Principle does not intervene in our use of the power of god's mind. Whether we make illusions, or creatively extend reality, we do so with god/mind, in which we live and move and have our Being.[175] The illusions we make are only appearances and have no substance; our creations are extensions of the one reality and are conserved in spirit.

Jesus made radical statements about what those who were committed to the inner invisible world would come to know. "You shall know the truth, and the truth shall make you free."[176] The clarity of Jesus' teaching in the New Testament is nearly smothered by the theology surrounding him.

In the early development of the Jesus movement, some writers relegated Jesus to the role of the one who was sent to meet the sacrificial need in the prevailing Jewish concept of god. This religion about Jesus cast him in the unique and separated role of a god. This divisive role had profound effect on how his teachings and sayings were later viewed. Jesus' teachings about the experience of the inner kingdom were unfortunately not believed to be universal in their application, and instead were restricted to what the early church perceived as his uniqueness.

'I am' statements in the gospel of John and many Gnostic teachings about the inner kingdom are perceived negatively by many of today's biblical scholars as part of a Trinitarian formula foisted upon Jesus by the early western church, in the attempt to prove his divinity. The actual mystical experiences of Jesus are treated as perceptions about the divine Jesus or Christ. The term 'Christ' lost its universal quality as an invisible anointing available to all – indeed, not only available but absolutely mandatory, if one is to achieve the joy, peace, and freedom that Jesus demonstrated.

As Houston Smith pointed out, the Jesus Seminar and the Scholars Version translation missed the point of the 'I am' statements of John's gospel. They are opposed to the traditional interpretations of Jesus' role. They negatively perceive the 'I am' statements as being early church additions designed to make Jesus appear unique. The scholars are thereby limited in understanding Jesus' attempt to teach a universal mystical truth.

---

[175] Acts 17:28
[176] John 8:32

In their translation, "The Five Gospels", a sidebar within the translation of John's gospel notes, "Many of the 'I am' sayings are designed, in the present form of the gospel, to expand on who Jesus is by adding identifying phrases. In virtually every case, the reader is being confronted with the language of the evangelist and not the language of Jesus."[177] It does make sense to suggest that the evangelist, who may be trying to prove the divinity of Jesus, would insert these words. However, one must consider the possibility, at least, that these *are* authentic words of Jesus, because they represent his own mystical experience, and were uttered in order to challenge us to experience the same. I believe that Houston Smith is correct in emphasizing the mystical aspects of the 'I am' statements.

Regarding the words of Jesus in John 10:38 "...so that you'll fully understand that the Father is in me and I am in the father." the Scholars Version states, "he does assert the unity of himself and his father (v, 38). The 'works' of Jesus and his unity with the father are Johannine themes that have no basis in the aphorisms and parables of the historical Jesus." [178]

It is tragic that there are none so blind as those who will not see. When Jesus made the claim that he was one with the Father, it was not because of any sense of his uniqueness. Jesus was simply stating that we are all to understand the reality of our oneness with the Father; and I believe that this knowledge will eventually come into the consciousness of us all, no matter how many lifetimes it takes.

In his book, "Honest to Jesus", Robert Funk, founder of the Jesus seminar and one of the authors of "The Five Gospels", makes a cogent plea that Jesus himself is not the proper object of faith. He states, "The proper object of faith inspired by Jesus is to trust what Jesus trusted. For that reason, I am not primarily interested in affirmations about Jesus but in the truths that inspired and informed Jesus." Again, "I want to discover what Jesus saw, or heard, or sensed that was so enchanting, so mesmerizing, so challenging that it held Jesus in its spell. And I do not want to be misled by what his followers did: instead of looking to see what he saw, his devoted disciples tended to stare at the pointing finger."[179]

I could not agree with him more; but I must confess perplexity that Mr. Funk could have such a passion to learn from Jesus and still fail to hear the mystical quality of what he so simply said. Perhaps, he is so caught up in debunking tradition, he is unable to see the woods because of the trees.

---

[177] The Five Gospels, Robert Funk: page 419
[178] The Five Gospels, Robert Funk: page 436
[179] Honest to Jesus, Robert Funk: item 6 pages 304,305

In summary, the major review of ideas covered thus far can be encapsulated in identifying Jesus' phrase 'born again', with the references to enlightenment by eastern sages.

To experience new birth is to move from an orientation with material space/time values at the center of our worldview, to recognition that the invisible things of the Spirit are the central focus of eternal reality. This is the transformation that brings about Spiritual healing.

The traditional view of the new birth in the Christian religion is in sharp contrast to a birth involving gestation and dynamic travail. Compare enlightenment, as an inner spiritual birth of transformed awareness, with the accepted legalistic concept involving a perfunctory spiritual birth certificate, signifying that an outside force has legally saved us.

The meaning of enlightenment once again can be expressed in the terms of the prologue to the Gospel According to John. The divine Logos expresses as the world. When the insight arrives that the Logos is expressing as 'you', one's own true Self, the coming of the Christ occurs. Logos is Spirit and Spirit is who we really are. Being born of the Spirit demonstrates the awareness of one's reality as Spirit. The logos gives us power (dynamic) to become sons of god.

God doesn't exist like one may think it does. To say that the reality of god is actually within nonexistence seems to be a contradiction, but god is not a thing. A thing is seen to exist, but that existence is only perception. Reality does not exist in perception. Cosmos is understood as the basic harmony and order of an intelligent universe. The potentiality of cosmos is within the reality of god, and can only exist in what we might consider non-being. God is Spirit and not a thing.

Perception needs to shift to a true understanding of cosmos. We perceive the sun setting. Cosmos says the earth rises. We perceive the cold of wintertime. Cosmos teaches the absence of heat. We can turn off the light, but we do not turn on the dark. Cold and dark are perceptions based on belief systems that are essentially in error.

We cannot truly turn off god or cosmos, but our false belief systems and our wrong perceptions can construct for us the appearance of chaos.

We believe that accidents happen, but what we perceive as accidents are the laws of cosmos being followed to the letter. We may believe that some event occurs at the wrong time or wrong place, but its time and occurrence follow the law of cause and effect. God exists as the Principle of cosmos – and in the order of cosmos we live and move and have our being.

God, is indeed, very personal as the base of our own existence. It is essentially god/force expressing Itself as our existence; rather than a separated personality god, who has made us apart from it, and only chooses to be friendly. The essential meaning and harmony of life is learning to allow god as Life Force to express as our very being. Our need is to overcome the perception of separation, which when we believe it, divides us from god, each other, and all expression of cosmos.

At the level of absolute reality, negative power in opposition to cosmos does not exist – chaos, separated from cosmos, does not exist. Love has no opposite in reality. But in perception, the appearance of the absence of love and love's awareness is experienced as fear. Chaos is a term that appears to have meaning only at the level of materiality. We can experience chaos just as we can experience darkness or the sun setting. We know that the sun does not set, even though for thousands of years our ancestors may have believed that it did. In fact, recent studies in apparent chaos, string theory, and fractal geometry, indicate a beautiful connective harmony in what was once assumed to be only dissociated and random.

Many of our perceptions about god, the world, and ourselves are based upon assumed traditions that have no basis in actual fact. The problem in believing an untruth is that wrong beliefs have profound effect upon our experience of the cosmos.

God is light; god is love – though the written words of Hebrew/Christian scripture affirm this to be true, it is true not because scripture acknowledges it so; rather, scripture based on experience confirms it because it is true. I believe that it is personal experience that truly establishes the concept of god as light, love and truth.

The concept that any written scripture is to be believed true is another matter indeed. There is a real problem in confusing the written words of scripture with what scripture itself calls the Living Word, or actual Mind/Voice (logos) of god.

The written word, in most cases and especially in the case of Hebrew/Christian experience, is a library of material giving witness to beliefs of particular ages and places. This library does not represent unanimous continuity. It does represent a wide variety of opinions, sometimes in support of opposing belief systems. The living Word, on the other hand, is the expression and experience of the law of the cosmos.

The prologue to John's gospel speaks of the Logos as god's expression, being in the presence of and having the same quality as god Itself. The *experience* of the expression, however, is not identical to the source that it expresses. It is at this point that the non-being of god Itself and the apparent being of the observable universe must be brought into focus. Inasmuch as we, too, are expressions of god, we, too, are part of the living Word. In him we live and move and have our being. Everything made that is made is an expression of cosmos. Even the molecular structure is alive – the very stones cry out. The question is how to listen to what the living universe is being, rather than to tell it our plans for doing. Most of us think that it is by our doing that we become. Rather it is in knowing our true being that we learn to allow appropriate action. There is much potential in the awareness of learning to be what we are, so that we can flow in an expression of effortless doing (*wei wu wei*). This is the Father within us doing the work.

To say that god expresses the world is to say that the real world is divine! Every once in a while the institutional church allows someone to take god seriously, and as a result they see differently. The heavenly kingdom, one becomes aware, is not located in space – it is not above the stars and beyond the galaxies. Likewise, the heavenly kingdom is not to be found within the bounds of time. It is not found in form or object, but in the experience of the timeless eternal spirit with which we are in our reality, one and the same.

We will know we understand enlightenment when we begin to replicate in our lives what Jesus accomplished in his. He said, "Greater works will you do."[180] The belief that Jesus is god has had great impact; in the religion about Jesus, he was supposedly capable of carrying out the entire divine work (external to us) directed toward salvation. The concept of Jesus as god is hopelessly inadequate to our need, if he is to be seen as a Way-Shower.

How can we hope to duplicate works attributed to a god? On the other hand, as a man who discovered the inner power of the kingdom, Jesus gives us a sense of direction and possibility. If we were to learn what he knew and understand what he understood, then we would be able to allow the energy in the mind of god to express its potential through us. We would escape the limitations of our body and intellect. We would become one in spirit with the One, and have no boundary.

There is no need to do; but there is a need to undo. Often it is a matter of who is in control. We need to undo all the attitudes and attachments that prevent us from experiencing an awareness of spirit. Being in control is a question of the direction of energy being utilized.

> *If you are trying to Tao, it is not the Tao.*
> *If you are trying to unfold, it is not unfolding.*
> *If you are trying to grow, it is not growing.*
> *If you are trying to flow, it is not flowing.*
> *The Tao that can be Tao-ed is not the Tao.*

To say, "I believe in god" may simply be belief as an intellectual assent, or it can be a gut wrenching conviction that demands behavioral change.

---

[180] John 14:12

Our very language demands that we state god as an object, as if we must say, we believe in he, she, or it. If we choose the wrong pronoun, present political correctness will raise some cause for objection. We get into a game of one-up-man-ship. Do we say Augus<u>tine</u> or Au<u>gus</u>tine? Is our theology merely a question of putting emphasis on the right or wrong sy<u>llable</u>?

To speak of the path to spiritual success is another oxymoron. Being spiritual is a given, it is not a matter of accomplishment. Life as we own it is a given; if we see life as a loan, or as our own accomplishment, it cannot be understood as a given. Awareness from beyond the senses is imported in the silence of the mind. Stephen Levine in his book "Who Dies?" says of healing, "It's like trying to give water to someone dying of thirst. You can either wring the fluid from your cells to give them something to drink, thereby becoming dry and wizened in the process. Or you can go to the well, the great source of sustenance, and carry buckets of clear water to those who need it, finding there's plenty to drink for yourself. Those who give from themselves burn out. Those who give from the source are nourished in the giving. Approaching the well, they enter intuition, sensing the subtleties of another, responding from the heart, not the mind".

From the separation of personal self we cannot find the inner Self. It cannot be found because that thought divides it and us. It cannot be found because it is not lost! The ego that searches must be dissolved, and in so doing, unfolds that for which we have been searching. When we undo the ego that looks for the Self, what remains is All-That-Is. To awaken from the dream is not an act of dreaming.

An actual journey to spirit does not exist; oneness with Spirit already is; god's given expression of life. Nor is the spiritual path of oneness a journey to outer success. Even in the garden of Gethsemane Jesus was portrayed as still groping to find the clarity of the Father's purpose.

One cannot be at the still point of the silence within while talking or writing about it! It is easier to talk about, than to experience. In simply knowing the truth of a statement like, "Thank you Father", an instant of stillness can be experienced in our daily activity.

Moses' experience on Mount Sinai was not mystical. Any mystic claiming to decree what is expected of others deserves to be suspect. The silence does not communicate well in pronouncements. It is evident that Moses, or more likely his editors, had an agenda. We need to be aware that the politics of the Sinai story do not necessarily reflect the intentions of god.

God has no needs, for god is Spirit and has no part in the space/time dimension of need. Perceiving god incorrectly as part of the space/time illusion can lead us down the road of attributing to god a sense of expectation. We begin to think that god is angry and that god has lost its center of eternal peace. We begin to think in terms of what god requires or even of what god demands, having lost sight of the fact that god is both whole and holy. We begin to believe that god has a need for us to worship and adore, as if god would not be complete without our action.

I once grievously offended a congregation, by stating that god didn't need their church and could get along without it. The point is this: we project our needs outwards and confuse our sense of reality by projecting a god in our image. God does not need our worship but we may well have a need for it; god doesn't need our money or gifts but others have needs and we may need to give. Churches, Temples and places of worship do not complete god but they may be of use in completing us. The negative reflection of this same mistaken picture is that we begin to believe that god is upset and angry at our mistakes and failures and, as a result, seeks to punish us or to exact retribution and vengeance. When our mistaken beliefs dim our awareness of god's presence we erroneously believe that god has pushed us away and built a wall between god's presence and us.

The discovery that god is love and so are we, opens a vista in us, from which we can understand both our purpose and god's. We discover who we are and in doing so, receive understanding of our neighbors and of god.

One of the reasons lay people have not been helped by organized religion is that both the institution and clergy are fearful of their status and position. It is dangerous to rock the boat, and the decision is made to safely tell congregations what they have always heard in the belief that this is what they need to hear. The 'old guard' is preserved along with its museum values. The consequence is that anyone searching for understanding is discouraged and driven away.

In a small town in Ohio where I was serving as a United Church of Christ pastor, our congregation participated in a Community Vacation Church School. The meetings were held in the evening at the local United Methodist Church. In order to provide for adults, who were bringing their children, I was asked to conduct an adult class for the parents and any others interested. In the first two or three classes, I used the two creation stories of Genesis as a resource. I covered the first story with a presentation in regard to the firmament bubble and its relation to the primeval waters above and below the bubble. We also talked about the differences between the two stories, and the suggestion that Genesis and the Pentateuch were made up as a collection from several disparate documents. The enthusiasm of the class was so great that our attendance kept increasing. On the fourth or fifth evening, a retired Methodist pastor attended, "To see what was going on".

After the class that evening, when I explained what we had been doing, he correctly identified the documentary hypothesis as the 'Graf–

Wellhausen' theory. He told how he remembered studying it some fifty years before, when he had attended Seminary. He then explained that it obviously had some merit, but he had decided after graduation to just preach Jesus. He was obviously proud of his decision, but I was saddened by the fact that in his ministry so many lay people had been kept ignorant of ideas that would have obviously increased their understanding of the Old Testament record. My own reaction, standing in the presence of so many adults thrilled with new insights gained from attending the classes, was simply "What a waste!" Was the retired minister's rationale that the information I had been presenting was too much beyond laypersons, or was his decision based on his, or institutional, fear of 'rocking the boat'?

Another area of interest garnered from the ancients, going as far back as Pythagoras, is the relationship between religion and the study of mathematics. Numbers were fascinating to what was an essentially enumerate people. Much religious symbolism was attached to belief in the early concepts of numerology. The number one stands for unity and was eventually referenced to god. Two stood for 'other' and signified the difference between the individual and the world outside. Three, represented by the triangle, was the smallest number of straight sides that could contain a whole, and manifests in the doctrine of the Trinity. The pyramid and cube were derived from the triangle and square. The triangle and other geometric figures were given deep mythological significance. The laws of geometric relationships were considered to contain deep mysteries, and those who understood them were given high honor. We still honor Pythagoras for stating the law of the hypotenuse.

We can readily understand seven days in the week, derived from the lunar month of twenty-eight days; but the twenty-eight day cycle doesn't coincide with the twelve months of the solar year (much closer to thirteen shorter months). Consider this illustration and its effect on religious myths. If one takes a sphere such as a billiard ball and then surrounds that sphere with other spheres of the same size, the number of spheres that can be drawn in contact with the original core sphere is exactly twelve.

Were there really twelve tribes of Israel? What did the number reference? Was it simple coincidence, or derived from mythological meaning? Were the twelve tribes referenced to the twelve months of the solar year, or to the twelve geometric spheres surrounding a center? If twelve spheres are positioned touching each other to form an outer sphere, then what is the significance of the space left in the middle? Did Jesus really have twelve disciples, or were some of their names fabricated to complete a mystic number? Could this explain why several of the disciples listed seemed to make no contribution to the early church?

I confess there are far more questions than answers in the above, but given the penchant to make the life of Jesus fit into an expected mold, it is interesting to speculate on the source of the twelve. We know that the number carries over yet today, in the members of a jury and the council heads of several religious groups. One can only speculate on other mythological, geometric effects on our society.

Traditional religion, for the most part, perceives god as an object separate from its creation. At the very heart of traditional Christianity, is the concept of the reconciliation of the creator god to the created world. This reconciliation can take place only in the healing of our minds, for in reality there is no separation. In traditional Christianity the relationship of the world to its separated creator has become adversarial. With this antagonistic outlook, god has condemned the world, passed judgment on it, and now sees it as full of sin. God is Prosecutor, Judge and Jury.

The earliest stories and sculptures in the Mediterranean area depicted Jesus as a teacher; there were no depictions of the crucifixion. Stories from Tibet demonstrate that upon death the bodies of many sages stayed in perfect condition for a period of time and then dissolved into dust, sometimes after three days. Was it this phenomenon that was celebrated on the first Easter? There is some evidence that in the early church, Easter was celebrated as the dissolution of the body and the resurrection of the Spirit. Mystical heroes prior to the Christian church were turned into gods. Later the Roman Catholic Church turned them into saints. (Deification became canonization)

In the early Jesus movement, the Gnostics strengthened in the east and the messianic literalists in the west. The Gnostics taught an inner kingdom, and the western literalists an outer political messianic expectation; because of their different approaches to god's reign, is it any wonder that the western church chose affiliation with the Roman Empire? The political structure of the Roman Catholic Church domination of Europe throughout the middle ages came to an end only with the Renaissance and Protestant Reformation.

Atonement or reconciliation, in the Hebrew tradition, is seen as being accomplished by blood sacrifice, as a legal payment for our debt. I charge that our western Christian cultural and religious traditions follow this same basic assumption. The established doctrine of the church holds the belief that *Jesus died for our sins*! Why did Jesus need to die? Is it to satisfy the need of a judgmental, bloodthirsty god? Very few theologians seem to have seriously asked this question. Yet every celebration of the Roman Catholic mass, and most observances of the Lord's Supper, are a re-enactment of Jesus' death and his blood shed for expiation of our sin. What is the nature of a god who requires blood sacrifice, and human sacrifice at that?

The movement away from that sordid idea perhaps began in the Hebrew Christian tradition, when Abraham refused to sacrifice his son Isaac, in disobedience to his culture's tradition and expectation. This refusal to accept religious tradition as reality, is the beginning of the path that eventually becomes the Way or Tao. Quoting a verse I learned as a child, "You shall hear a word behind you saying, this is the Way; walk ye in it."[181]

Our life does not consist in the abundance of the things we possess. Our life, as we experience the world around us, consists in the effect our attitudes and beliefs have reflected back to us. Our outer environment is the result of what our inner minds have projected outward. What we have sown, we now reap. Because all minds are joined, the group consciousness of a given society also reflects back its attitudes and beliefs at the group level, as surely as the same law works at the individual level.

The things that happen around us are a result of projected outward beliefs. World circumstances are the result of the beliefs and attitudes of our total community and society. The things that happen to us are a result of our own individualistic attitudes and belief creations. My best understanding of this law at work comes from an awareness of our mental and emotional continuum, and the effect it has on the various aspects of mind and its creative force. These are the things that happen in us; and what happens in us is the key to the kingdom. What we sow we reap, and vice versa.

After World War I, when Germany was defeated, the allies ravaged that nation with reparations and other negative economic pressures. The result was terrible inflation and severe economic depression. As a result Germany became fertile ground for such as Adolph Hitler. He came to power on the political lie that Germany had not been defeated; the Jews had betrayed it. The result was a second global war.

Following World War II the allies, with a greater sense of humanitarian aid, rebuilt the Axis powers. Such programs as the Marshal Plan aided provisional governments in the defeated countries. The result was an eventual economic reconstruction and democratization.

Someone had finally listened to Karmic Law and the words of Jesus, "Love your enemies and do good to those who despitefully use you". Ancient enemies had become allies at last.

Andrew Young recently stated in regard to the war against terrorism that as a pacifist, he was pleased to hear the reports that after dropping bombs during the night, our planes were dropping food supplies during the day; to his mind, a step forward in global consciousness.

---

[181] Isaiah 30:21b

As it is in the microcosm, so also it is in the macrocosm. As a global community, we express and form our society according to our worldview. Any madness and terror that we see is a reflection back to us of our attitudes and intentions that we have expressed outwardly.

Some have supposed that the tragedy of the World Trade Center is a judgment and punishment from god because of what they perceive as corrupt and immoral behavior, the sins of the flesh in particular. I would suggest, however, that it is not judgment from an external deity but rather a reflection of our collective injustice in the world, our greed to consume the earth's resources, and our judgment and anger toward societies with whom we are unfamiliar. We may haply say that the cold war is over, but do we really believe that the entrenched fears and nuclear threat of the past fifty years has had no effect upon our global community?

We have judged harshly the terrorist activities of occupied Palestine, but have armed to the teeth the occupying armies of Israel, basically in support of the fundamentalist belief that Israel is god's chosen people. Can the 'truth' of our religious arrogance toward those of another faith have no effect on the millions who see our awesome military as life threatening?

Does our might make us right when we wage war in order to preserve the status quo of the world's oil supply? Do we really believe that our national involvement in the tragedy of Vietnam has had no bearing on the divine law of cause and effect? "Don't kid yourselves, god is no fool! Whatever we sow we will reap; of the flesh – destruction; or of the spirit – life."[182] We can only pray that our good intentions for the welfare of the world will to some degree offset our negative karmic debt.

On the personal end or polarity of this continuum is our own individual set of belief systems and their emotional structure. This is the baggage we carry in our own personal worldview. On the other end of the continuum is the Source of all, divine Principle. These polarities act as the source program for our unconscious computer. Between them is the vast area we generally label as the unconscious and subconscious mind. This is a part of the mind that, as a result of the program, affects outwardly the circumstances of our life as a result of guidance from the two polar sources. These two directive aspects, which we have called conscious mind and divine principle, could also be referred to as the divine mind source and the physical mind source. Healing occurs as this split-mind is unified.

Principle states the law that two plus two equals four. The conscious mind, in its freedom to choose separation, and with its power derived from the divine mind, can choose to program the unconscious in error. The

---

[182] Galatians 6:7-8

unconscious, will then construct a world from the choice to believe error rather than divine principle, i.e. the conscious mind can choose to believe that two plus two equals five. Given this scenario, the unconscious mind constructs an outer world based upon an inner conflicting worldview, and as a result, the outer appearance will be calamity. What we are now seeking to do as individuals is to live by a self-imposed law or belief that two plus two equals five. What we seek to do as individuals is also structuring the global community. The result, in its simplest terms, will be suffering and pain. The other pole of the mind, Principle, knows the truth, and its truth is not altered by our personal mistaken equations. Principle simply waits and gives us opportunity to learn from the calamitous world that we have made.

It is important to understand that Divine Principle is not simple, cold, intellectual logic. While it is vital to move our concept of god away from the ideas of object and personality, it is imperative that we know that the truth of god expresses the total energy of our being, which includes Love, Peace, Hope, and Joy. Although we usually limit these feeling attributes to a concept of personality, Spirit contains the positive relationship of all of these including a sense of humor. Can Principle laugh and enjoy its Reality? Absolutely!

To restate this law of manifestation, the production of outer effect is from inner cause. We can only change this effect by changing the belief systems that are its cause. The inner mind, that builds or manifests the outer experience, receives its instruction from the two polarities of mind. The one is the source of the law of perfect Principle and the ground of being itself. The other is our own will, making a choice to function either in separation or in unity. The experience we encounter in our lives from our projected outer, or world circumstance, becomes the teacher that life offers to us, as a continual array of lessons to be learned. As David Spangler wrote in "Laws of Manifestation", "True abundance is a consciousness of wholeness, oneness and quality, not of separateness, multiplicity and quantity."

The sages of the world have tried to point us in the direction of the healing of this conflict, which occurs between personal and corporate beliefs and divine principle. Sometimes we have listened, but more often than not we have not been ready to learn until the suffering made by our beliefs and attitudes causes us to finally cry out in pain, "There must be a better way." This plea opens an opportunity for change. When we cry out for a better way, the Universe responds. The spirit always sends a teacher. It may be a direct insight, an exposure to a new outlook as a result of a conversation, a book, or any other source for new vision. After the tragedy of 9/11/01 the world is beginning to cry out for a better way. We are faced with the opportunity to change our beliefs, resulting in a change in the outer experience and circumstances of what our minds have built.

Instead of a "War on Terrorism", couldn't we invest in understanding the cause of terrorism, and discover what might bring healing to those who perpetrate it; instead of thinking the only solution is bombing dissident Muslims back into the Stone Age, might we try bridging our profound gaps of ignorance as to why we are hated so vociferously? There must be a better way. We can listen to the lessons life will teach, or continue to shut off 'the better way' we have cried out for, and as a result continue in our suffering. How long we delay is our choice.

Sometimes, our familiar pain seems less threatening to us than opting for change and the risks we think we see in a new venture – what seems to us to be the unknown. Until we learn to trust the Universe, we have all the time it takes. Principle is not upset that we are slow learners. The problem is ours, and the Spirit as teacher always reveals the next step in life's progress.

The time when we will decide to take the next step is always our decision. As an old gospel song has put it, "God doesn't make us go against our will, god just makes us willing to go".

Eventually, inevitably, we will learn to correct our mistakes, and let go of our errors of judgment and separation. Our split-mind will be healed, and the separation will be dissolved. We will learn to live in harmony with divine principle, and the integrated mind will then build for us the Peace, Joy, and Bliss, that the sages of the world have promised. Jesus, as a man like the rest of us, struggled in his life to discover the nature of god. He then learned to stop struggling and trust. The gospel record attempts to disclose what he found. I don't know if he was always right; I'm sure he had to learn from his mistakes as do the rest of us. With Jesus as Lord, the challenge is simply, are we demonstrating in our lives what he presented in his?

Over 50 years ago, I remember a discussion to the effect that god could not have transtemporal perception and could not look back on the future, for this would mean that time was not real. This followed the atomic events of World War II, but was well before the space/time ideas of Albert Einstein were generally acknowledged.

Based on the illusion of space/time, the perceptions of time and space are simply memories of a past that does not exist. Our reality as the son of god is timeless unity with All-That-Is. I am but there is no me. In terms of the Real, I am; but in terms of the illusion of space/time, there is no me. There is a Real World but there is no objective, space/time world.

The essential miracle of "A Course in Miracles" is the awareness that all the grievances that we hold are based on past memories that do not exist.

What we perceive in the space/time world around us is simply an instant that happened long, long ago, an ancient illusion of memory. The past does not exist, and the grievances we hold in our perception of the now are based on nothingness. As we let go the past by means of forgiveness of the apparent now, we see the world through Christ's eyes, perfect, Holy, and innocent. We see our brothers with the same vision as Christ and know that we are one with them in the timelessness of god. In the silence of the Eternal Now, without judgment, we trust our brothers, for we are no longer separated from them, as the sonship is now one. What god is we are, what we are God is. What our brothers are we are; what we are our brothers are – One. Because minds are joined as one, when we 'see' the Oneness of all, we gift our brothers as well. Those who see differently, make vision possible to those who temporarily do not see. This is the miracle of Love, which is the essential message of the course. We are in the world but not of the world. In the real world, beyond time and space, the justice of god prevails.

We must be actively involved in undoing our own constructs, our own attachments to the space/time world of illusion. It is not our job to construct an inner kingdom that is already there. The kingdom will assert itself in what appears to be the fullness of time, as a disclosure of time-less-ness. Ours is the task of letting go the outer, which has no real value, and accepting the gift of the inner, which is the only value that truly exists. By removing the barrier of externals, we open ourselves and become willing to allow the inner to express that which it has always been.

I have puzzled, why it is, that an individual with a disease or handicap can have faith in a healer, and be cured of a physical problem, when the individual's faith alone, seems to be inadequate to effect the needed transformation.

Perhaps, the co-operative effort of the healed with the healer creates a tangible unity, which brings about clearer dimensions of spiritual reality. Jesus taught that where two or three are gathered together, the Christ would be in the midst of them, and when two agree it shall be accomplished[183].

I am reminded of Marlo Morgan's story in the last chapter, of the healing of an Aboriginal man's compound fracture. The community gathered around and sang to the bone, reminding it of its perfect potential, and the ability to become stronger than it was before the break. The combined strength of the community was obviously a factor needed in order for the leg to regain its strength as quickly as it did.

---

[183] Matthew 18:19,20

Certainly, there is ample evidence that when the doctor/patient relationship has a context of trust, the healing of the patient is more quickly achieved.

Ready – Set – Be!

Some years ago I had the opportunity of attending a Yoga retreat in the northern part of New York State near the St. Lawrence River. There was a carload of us who traveled from western New York, where I was living at the time. The retreat was at an old farmhouse that did not have running water or inside plumbing. There were probably about fifty or sixty people in attendance, and seven or eight persons who acted as staff. The staff directed the discipline of the retreat and was responsible for cooking the strictly vegetarian meals. We were all asked to leave our watches and other particulars locked in our automobiles. We were under the complete direction of the staff that gave us the rules for participation in the retreat.

The retreat was based almost entirely on the question "Tell me who you are?" which led to necessary reflection on the more personal question, "Who am I?" Participants were instructed to choose a partner, sit facing one another on the floor, and take turns asking the primary question, "Tell me who you are?" After one partner took a turn for several minutes, telling who they believed they were, a bell was rung and we were instructed to reverse our roles. After another several minutes of expressing ideas about who we thought we were, we were again instructed to change roles, by the ringing of the bell. When we had spent some length of time exchanging roles with the same partner – probably twenty or thirty minutes – we were instructed, again with the bell, to change partners. Except for short stretch breaks and meals, this was the entire program until we retired for sleep. The entire group slept in sleeping bags, in one large room on the upper floor of the farmhouse. After being involved in this exercise for a good part of three days, there was little question that we had exhausted every intellectual concept of who we thought we were. I expect the one result of the exercise was the simple awareness that our own being was something greater than our explanations of it.

On the final day, toward the end of our exercises, I was partnered with a young man of about thirty years of age, who was just a few years younger than I was at the time. We had exchanged the role of asking and listening to the question "Tell me who you are?" several times. I was just finishing making a statement of who I felt I was when we heard the bell ring, but did not understand whether it was a signal to reverse roles or to exchange partners. On query, we discovered that we were to reverse roles. As it was my turn to begin again with the question, I began to reflect on what I felt we were actually doing. As a result, I said to my partner "Ready, Set, Be!" instead of the expected question. This of course is a take off on the words every child has used to begin an action or contest, "Ready, set, Go!" My partner was not only able to see the depth of meaning in the changed statement but was also able to respond with a tremendous sense of humor. Needless to say, when he broke into gales of laughter, I responded in like kind. We both broke up and hugged each other while tears rolled down our cheeks. After we were able to stop laughing, my partner said he wanted to thank me for the gift he had received by means of the comment. Life is, after all, Being and not Doing. If the words of this book have helped you gain any insight into the nature of your reality, then know that god is saying from within you, "Ready, Set, Be!

The Quest for the Historical Jesus

He comes to us as One unknown, without a name, as of old, by the lakeside, He came to those men who knew Him not. He speaks to us the same word: "Follow thou me!" and sets us to the tasks which He has to fulfill for our time. He commands. And to those who obey Him, whether they be wise or simple, He will reveal himself in the toils, the conflicts, the sufferings which they shall pass through in His fellowship, and, as an ineffable mystery, they shall learn in their own experience Who He is.[184]

Albert Schweitzer

---

[184] The Quest For the Historical Jesus, Albert Schweitzer: page – 403

Glossary

Acosmic pantheism – (a-cosmic – not cosmic) The cosmos is illusion, the rest god.

Advaita – non-dualistic

Atman – the essence of the individual soul

Brahman – universal being, All-That-Is, non-object god

Daemon – the true Self

Dualism – To believe that both the world and god are real, or hold the position of having two gods and two powers such as good and evil, god and Satan.

Eidolon – individuated self.

Glory – Greek *boka* translated glory or righteousness means honor and distinction, an imprint of god's nature and a reflection of god's image within. The inner Christ is the imprint of the engraved Word, particularly at the spiritual level.

Karma – The law of cause and effect (action/reaction).

Law of One – acosmic pantheism is practically identical.

Logos – Greek term translated as word, message or content

Non-dualism – There is only one Presence and one Power in the entire Universe. Spirit is real and matter is illusion, unless we accept that the world is god, the concept of cosmic pantheism.

Maya – illusion, the projection of memory and judgement outward upon space/time appearance.

Panentheism – (all is in god) all things are in god, also, **acosmic pantheism** (not the world) (a-cosmic – not cosmic) The world is illusion, the rest is god

Pantheism – (all-god), also, **cosmic pantheism**: (the world) is god. In cosmic pantheism the changing world is defined in its totality as god.

Paradigm – A framework of understanding, i.e. Dividing 3 into 10, will give a different result, depending on decimal or fractional arithmetic

Tat tvam asi – (thou art that) the Impersonal Self is fundamentally identical with universal being; and that the outer world of personal experience has no independent reality, for reality is a single principle.

Upanishads – Hindu esoteric and mystical part of the Vedas, the basis of Vedanta. Their major view is the identity of the individual Atman with the universal Brahman.

Vedanta – fulfillment of the spiritual teachings of the Vedas

Shankara developed the system of Vedanta in Hindu thought. His central message is that the essence of the individual soul (atman) is fundamentally identical with universal being (Brahman). He believed that because Brahman is absolute and undifferentiated from the individual soul, the entire world of physical experience is *maya* or illusion and has no independent reality.

Vedas – From Vedic, an earlier form of the Sanskrit language. Ancient Spiritual writings of the Hindus

Bibliography and Recommended Reading

Karen Armstrong – A History of God

Roberto Assagioli – Psychosynthesis

Marcus Bach – Spiritual Breakthroughs for Our Time

Richard Bach – Jonathan Livingston Seagull (A delightful parable)

J. Allen Boone – Kinship with All Life (animals have spirit too)

Marcus J. Borg – Jesus at 2000

Harmon Bro – Edgar Cayce on Dreams

Tom Brown, Jr. – Awakening Spirits

Paul Brunton – The Wisdom of the Overself

Richard M. Bucke – Cosmic Consciousness

Eric Butterworth – Discover the Power Within You

H. Emilie Cady – Lessons in Truth / How I Used Truth

Joseph Campbell – The Hero With A Thousand Faces / The Masks of God
(Also PBS tapes with Bill Moyers)

Deepak Chopra – The Way of the Wizard / The Seven Spiritual Laws of
Success / The Return of Merlin / Quantum Healing

Robert Conklin – Reach for the Sun (A delightful small book.)

Pierre Teilhard De Chardin – The Phenomenon of Man

Larry Dossey – Healing Words

Wayne Dyer – The Sky's The Limit / Spiritual Solutions

Nels F. S. Ferre – The Living God of Nothing and Nowhere

Arthur Ford – Nothing So Strange (autobiography)

Anne Frank – Diary of Anne Frank

Viktor E. Frankl – The Will to Meaning

Timothy Freke and Peter Gandy – Hermetica

Robert W. Funk – Honest to Jesus / The Five Gospels

Fynn – Mister God, This is Anna (One of the finest I have ever read!!)

Eileen Garret – Many Voices, Autobiography of a Medium

Joscelyn, Godwin – Mystery Religions in the Ancient World

Joel S. Goldsmith – The Infinite Way / The Mystical I / The Thunder of
Silence / A Parenthesis in Eternity (Excellent metaphysics)

Joan Grant – Far Memory (how Winged Pharaoh was written)

Winged Pharaoh (fascinating posthumous autobiography)

Denys Kelsey and Joan Grant – Many Lifetimes

Stuart Grayson – Spiritual Healing

S. Ralph Harlow – A Life After Death

Willis Harman & Howard Rheingold – Higher Creativity

Joseph Head and S. L. Cranston – Reincarnation – An East-West Anthology (The Phoenix Fire Mystery)

Thomson Jay Hudson I – The Law of Psychic Phenomena (recommended by Edgar Cayce)

Aldous Huxley – The Perennial Philosophy

William James – The Varieties of Religious Experience

Gerald G. Jampolsky – Love is Letting go of Fear (based on "A Course in Miracles")

Raynor C. Johnson – The Imprisoned Splendor

Shafica Karagulla – Breakthrough to Creativity

Helen Keller – My Religion

John C. Lilly – Man and Dolphin / The Center of the Cyclone

Franklin Loher – The Power of Prayer on Plants

Shirley MacLaine – Out on a Limb

Catherine Marshall – Christy (excellent)

Abraham H. Maslow – Religions, Values, and Peak-Experiences

D. Patrick Miller – The Complete Story of the Course ("A Course in Miracles")

Stephen Mitchell – The Enlightened Mind / The Enlightened Heart

Marlo Morgan – Mutant Message Down Under (the 'Real' people)

F. W. H. Myers – Human Personality and its Survival of Bodily Death

Robert Ornstein – The Roots of the Self

Elaine Pagels – The Gnostic Gospels

Phoebe D. Payne and Laurence Bendit – The Psychic Sense

William R. Parker and Elaine St. Johns – Prayer Can Change Your Life

Joseph Chilton Pearce – The Crack in the Cosmic Egg

J. B. Phillips – Your God is Too Small

Herbert Bruce Puryear – Reflections on the Path

Louisa Rhine – Hidden Channels of the Mind

Jane Roberts – The God of Jane: A Psychic Manifesto / Seth Material

Elizabeth Kubler-Ross – Death, The Final Stage of Growth

David St. Clair – Watseka (You need to read it to believe it)

Antoine de Saint Exupery – The Little Prince

Helen Schucman – The Gifts of God (scribed "A Course in Miracles")

Albert Schweitzer – The Quest of the Historical Jesus

Bernie Siegel – How To Live Between Office Visits

David Spangler – The Laws of Manifestation (no one who wants to understand prosperity should miss it. On the mark)

Walter Starcke – This Double Thread, (A remarkable guide to modern mysticism)

Jess Stern – Edgar Cayce – The Sleeping Prophet

Ian Stevenson – Twenty Cases Suggestive of Reincarnation (the best)

Thomas Sugrue – There is a River, The Story of Edgar Cayce

Emanuel Swedenborg – dozens of books both in English and Latin

Michael Talbot – The Holographic Universe

Peter Tompkins and Christopher Bird – The Secret Life of Plants

Chogyam Trungpa – Cutting Through Spiritual Materialism (excellent)

Kenneth Wapnick – Absence from Felicity (story of Helen Schucman scribe for ("A Course in Miracles"))

Allan W. Watts – The Wisdom of Insecurity / The Book

Leslie D. Weatherhead – The Christian Agnostic / Psychology Religion and Healing

Wei Wu-Wei – Open Secret / Posthumous Pieces / The Tenth Man: The Great Joke

(Which Made Lazarus Laugh) mind blowing

Stuart Edward White – The Unobstructed Universe / Across The Unknown

Ken Wilber – No Boundary, Eastern and Western Approaches to Personal Growth (One of the best Yet) The Atman Project

Marianne Williamson – A Return to Love (based on "A Course in Miracles")

Elia Wise – Letter to Earth (One of the best ever.)

Franklin Merrell-Wolff – The Philosophy of Consciousness Without an Object / Pathways Through to Space

(Absolutely the greatest, if you can stretch your mind to follow a mathematician's logic.)

Paul Woodruff – Reverence Renewing a Forgotten Virtue

Ambrose A. Worrall and Olga N. Worrall – The Gift of Healing (An amazing story)

Paramahansa Yogananda – Autobiography of a Yoga

Foundation for Inner Peace – A Course in Miracles

The Bahagavad Gita
Rumi, Works of
Chaung Tsu, Works of
Lao Tsu – Tao Te Ching and other works

About The Author

George Fandt has written a superb work of spirituality. He traces his spiritual journey, his education (both inner and outer) and presents a view of the truths of Jesus Christ in a way that honors Christianity and other paths as well. This is a book of inspiration, a book of history, a book of truths that help to set the soul free. Mr. Fandt is a courageous spiritual seeker and a masterful writer. I found this book to be insightful, forward thinking, and uplifting. I believe this book can be a tremendous help to all who are searching for light through spiritual study and meditation.

John Strickland, Senior Minister—Atlanta Unity Church

He holds a Bachelor of Arts, (1952); from Houghton College, a fundamentalist school in upstate New York. He received a Master of Divinity, (1955) from United Theological Seminary, a former Evangelical United Brethren school in Dayton, Ohio. He was a student in the School for Ministerial and Religious Studies, (1975) at Unity School for Practical Christianity in Lee's Summit, Missouri. He has attended numerous seminars and workshops, including those sponsored by Edgar Cayce's Association for Research and Enlightenment, Spiritual Frontiers Fellowship and has been a student of A Course in Miracles for over a quarter of a century.

As the academic listing would suggest George has chewed his way through fundamentalism, more liberal forms of Christianity and ultimate discovered the need to Move beyond the religion of the Institutional Church toward awareness of a universal experience of the god within, referred to as Buddhahood or Christ consciousness.

George retired in 1992 as a Pastor/Teacher from The United Church of Christ. He served churches in New York, Ohio and South Dakota.

George and his wife Lillian were married in 1952; they live in a Senior Citizen facility in Xenia, Ohio. Their daughter Kara and her husband Dennis live in nearby Jamestown, Ohio. Their son Kevin and his wife Renee live in Renton, Washington. The grand children and great grandson are mentioned in the Preface of this book.

Printed in the United States
1162500003B/1-51

9 781410 710260